FIRING AT WILL

A MANAGER'S GUIDE

Jay Shepherd

Apress®

Firing at Will: A Manager's Guide

ISBN-13 (pbk): 978-1-4302-3738-9

ISBN-13 (electronic): 978-1-4302-3739-6

Trademarked names may appear in this book. Rather than use a trademark symbol with every occurrence of a trademarked name, we use the names only in an editorial fashion and to the benefit of the trademark owner, with no intention of infringement of the trademark.

Distributed to the book trade worldwide by Springer-Verlag New York, Inc., 233 Spring Street, 6th Floor, New York, NY 10013. Phone 1-800-SPRINGER, fax 201-348-4505, e-mail orders-ny@springer-sbm.com, or visit www.springeronline.com.

For information on translations, please contact us by e-mail at info@apress.com, or visit www.apress.com.

Apress and friends of ED books may be purchased in bulk for academic, corporate, or promotional use. eBook versions and licenses are also available for most titles. For more information, reference our Special Bulk Sales–eBook Licensing web page at www.apress.com/bulk-sales.

To Heidi,
for standing by me all these years
and allowing me to pursue my dreams

Contents

About the Author

Photo by Gregory Segall

Jay Shepherd is a writer and speaker focused on fixing workplaces so that individuals are free to do their best work.

For 17 years, he worked as an employment litigator and adviser helping companies stay out of trouble. He had something of a knack for it: *Law & Politics* magazine named him one of the Top 100 Lawyers in New England. One thing he didn't have a knack for was tracking hours, so in 2006 he banned timesheets from his Boston law firm, Shepherd Law Group. This made some waves around the country and the world, which led Jay to write and speak about the subject. In 2011, he closed the law firm after 13 years and opened Prefix, LLC (prefixllc.com), a firm that helps professionals learn how to price their knowledge.

Jay writes two award-winning blogs. *Human Resource Executive* has called Gruntled Employees (gruntledemployees.com), his workplace blog, the "top HR web site." The American Bar Association has twice listed The Client Revolution (clientrevolution.com), which focuses on reinventing the business of law, as one of the top 100 lawyer blogs. He has also been a widely read columnist on Above the Law (abovethelaw.com/author/jshepherd), the world's most popular law blog.

Jay is married to the chief human-resources officer of a top Boston law firm, and they have two amazing young daughters who enjoy reading so much that they might even read this book. Eventually.

Follow Jay on Twitter at @jayshep, or e-mail him at jay@prefixllc.com.

Acknowledgments

My father, Norm Shepherd, has been telling me to write pretty much this exact book for the last 15 years or so. I always knew he was right, but I needed to get to this point in my life to be able to do it justice. My mother, Geri Shepherd, has been a force of encouragement my whole life. Without the love of these two amazing people, I never would have been able to acquire the experience, knowledge, and judgment that I now share in this book. Thank you, Mom and Dad.

I also owe a huge debt of gratitude to my grandparents, now gone but never forgotten. Jim Whalen was the biggest supporter of my going to law school; Evelyn Whalen taught me about unconditional caring and compassion; Norman Shepherd, a banker and an author in his own right, got me interested in business; and Rose Shepherd, a schoolteacher, taught me the value of teaching others.

Heartfelt thanks to my parents-in-law, Jack and Lily Goldstein, whose support for and interest in my career and business were indispensable. I am so grateful for being welcomed into their quintessentially American family.

I have been incredibly fortunate to become involved as a senior fellow with the VeraSage Institute (verasage.com), a think tank devoted to improving the professions and trashing timesheets. I have learned so much from my fellow fellows and colleagues, and much of their wisdom adorns these pages. Three of my VeraSage friends merit special attention:

Ron Baker, the founder of VeraSage, is the smartest individual I have ever met. I have learned more from him in a few short years than I have from anyone outside my family. His visions for improving the lives of professionals are revolutionary. I'm humbled by the wonderful Foreword he's contributed to this book, and I am honored by his invaluable friendship.

Along with Ron, VeraSage senior fellow Michelle Golden helped guide me through my "pivot" from running a law firm to becoming a writer and speaker. Michelle has the uncanny ability to mesh business strategy with openness and compassion. As a social-media expert, Michelle has taught me countless lessons about being connected. (And without social media, this book never would have happened.) As published authors, both Michelle and Ron also provided me with enormous support toward completing this book.

In Australia, VeraSage senior fellow John Chisholm welcomed me into his home and hosted me on a speaking tour of law and accounting firms. It was that trip last year that proved to be the tipping point for my pivot into this new phase of my life. John's humor and friendship more than make up for his stinginess with the Shiraz.

Back home in the States, I owe my legal career and much of the wisdom that I learned and now share with you to two amazing employment lawyers. Ellen Kearns and David Rubin were my first (and, as it turned out, only) bosses in the legal profession. Ellen taught me how to build up a boutique law firm and a national reputation in the law. She was a wonderful role model for me. I've always said that Dave was the best employment lawyer in Boston whom nobody knew. That's an exaggeration—more people know him than he realizes. But Dave is a top-notch labor and employment lawyer who eschewed the limelight. His dry sense of humor and great good sense helped make me the lawyer I became.

I also owe a gigantic debt to the professionals I worked with at Kearns & Rubin and Shepherd Law Group: Steve Reed, Debbie Cohen, Lurleen Gannon, Sarah Turner, Mike Pacinda, Mike Bertoncini, Annie Ladov Eisemann, Nicole Corvini, Shannon Lynch, Lara Czerwinski, Jennifer Becker, and Jonathan Duke.

I could not have written this book without the incredible support of the wonderful group of people at Apress. Senior editor Jeff Olson, a true professional, came across my Gruntled Employees blog and thought I might just be able to write a book. Despite all I did to disabuse him of that, he stuck with me. I truly appreciate his patience, faith, and professionalism. Thanks, too, to coordinating editor Jessica Belanger, who kept the trains running despite numerous author-related delays. And my deep thanks to everyone else at Apress who worked so hard to put this book together in an amazingly short time.

Very special thanks to Nicole Corvini for serving as the technical reviewer of this book. I had the privilege of working with Nicole at Shepherd Law Group for three years. She is the most gifted employment lawyer I worked with in my career, and one of the most wonderful people I have had the honor of calling my friend. Thank you, Nicole.

I never could have finished this book if Jan Coupe hadn't kept me in one piece, physically and mentally. Jan is one of the most caring, amazing people

I have ever met, and it is not overstating it to say that she changed my life forever.

When you spend most of your career as your own boss, it's very difficult to have anyone fulfill the classic mentor role. Instead, I had an incredible team of business and career advisors without whom I never could have succeeded:

Martin Ebel was my law partner for four years (when the firm was known as Shepherd & Ebel). I have never met a more inspiring person. So much of what I learned as a lawyer came from working side by side with Marty, and his wisdom and judgment permeate this book.

Christopher Mirabile has been my *consigliere* for nearly two decades. Much of my career was mapped out in monthly breakfast meetings with Christopher at the Knotty Pine in Auburndale.

Russell Beck is one of those rare individuals who becomes a closer friend than the time spent together would seem to warrant. Russell's advice and support as I transitioned from practicing lawyer to my new role were hugely helpful, as was his stewardship of my firm's remaining clients.

The closest person I ever had to a mentor was my practice-management and marketing coach, the incomparable Dustin Cole. For more than six years, Dustin has guided me through the ups and downs of running a law firm, helping me get out of my own way, and stopping me from "preparing to prepare." He was also instrumental in the decision to write this book. I am forever indebted to Dustin, and I am privileged to call him my friend.

My most important business adviser is also my oldest friend: my brother Bill. A genius at sales, Bill has offered me support, advice, and love my entire life. Younger brothers aren't always naturally suited for that role, but Bill is an exceptional human being. I absolutely would not have made it without him.

I have talked about shifting my role from lawyer to writer and speaker, but the most important role I've ever held is that of father. The greatest joys in my life are my incredible and beautiful daughters, Rebecca and Samantha. They are my everything. Rebecca's passion for reading and skill at writing has led her to say that she would also like to become an author; she'll certainly be able to do that. Samantha's amazing mind is a marvel; whatever she chooses to do in her life, she will excel at it. Girls: I love you more than life itself.

More than anyone, I owe my deepest gratitude to my lovely, incredible wife Heidi. To say that I could not have done it—my career, my business ventures, this book—without her is a ridiculous understatement. To say that she stood by me and supported me all this time is to trivialize the unbelievable gift that she has given me. Besides our wonderful daughters, she has given me the ability to be who I am. I love you, Heidi, and I thank you heart and soul.

Foreword

Albert Einstein's research assistant–turned-philosopher Michael Polanyi drew a distinction between *tacit* and *explicit* knowledge. To illustrate tacit knowledge, he said, try explaining how to ride a bike. You know more than you can tell.

Tacit knowledge is "sticky," in that it is not easily articulated. It is complex and rich, whereas *explicit* knowledge tends to be thin and low-bandwidth, like the difference between reading the employee manual and spending some time chatting with a coworker about the true nature of the job.

Reading *Firing at Will* is the opportunity to have an extensive chat with its author, Jay Shepherd. You are about to gain 17 years of tacit knowledge from an unapologetic management-side lawyer, which will pay you dividends for years to come.

You should know upfront, I have an alignment of interest. Jay is not only a colleague, a senior fellow at VeraSage Institute—the think tank I founded— and the author of the Foreword to my latest book; he has also become a good friend.

In my book, I discuss what's become known as Baker's Law: *Bad customers drive out good customers.* The corollary to that law is: *Bad employees drive out good employees.*

Bad team members have a toxic and demoralizing influence on the performance of an organization. It is simply unacceptable to other team members to keep people in the organization who are not meeting expectations. The effects of negative morale are significant, and will ripple throughout the company.

When it comes time to let substandard performers go, it is a task that must be carried out with dignity, respect, compassion, and precision—sometimes a surgeon must cut in order to cure. We do people no favors when we let them languish in jobs they are not capable of performing well or for which they have no heart.

Yet as Jay points out, firing people sucks. No employer worthy of being human enjoys the deed. It creates anxiety and stress, and stress can make us stupid. *Firing at Will* is like having an insurance policy guarding you against the potentially perilous risks of terminating employees.

Even though most workers in the United States are employees at will—meaning they can be fired for any reason, or no reason at all, with or without warning—there are exceptions to this doctrine, and they have grown over the years.

You'll learn the three major exceptions to the at-will doctrine, with the most insidious being the implied-contract exception. These contracts can severely limit your ability to fire at will. But if you must have one, do you know why a mandatory-arbitration clause is a terrible idea?

Do you know the 30 riskiest employees to fire; the seven deadly workplace sins that require immediate termination; and the number-one leading indicator that predicts whether or not you'll be sued? Jay walks you through the minefield of a typical discrimination case. You'll want to read this book if for no other reason than to avoid this debilitating, no-win predicament.

Firing at Will also provides an abundance of counterintuitive advice that flouts the conventional wisdom, which is usually far more conventional than actual wisdom. For example: why you should not give written warnings; why performance-improvement plans are a poor substitute for good management, especially since so many are based on mindless templates.

My favorite example of his counterintuitive counsel, though, is why performance appraisals are the dumbest managerial tool ever devised. His advice invalidates one of the biggest justifications for this anachronistic, inhumane, and demoralizing paper-shuffling ritual. Have you ever met anyone who believes they are effective at increasing performance? Jay even shows how they can actually hurt you in court.

Jay is a lawyer who also understands economics. And the first rule of economics is: incentives matter. No one washes a rental car or asks their barber if they need a haircut. When it comes to pointing out the irrationality of his own profession, Jay is fearless. Nowhere is this more evident than the perverse incentive created by the billable hour—the predominant method used to charge for legal services.

He once wrote a blog post titled "A One-Question Test for Your Law Firm" to determine how good your lawyer is: *How much will this cost?* If your lawyer can't correctly answer this question, you have the wrong lawyer. As a client, this is sage advice you can implement immediately. Demand fixed prices from your law firms.

Most importantly, Jay expresses the importance of being compassionate when firing fellow human beings. This is not the time or place to be efficient. His concept of "Retained Dignity" is pure genius.

To keep poor performers in place is to risk the future of your organization. Comedian Steven Wright once sardonically quipped, "The problem with the gene pool is there's no lifeguard." *Firing at Will* is all the tacit knowledge you'll need to ensure your lifeguards perform one of the most unpleasant— but vital—jobs with the dignity and compassion worthy of the human spirit.

—Ronald J. Baker
Founder, VeraSage Institute

Introduction

I've been hugged by employees I've fired. On more than one occasion.

I once got an e-mail from an employee I fired, thanking me for the employment and calling my firm "truly a great place to work."

I'm not telling you this to brag about my skills at firing. Quite honestly, I don't ever want to be known as a good terminator (non-cyborg division). I never wanted to fire anybody, and I never want to have to do it again.

In fact, no one *wants* to fire employees—certainly no one who would ever pick up this book. But it's an unfortunate certainty in life—along with death and taxes—that an employer will have to fire an employee at some point in his or her career. This book will help you do it right.

You could say that the possible reactions of a fired employee fall along a spectrum. At one end are the hugs and the grateful e-mail I mentioned. At the other end are employee lawsuits. Trust me: you want the hugs, not the lawsuits. And this speaks to one of the central themes in *Firing at Will*:

People don't sue people they like.

Employee lawsuits are the weapon of last resort for disgruntled employees. For this reason, much of my advice centers on keeping your employees "gruntled."

Employees don't sue their employers just for money. They sue them because of emotion: anger, hurt, sadness, betrayal. Because of this, I'll talk a lot about emotion in this book.

Now before you get all concerned that this is a touchy-feely book about having happy employees, let me explain where I'm coming from.

For 17 years, I defended and advised companies as an employment litigator. I've represented all kinds of employers, small and large, from individuals hiring nannies to multinational corporations with billions of dollars in revenue. I've fought in the trenches against the lawyers of angry employees in state and federal courts and agencies all over the United States. So I was very much a management-side lawyer. I hold no brief for employees.

But even though I've written this book for employers and managers, it is very much a *pro-employee* book. Despite spending most of my adult life in the adversarial legal system opposing employees, I don't believe that employees and employers should be adversaries.

One of the common factors among the best employers I represented was a sense that the employers and the employees respected each other and worked together toward a common goal. The companies who had more than their fair share of problems and lawsuits were inevitably places that treated their employees poorly. And those problems and lawsuits increased their expenses, and thus lowered their profits. So forget about touchy-feeliness: this is a book designed to help companies be more profitable.

Let me talk about lawyers for a moment. I understand that people don't have a high regard for lawyers, and deservedly so. One of the problems with lawyers today is their tendency to write and speak in way that makes them sound … well … *lawyerly*.

Lawyers have an unfortunate tendency to say things in an unnecessarily complicated and overly formalistic way. That's the last thing I want to do. It makes for boring reading, and causes the important messages to get lost. And lawyerly writing tends not to be fun. This entire topic lacks for fun, so we might as well have a little while we discuss it.

Lawyers also tend to shy away from firm opinions and straight answers. The classic lawyerly answer is, "It depends." But I found that clients prefer straight answers, and straight answers require the lawyer to state an opinion. In this book, you will get my opinions. You don't have to agree with them, but at least you'll know where I stand. I'm bound to tick some people off, because I take a lot of shots at conventional managerial and HR practices. Spoiler alert: annual performance appraisals, employee handbooks, and performance-improvement plans do not fare well in the pages that follow.

What really excites me are workplaces where individuals are free to do their best work. Paternalistic work rules and micromanagement stand in the way of this. So does slavish adherence to outdated business methods just because "we've always done it this way." In the legal world, this was the primary justification for timesheets and hourly billing. I got so fed up with this old way of doing business that I closed my law firm and opened Prefix, LLC (prefixllc.com), a firm that helps professionals learn how to price their knowledge instead of just billing their hours. This way, I can help more firms free up their employees to turn in their best performances.

And that's the mission of *Firing at Will*: to help companies large and small create workplaces where their employees will be happy and productive instead of disgruntled and litigious. My experience defending and advising employers has shown me that this is the most effective way to reduce the risk of debilitating employee lawsuits.

Being an employer or a manager is an incredibly difficult job. And firing employees is the single hardest and riskiest part of that job. But after you've finished reading this book, I'm confident that your job will get considerably easier.

The Book and the Web Site

Firing at Will is laid out in four parts. Part I covers the risks of firing, both general and specific. Part II goes through the whys and hows of firing in great detail, offering you a roadmap for making and carrying out these difficult decisions. Part III describes the worst-case scenario you're trying to avoid: the various kinds of employee lawsuits. And Part IV gives you concrete methods for reducing your risk in the first place.

There are also three appendixes. The first, Appendix A, provides a checklist for before, during, and after the termination. Appendix B gives some brief highlights of how firing differs in other countries. And Appendix C offers some sample documents that you can adapt for your workplace.

There is also a companion web site to the book at firingatwill.com. At the web site, you will be able to download the checklist of Appendix A and the sample documents of Appendix C. You will also find other resources and news that you might find helpful. You can also arrange to have me to come and speak at your organization or company. I'm even more fun in person, and people rarely throw things.

I was asked to write this book in part because of the blogs that I've written. Some of the material in *Firing at Will* has appeared in different form in my blogs, but all of it has been updated specifically for the book.

You Are My Reader, Not My Client

Somewhere on the copyright page there is a disclaimer about not relying on this book as advice. My excellent publisher wrote that, not me. I'm not a fan of disclaimers, because lawyers tend to put too much stock in them.

Instead, I prefer to give you credit as an intelligent, thoughtful reader. (You wouldn't be reading this far into the Introduction if you weren't.) You are my reader and I am your author, and I am honored by that. But I am of course not your lawyer, and you are of course not my client. Part of the reason is that I've stopped practicing now, so I don't have any law clients. But part of it is that you and I haven't sat down and formalized a lawyer-client relationship.

I stand by the advice I give in this book and the experience it's based on. But this is general advice for all the readers of *Firing at Will*. If you or your company needs employment-law advice for your own specific circumstances, I'm sorry that I can't help you with that. I urge you to get yourself an excellent employment-law specialist who can give you the attorney-client attention that you need. Chapter 15 tells you how to do this.

The Risks of Firing

Firing employees is the riskiest thing you can do at work with your clothes on. In Part I, we'll go through just what these risks are, and why it's so important to get right this difficult part of your job. We'll talk about the most important — and most squandered — tool of employers: the concept of at-will employment. We'll cover why it's so important for employers to have the freedom to fire the people they need to. Then I'll tell you about the 30 riskiest kinds of employees to fire.

"At Will" Is Alive and Well

I love baseball. I'm from Boston, so being a member of Red Sox Nation is a birthright. I don't get to Fenway Park as often as I'd like, so I watch a lot of games on TV and listen to many on the radio. Because baseball has a distinct rhythm to it, it's easy to have the game on and still work on something else (like writing this book). I can bang out a sentence or two between pitches, and then look up at about the right time to see the next offering to the plate.

When you listen to a lot of games on the radio, you pick up a lot of the sayings and automatic jokes that the announcers use. For example, if a player gets injured and comes out of the game, the team will often make an announcement that the player is listed as "day-to-day." In other words, he's not expected to go onto the disabled list, but it's uncertain whether he'll play in tomorrow's game. Almost inevitably, after telling the radio audience that so-and-so is day-to-day, one of the announcers will add the following quip: "As are we all."

That might get a knowing chuckle, but in many ways it's true. In the American workplace, nearly all workers are listed as "day-to-day." And it's true in a sense. Unlike baseball players, who sign contracts for one or more seasons, most American employees do not work under contract. Instead, they work day-to-day, with their next day's employment at least metaphysically uncertain.

This is because most US workers are employees *at will*.

Employed at Will

Being an at-will employee means that you are subject to the ancient, common-law, at-will doctrine. In other words, you are employed as long as both of you—the employer and the employee—wish you to be employed. Neither one of you owes the other any commitment about the future. The employer can fire the employee for almost any reason or for no reason at all, with or without warning. The employee can likewise quit for any reason or for no reason at all, with or without warning. It might sound a bit harsh and unfeeling, but it actually is a very fair arrangement. Both the employer and the employee have equal discretion to end the employment relationship.

The opposite of an at-will employee is a contractual employee. Most American workers operate without an actual contract for a specific term of service. Exceptions include professional baseball players and other sports figures, movie stars, and senior corporate executives. Also, employees in a unionized workshop who are subject to a collective-bargaining agreement are also considered contractual employees. But the overwhelming majority of US employees are employed at will.

A Dying Doctrine?

Many commentators think that the at-will doctrine is an antiquated concept, that it is under attack from courts and legislatures, and that it will soon be extinct. A Google search for the phrase "employment at will" with the word "death" made at the time of this writing (September 2011) yields more than 100,000 hits, many of them law-review articles and blog posts that are either advocating for its demise or bemoaning it. Over the years, I've had many employer clients tell me that they thought the at-will doctrine was dead or dying. It's understandable why they'd come to that conclusion. But it's also wrong.

The at-will doctrine is alive and well and living in the United States (almost exclusively; unlike Coca-Cola and rock 'n' roll, it has not been one of our more successful exports). But the scope of the doctrine has narrowed over the past few decades. Or to be more precise, the exceptions to the at-will doctrine have grown. This has led many people (especially frustrated employers) to wrongly conclude that the concept has weakened or failed altogether.

Understanding the exceptions to the at-will doctrine will help employers lower their risks of employee lawsuits. There are three major exceptions, and employers need to consider them before firing an employee. They are the public-policy exception, implied-contract exception, and statutory exception.

Blowing the Whistle

The public-policy exception is a pretty narrow one. Think "whistleblower." If an employee drops a dime on your company, telling the government that you're hiring illegal immigrants, or selling arms to terrorists, or filling your hamburgers with sawdust, you're not free to fire the employee for that. The thinking behind this is that society wants people to report bad things happening, and it figures that people would be less likely to do so if they thought that their employers would legally be able to fire them for it. In this case, the public-policy concerns for preventing lawbreaking outweigh the freedom to fire at will.

It doesn't have to be something particularly serious, either. Let me give you an example from one of my past cases. I once had a small engineering company as a client. They had a guy—let's call him Calvin—who worked as a fairly low-level clerk.

A Royal Pain

Calvin wasn't a great employee; in fact, he was a royal pain. We've all known a Calvin or two in our day. He was always moping around, complaining about pretty much everything, and dragging down workplace morale. His life, according to him, was an endless series of minidramas in which everyone else played the roles of the bad guys. He was always the victim. Calvin was competent enough at his job; his performance always hovered above the level of "barely acceptable." It was his attitude that was the big problem.

Unfortunately, the owners of the company were nice guys, and a little too timid as managers. Like so many people, they preferred to avoid conflict and just focus on the work they were doing. If Calvin's performance had been worse, they might have fired him a long time before. But he coasted along, complaining all the way.

Finally, after years of putting up with this, Calvin's attitude started to decline. He didn't like his assignments. He didn't like his pay raises (they were minimal). He didn't like his coworkers (that feeling was surely mutual). The owners' patience also declined. They finally made the decision that it was time to let Calvin go because of his declining performance. Unfortunately, they procrastinated and delayed having the meeting with him to discuss it. In fact, it took more than a month for them to actually do it.

But in the meantime, there was a foul stench in the workplace. Not figuratively. Literally.

The Rotten-Egg Smell

One of the particular bees in Calvin's bonnet was that on certain days, an unpleasant odor like that of rotten eggs would waft up from the building's basement. The building was over a hundred years old in a crowded neighborhood just outside Boston. There seemed to be no rhyme or reason as to when the smell would worsen; sometimes on hot days, sometimes on cold days. It didn't smell bad every day. It was actually a rare occurrence. Everyone noticed it from time to time, but it only became a *cause célèbre* for Calvin.

The company's management had taken it seriously. They'd hired a contractor specializing in molds and whatnot to come in and check it out. Then they had hired a special kind of plumber who specialized in sewer stuff (now there's a career for you). They put in fans and humidifiers and dehumidifiers. Nothing seemed to work. And nothing would stop Calvin from complaining about it.

Finally, during the month in between the decision to fire him and the actual termination, Calvin decided to take matters into his own hands. Without his bosses' knowledge, he placed a phone call to the city's board of health. They sent an inspector to come check it out. The company owners weren't thrilled at the surprise visit, but they granted the inspector access to the basement and openly answered all his questions. The inspector came to the same conclusion that the other experts had: that it was a weird phenomenon, certainly unpleasant, but not dangerous. He then departed, satisfied that the company had done everything it could have.

Calvin's boss made it clear that he was angry at Calvin's decision to call the health board without consultation. It had created an embarrassing situation, and it had been disrespectful. But he didn't punish Calvin in any way, and that was the last time they discussed the call.

A short while later, the previously scheduled performance-review meeting took place and Calvin was fired.

A Situation That Stinks

You can see where this is headed. Calvin, of course, lawyered up, and his story was that the company fired him because he "blew the whistle" about the rotten-egg smell. The case was litigated in federal court for two years.

Legally, we had a pretty good argument in defense. Complaining about a rotten-egg aroma isn't what the law usually contemplates for the public-policy exception to the at-will doctrine. Public policy protects an employee who is fired for asserting a legal right, doing what the law requires, or refusing to do what the law forbids. Merely complaining about a smelly basement that was not a health hazard didn't cut it.

What is more, Calvin had to prove that the real reason he was fired was because of his dime-dropping; not because of his lousy performance and attitude. This was going to be hard for Calvin and his lawyers to do, because the employer had documented his shortcomings and because the termination meeting had been scheduled before Calvin called the health department.

But even with the law on our side, the federal judge was unwilling to dismiss the case. He concluded that a jury could possibly find that the real reason the company fired Calvin was because of his so-called whistleblowing. So the judge allowed the case to head toward trial, but warned Calvin's lawyer that a jury would probably rule against him. At the judge's urging, we went to mediation, and ended up settling the case. Between legal fees and the settlement, the employer spent a ton of money. Bottom line: defending a lawsuit relating to the public-policy exception can be very expensive.

Unintended Consequences

The second major exception to at-will employment is the implied-contract exception. This is where the employer has effectively created a contract with its employees, even though it didn't mean to. In a word: oops.

You'd be amazed how often this happens. And it's usually a situation where a well-meaning employer (or its human-resources team) thought that it was merely laying down some rules to improve the workplace. Maybe you've spent time in a workplace like that. Maybe your company is like that now.

These are the workplaces where the employers try to legislate behavior with complicated, detailed rules and codes of conduct. Typically, they have felt burned in the past by problem employees who have taken advantage of their good nature or largesse. *Never again,* they say, as they set about crafting the personnel manual to end all personnel manuals.

Manual Overdrive

I can generally tell that this has been the case as soon as I start reading a company's manual. For example, they'll have an overly detailed bereavement-leave policy, explaining exactly what degree of relatedness is required for an employee to get time off to go to a family funeral. One of the most amazing examples I ever encountered was the bereavement policy at Alabama Agricultural and Mechanical University back in 2007 (the language dates back to 1993). Here it is verbatim in all its glory:

> Staff members shall, upon request, be granted up to three (3) days annually of bereavement leave for the death of a parent, spouse, child, brother or sister, grand parents [sic], grand parents-in-law, grandchild, son or daughter-in-law, mother-in law, father-in-law, brother-in-law, sister-in-law, step children, children-in-law, aunts, uncles, nieces, nephews, and first and second cousins. Other relationships are excluded unless there is a guardian relationship. Such leave is non-accumulative, and the total amount of bereavement leave will not exceed three days within any fiscal year. If additional days of absences are necessary, employees may request sick or annual leave, after providing an explanation of extenuating circumstances.

The AAMU bereavement policy is robotically impersonal. Imagine being a valued member of the faculty or staff, losing a family member, and then having to parse that gobbledygook. Imagine an employer docking an employee's pay after she lost her father because the travel involved pushed her over the "nonaccumulative" three-day limit? Absurd.

Another area where this sort of ridiculousness crops up is in dress codes. It happens when bad HR directors or clueless managers become flummoxed by the revealing or otherwise inappropriate outfits of their employees. *Uh-oh, we can't have that.* And then they start typing up a dress code, trying to regulate against every possible fashion faux pas. I once read the dress code of a banking association that actually specified what kinds of underwear could and could not be worn (thongs: no; granny panties and tighty-whiteys: yes; boy shorts: not yet invented). The Swiss banking giant UBS famously banned employees from having garlic at lunch or wearing "socks with cartoon motifs."

Progressively Worse

The worst type of personnel policy is the progressive-discipline policy, where the HR folks have legislated what type of bad behavior will get you in trouble at work, and what that trouble will look like. It's called "progressive" because the level of punishment tends to increase with the number and seriousness of the offenses. A first offense might merit a "verbal warning." ("Verbal" in this sense means "spoken," as opposed to "having to do with words." Otherwise, all warnings would be verbal, unless they were spelled out in handy pictograms as on an airplane's flight-safety card.) A second offense might lead to the so-called "written verbal warning," a fine piece of redundancy if there ever was. Subsequent offenses might merit probation, suspension, or termination.

Doesn't sound like a problem at first, does it? I mean, you can't have employees running around helter-skelter, willy-nilly, and pell-mell. (And why do we like these rhyming words to describe chaotic behavior? Never mind.) This is a place of work; we need to enforce certain codes of conduct so that people act professional. Right?

I get the underlying sentiment; I really do. But HR folks, well-meaning as they are, sometimes go too far with the legislating. This usually happens at places that have been burned by bad employees. Managers and human-resources people will long remember when a bad employee has taken advantage of the company's permissive atmosphere. And they'll vow to prevent it from happening again.

One of the problems with this is that you end up throwing out the baby with the bathwater. You're playing defense instead of offense. You're worrying more about the bad employees (who I trust make up only a small part of your workforce) than about the good employees (who make up the bulk of your team). Worse, you end up restricting or even effectively punishing the good employees in your quest to stop the behavior of the bad employees. You end up making it a less-fun place to work, which then makes it a bad place to work, which then drives away the good employees. Oops.

But the biggest problem with progressive-discipline policies is that they have the tendency to create semicontractual relationships between the company and the employees. Many courts around the United States have concluded that the presence of a progressive-discipline policy alters the at-will status by changing the terms and conditions of employment. In essence, the employer is setting forth the disciplinary policy and the employee is (at least implicitly) agreeing to be bound by it. Presto! You have a contract. Ish.

By creating this paradigm of discipline, you've now lessened your ability to fire employees at will. Ironic, isn't it?

A Customer-Service Breakdown

This scenario came back to haunt a coffee stand that had created a progressive-discipline policy for its workers. Host Marriott Corp. held the Dunkin' Donuts franchise in Terminal B at Boston's Logan Airport. This was a small, busy location serving harried air travelers before they headed through security.

One of their employees, a guy named Ferguson, apparently had a poor attitude and deficient customer-service abilities. One customer, unfamiliar with the Dunkin' offerings and out of step with the rush-hour bustle, asked a few too many questions of Ferguson. "What is the special coffee today?" he asked. Ferguson replied, "Nothing much." The customer stormed off, and a supervisor went after him to apologize. Afterward, the company fired Ferguson, understandably deciding that this was not the proper way to treat customers. Naturally, he sued.

Unfortunately for Host Marriott, its discipline policy was too specific, listing 11 specific acts that would lead to an employee being summarily dismissed. This list included things like fighting, drunkenness, gambling, and weapons possession. Strangely, it did not include mistreating customers. For this reason, a Massachusetts court allowed the lawsuit to proceed, concluding that the company should have first given Ferguson a warning under the policy. While the case eventually settled, it ended up taking years and costing hundreds of thousands of dollars to litigate. All because of a progressive-discipline policy.

In this case, a well-meaning HR department came up with a list of what it wanted to prevent—namely, drinking, fighting, gun-toting gamblers (apparently, they thought they were in the Wild West instead of a major metropolitan airport). But in drawing up their list of cardinal sins, they overlooked the basic concepts of being a good employee and treating customers right. They could successfully fire an employee for something as obscure as gambling (not a lot of room for a craps game in the tiny airport coffee stand) but not for interfering with the company's sole mission of serving customers well. This is a problem with progressive-discipline policies and many personnel policies in general. Better to treat your employees like grown-ups and focus on the company's purpose.

The Letter of the Law

The third and final major exception to the at-will doctrine is the statutory exception, where state or federal laws have explicitly limited an employer's ability to fire workers. These statutes generally prevent employers from firing people because of what type of person they are, or because they've done certain things.

The most common type of statutory exception comes from state and federal antidiscrimination laws, which make it illegal for an employer to fire a worker because of the employee's membership in a certain protected category. These categories vary among the states and the federal government, but they generally include race, color, national origin, religion, gender, age, disability, pregnancy, and sexual orientation. Firing someone for any of these reasons is illegal, and these laws give rise to many lawsuits. I discuss these categories in greater detail in Chapter 4.

Then there are the statutes that give employees freedom to do certain things without fear of termination. For example, the federal and state governments feel so strongly that employers must properly pay wages that employees are free to question and complain about wage issues without any risk of retaliation. Often, an employee who has a weak wage claim will have a successful retaliation case because the company mishandled the complaint. Employees who complained about discrimination enjoy the same protection.

Similarly, there are various whistleblower statutes that guarantee employees freedom from retribution if they report certain things to the authorities. (This is similar to the public-policy exception discussed above.)

Employers need to be aware of these statutory exceptions before deciding whether to fire an employee. I'll discuss many of them in the chapters to come. But your employment counsel will be able to explain all the different exceptions that apply to your company under the laws of your jurisdiction.

Conclusion

Most US workers are employees at will. And contrary to what you may have heard, the at-will employment doctrine is still alive and well. Of course, the freedom to fire at-will employees is not unfettered. Managers need to be aware of the public-policy exception, implied-contract exception, and statutory exception to doctrine. But as long as they keep them in mind, employers remain largely free to shape and refine their teams as they see fit.

The Freedom to Fire

These days, many people have developed a funny attitude about employment. They look at employment as a right, and they look at their jobs as entitlements. But that's not how our system works. You might have a right to work in general, but you don't have a right to a particular job. And when you start thinking about your job as an entitlement, you tend not to care as much about doing what it takes to keep that job.

What Is a Job, Anyway?

A job is a role within an enterprise that is generally necessary, at least to some degree, to that enterprise's survival. Jobs that are unnecessary tend to be eliminated over time.

The enterprise itself is the undertaking of the business owner; the word comes from the French word *entreprise*, meaning *undertaking*. The business owner (the entrepreneur) has undertaken risk to create a company that will make a product or perform a service for which the marketplace will pay a high-enough price to generate a profit. Yes, the enterprise needs the employees to do the work. But people too often forget that the employees need the enterprise—the entrepreneur's risk taking—to have those jobs in the first place.

In 17 years as an employment lawyer, I represented hundreds of employers in their dealings with employees. My bias is clear: I am a management-side lawyer. But even though my job was to litigate cases against employees, I never believed that the employment relationship should be an adversarial one. The best employers and managers I dealt with were always the ones who treated their employees respectfully and fairly.

But that doesn't mean that employees run the show. The employer has to be the one to set the direction of the enterprise, and the employees have to be willing to follow it. If they don't like that direction, they are free to leave. If that's how they feel, then they probably shouldn't be there in the first place.

It's not up to the employer to accommodate the whims and wishes of the employees. Their job is to do what the company needs them to do. And that all depends on why the company exists in the first place.

Finding Your Why

All the best companies have a well-developed sense of purpose. A mission. A reason for their existence. This isn't about some committee-developed mission statement filled with jargon and bromides. Instead, I'm talking about the reason that company does what it does, simply stated.

Southwest Airlines has a well-known mission: to make air travel accessible to almost everyone. (This was well stated in a recent ad campaign with the tagline, "You are now free to move about the country.") Every decision Southwest makes—about adding routes or buying planes or not charging for checked bags—is based on this underlying mission.

Apple also has a well-defined reason for being, best summed up in its classic "Think Different" campaign. Where other computer companies tried to make the user experience standard and uniform, Apple set about to focus on the individual and his or her natural creativity.

The importance of having a company understand and focus on its mission is best described in Simon Sinek's book, *Start with Why* (Portfolio, 2009). Sinek, a marketing consultant, explains that customers don't buy *what* you do; they buy *why* you do it. What you do and how you do it should flow from the why that underpins your company. Too many companies approach this backward.

Once you've figured out what your company's why is, your next task is to figure out who's going to help you fulfill that mission.

The Right Team

It's not enough to find employees who are qualified to do the job (and willing to take your money). Instead, you need to find people who believe what you believe, what your company believes. That's much more difficult to do. Anyone can hire someone willing to work for a paycheck. Even in periods of low unemployment, you should be able to fill just about any job as long you pay enough. But is that what you really want? I say no.

During my 13 years as an employer (as the owner of a small Boston law firm), I hired a total of 20 people: lawyers, receptionists, office managers, and a bookkeeper. Looking back, the biggest lesson I learned over that period was that you were far better off hiring people who actually believed in the mission of the firm, instead of people who were merely looking for a way to pass the days while earning some money.

Likewise with people whose only motivation is to advance their own careers. (Don't get me wrong: I have nothing against goal-oriented people who want to improve their standing in the world by excelling at their vocation. They are certainly worthy of respect.)

No, instead, you are much better off finding people who *really* want to work there, ideally because working there fulfills a need inside them to be a part of something bigger than themselves. Too touch-feely for you? I get that. But give me some leeway here for a moment. I'm not going to break out the guitar and start strumming folk songs for you. I consider myself a hard-core capitalist. I defended "The Man"—employers—against workers in court. I'm no softie for employees.

But I also learned the hard way about what works and what doesn't. Between my own experiences as an employer and my years of counseling employers in dealing with thousands of employees, I've learned a thing or two.

An employee who works solely for a paycheck or to advance his or her career will generally do what's necessary to get the job done. That employee—the hired gun—will show up at the right time, leave at the right time, complete the necessary assignments, and usually not cause problems. The hired gun can be a valuable member of your workforce.

But the hired gun will never be a great employee. Because at some point, he or she will tire of the work, or will want more money, or will want to move on to the next personal career stage. This is fine, all in all. Respectable, even. But not ideal for you, the employer.

Better for you and your business is the person who is *committed* to your company. But how can someone be committed to some kind of corporate entity? By believing in the same thing that the company itself believes in. That's the "why" of Simon Sinek that I mentioned earlier.

If you can identify the mission, the purpose, the driving force behind why your company exists, and if you can build your company around that why, then you can attract people who share that purpose, and who will want to work there because of what it says about them. People like that work harder, longer, and for less pay than people only working for a paycheck or to advance their careers.

What is more, they will be people whom you are less likely to ever need to fire.

Every company can be improved by figuring its why, aligning its business with that why, and hiring people who share that why. Jim Collins famously talked about getting the right people "on the bus" in his management classic, *Good to Great* (HarperCollins, 2001). But what if you have the wrong people on the bus?

Getting People Off the Bus

In the real world, your company is going to have some of the wrong people on the bus. So be it. And you'll be able to muddle along with these wrong people for quite some time. Eventually, some of them will quit, having become bored with their jobs or with your company, or having found something with higher pay or a better steppingstone for their careers.

But some of them won't. Some of them will linger, their work quality or quantity dropping off, their attitudes deteriorating. And their malaise will spread, infecting their coworkers and your workplace. And they'll keep collecting their paychecks.

These are the people you need to be able to get off the bus. These are the people for whom you need the freedom to fire.

(By the way, there's a whole other category of people that you need to be able to fire: the ones who commit certain acts. We'll discuss these people in Chapter 5.)

Basically, what we're talking about here is getting rid of the wrong people— the people who are wrong for your company. Now maybe they were wrong from the start, and you (or someone in your company) made a mistake in hiring them in the first place. Or maybe they were OK hires, but eventually went bad for whatever reason (they got bored or dissatisfied, they encountered personal problems, they had a midlife crisis). Either way, they're now wrong for your company and you need to get rid of them.

Nothing sucks the life out of a company faster than a wrong employee. They make work less fun for their coworkers. They give off bad vibes that customers can pick up on. They might not mean to do any of this, but they do it nevertheless.

They need to be fired.

No One Likes to Fire People

Just about every adult has been an employee at some point in their lives; most people spend most of their lives as employees. By contrast, very few people ever assume the role of employer. So there tends to be some misconceptions and stereotypes about what it means to be an employer.

Sitcoms and soap operas and comic strips and movies help perpetuate the myth of the unfeeling, callous, money-obsessed, slave-driver boss. When a fictional employee gets fired, it's usually at the hands of "The Man." The poor downtrodden employee gets his pink slip, and the uncaring boss goes off to the country club for martinis.

But in the real world, it's not like that at all. Firing people sucks. I have never once encountered an employer or manager who actually enjoyed firing people. It's highly stressful.

Now don't get me wrong; I'm not looking for people to sympathize with employers here. Obviously it's much more stressful for the person getting fired than it is for the person doing the firing. But don't underestimate the stress that firing causes the manager.

One of the things that helped me as a management-side employment lawyer was my own experiences as a manager and an employer. Over the years, I've had to fire six people: one when I was a branch manager at a bank (back before I became a lawyer); four as the owner of a law firm; and one as a household employer (I had to fire a nanny after five years of employment). Each one of those terminations caused me sleepless nights. (Again, to be clear: not looking for sympathy here. Yes, it was harder on the employees than on me.)

Theoretically, there must be some employers or managers who don't mind firing people; maybe some who even like it. But people like that wouldn't qualify as clients of mine, and people like that would never bother to read a management book like the one in your hands. So I think it's safe to assume that if you're still reading this and you're an employer or manager, you're going to find terminating employees to be one of the most stressful tasks you can undertake in your job.

Because of this, we had a rule at my law firm: we would never try to talk a client out of firing an employee. I believe that once a manager has made the difficult decision to fire someone, the relationship with that employee is already irreparably broken. At that point, it would be a mistake to try to talk the manager out of it. Instead, our advice would focus on how to do it the right way and minimize the risk of an expensive lawsuit.

We also had a corollary to that rule: we would never try to talk you *into* firing an employee. For all good managers, firing someone is a very difficult decision, not to be made lightly. Instead, we would advise the manager on how best to handle the situation, and wait until he or she comes to the termination decision naturally.

So when I say that you need to be free to fire wrong employees, I say that without fear that you will exercise this freedom willy-nilly. No one likes firing people. But when it becomes clear that it's time to let someone go, you need to be free to do it.

Taking Out a Contract

As we discussed in Chapter 1, this freedom is already tempered by the exceptions to the doctrine of at-will employment. There isn't anything you can do about the statutory or public-policy limitations. But you can avoid saddling your company with implied contracts that limit your ability to fire employees when you need to.

Similarly, you should also resist the temptation to enter into employment agreements with your employees. Some employers have their workers (usually executives) sign agreements because they think it's necessary. Others do it because they think they're buying protection for the company. But the problem with most employee agreements is that they limit—sometimes severely—the company's ability to fire the employee when it becomes necessary.

Many employee agreements have a term built in, often for a year with an option to renew. This is a problem, because decisions to fire don't necessarily coincide with employees' anniversaries. If your contract includes a promise to keep an employee for a certain period of time, you've just made it harder to fire that person if it becomes necessary.

The other big problem in employee agreements is the "for cause" provision. This is common (often boilerplate) language that defines the circumstances under which the employee can be fired without consequences. The problem is that cause is usually defined as intentional acts of fraud, embezzlement, or theft; intentional damage to company assets; conviction of a crime involving moral turpitude; or (my personal favorite):

> Willful misconduct or gross neglect of duties which, in either case, has resulted, or in all probability is likely to result, material economic damage to the company; provided that within 30 days after receiving notice of such misconduct or neglect, on which the board is relying to terminate you for cause, you are provided the opportunity defend yourself before the board.

The problem is that it's very difficult, if not impossible, to fire someone for cause under these definitions. For example, waiting for a conviction of a crime involving moral turpitude means you might have to wait months or even years before you can act, and you've basically imported the criminal-justice standard of "beyond a reasonable doubt" into the workplace. And the "willful misconduct or gross neglect" language with all the opportunities for notice and defense makes it almost impossible to satisfy the cause test.

What ends up happening in situations where an employee has cause provisions like this is the following: the company fires the guy anyway, claiming that it's a termination for cause even though it knows it can't make it stick. The guy lawyers up and sues for breach of contract, saying that the company actually fired him *without* cause, entitling him to some foolish severance package, including maybe a year's pay. The lawyers fight it out, costing the company time and money, and then the company settles for too much money. A good deal for the employee, a bad deal for the company.

The better course is to keep your employees at will, retain them for as long as they are good contributors, and fire the ones that go wrong.

Conclusion

To be able to run the kind of company you want to run, you need to have the right people on board. If you can find the right people at hiring time, all the better. But sometimes you will end up with the wrong people, and you need to be free to fire them, as painful as that is.

Of course, all firings have risk. Next, we'll talk about what these risks are.

Risky Business

The Perils of Employee Lawsuits

We've talked about why you need to be free to fire people, as unpleasant as that might seem. Now we need to talk about the downside to firing people, and the serious risks it brings to your business.

The point here isn't to dissuade you from firing the employees you need to fire; that would go against the central premise of *Firing at Will*. Instead, the goal here is to let you go into that important decision-making process with your eyes wide open, and to prepare you for the consequences. Because there will be consequences.

Let's start with the lesser consequences, and work our way up. First off: gossip.

Watercooler Talk

Employers hate gossip. There are few things that irritate managers and business owners more than the notion of employees standing around gossiping about what's going on within the company. These are employees getting paid for idle chitchat about things that are really none of their business.

But it's human nature to gossip—and no amount of policy drafting is going to change that fact. The truth is that people are always interested in stories, and drama, and conflict. And it's more interesting when they know the players involved or when they can easily relate to the dramas of strangers. People love soap operas—especially when they take place at their own workplaces.

I've had clients go overboard with trying to repress gossip. One employer I worked with insisted that an e-mail had to go out to everyone in the company explaining why a particular individual was fired. I thought this was a terrible idea, and I said as much. The executive told me that he was afraid that other coworkers would call looking for the departed employee, find him gone, and then start speculating and gossiping about what had happened. This was intolerable to the company official.

To avoid this, he drafted a defensive, self-serving statement about why the employee basically sucked, and why the company had decided to fire him. I told the client that if he sent this out, that e-mail would be Exhibit A in the fired employee's lawsuit. The client partially relented, removing some of the more-offensive parts of the explanatory e-mail. But he still sent it out, and I stopped doing any more work for that client.

Yes, gossip is a pain. But imagine the reaction of your employees if they suddenly received an e-mail saying that one of their own was fired, and why. What's the first thing they're going to think?

That could happen to me.

And no one wants to imagine their colleagues getting an e-mail saying why he or she was fired. An e-mail like that shows an amazing lack of sensitivity on the part of the employer. One of the themes throughout this book is that firing needs to be a private tragedy, not a public spectacle. Yes, nature abhors a vacuum, and if people don't have all the facts, they are apt to speculate. But that's life. Publicly dumping on a fired employee—even if it's totally justified by the facts—is a foolish way to avoid idle gossip.

Instead, it's better to work at cultivating a workplace where employees respect each other, and each other's privacy. But you can't do this by legislating policies. In fact, doing that could get you into a different kind of trouble.

Don't Hit the "Like" Button

Private, nonunionized employers usually don't need to worry about the National Labor Relations Act or the federal agency that enforces it, the National Labor Relations Board. The NLRB's purview primarily extends to disputes between employers and unions. But one of the times when the NLRB sticks its nose into the private, nonunion workplace is when an employer creates rules that prevent employees from talking with each other about their working conditions.

Section 7 of the Act gives all workers the right to engage in "concerted activities," a term that sounds ominous to employers and management. It's a broad term that usually refers to employees' getting together to form a union or engage in labor-related activities.

But it can also be used to describe workers' informally complaining about bosses or pay or other goings-on at work. Employees have a right to do that, and employers—even those in nonunionized workplaces—can't create policies restricting that right.

This has come up a lot recently with Facebook-related incidents. The scenario is increasingly common: an employee gets into some kind of beef with her supervisor, then logs onto the social-networking site and complains about her boss. The company then fires her. Problem? According to the NLRB, it may well be.

In a nonunion environment, an employer can fire an at-will employee for any reason, including an angry Facebook rant. (And before you start squawking about the First Amendment and freedom of speech, remember this: there's no such thing as the First Amendment in a private employment context. You need a state actor—a person acting on behalf of the government—to have First Amendment concerns.) But Section 7's concerted-activity clause creates a type of free-speech protection. And this is where Facebook comes in.

In the rash of recent Facebook cases the NLRB has brought against employers, the workplace was either unionized or the employer created a policy that restricted workers' concerted-activity rights (or both). Well-meaning employers created policies that prohibit employees from saying mean things about coworkers or supervisors on Facebook or Twitter or some other social-media site. By doing this, the nonunionized employer gave the NLRB a hook to go after it, because a policy like that can be seen as squelching concerted activities among the workers. (One employee bitching about his boss is a terminable offense, but two employees complaining together can be protected concerted activity. Makes sense, right?)

So far, most of these NLRB Facebook cases have ended up with the employers settling to avoid costly and distracting litigation. And in my opinion, the NLRB has been overreaching and outstepping its proper authority. But the main takeaway is that you'd better be careful about creating workplace policies that prevent employees from discussing work. Idle gossip may be a negative influence at the workplace, but trying to legislate it away with policies may get you into hot water.

The Morale of the Story

While concerns about a firing leading to office gossip might be overblown, terminations can hamper workplace morale. An employee getting fired is a high-stress event: obviously for the fired employee; less obviously, but nearly as much for the firing manager, and also for the employees who remain after the termination.

In a small office, the firing of an employee can send shockwaves throughout the workplace. If people don't know the reasons behind the termination, they will be filled with questions, uncertainty, and even fear. *Why did this happen? Will it happen to me? Is the company in trouble? Should I be looking for a new job?* It's natural for coworkers to worry when one of their own gets shown the door.

Even in a larger workplace, one or more terminations can lead other employees to wonder. And when there are questions and fear, employee morale can suffer. With a decline in morale, a team's productivity can decrease, causing real losses measurable in dollars and cents.

So a balance needs to be struck, and carefully. On the one hand, as I said, a termination should be a private tragedy. It's bad enough for an employee to lose her job; it's worse if she feels like everyone is talking about it and about her. On the other hand, you don't want to create an atmosphere of fear and doubt in your workplace. So what to do you do to strike that balance?

Pretend you're in the CIA.

No, seriously: one of the guiding principles in any intelligence agency is "need to know." In other words, you limit the output of information to those who have a need to know, and you only tell them as much as they need to know and no more.

In the real-world situation with the client I described earlier, the wrong-headed executive expressed concern about what salespeople would think when they called the fired employee to report an order and found that he was no longer there. Seriously, who cares? In that circumstance, those salespeople would happily give their orders to another employee without missing a beat. They might have a moment's curiosity about the other guy's fate, but life would go on for them.

But for the departed employee's close coworkers, the ones who worked side by side with him every day, their need to know would probably be greater. In their case, they probably need to know a bit more, but not everything. "We had to let John go," they might be told. "It just wasn't working out. I'd appreciate it if you'd respect his privacy on this." And you're done.

By the way, that conversation must be done one on one and face to face. You don't announce it in a meeting and you certainly don't send out an e-mail blast. Yes, meetings and e-mails might seem more efficient, but they are inappropriate and tone deaf.

After the Lawsuit Hits

Even if you take all the right steps, your termination of an employee may still lead to a lawsuit. The most obvious downside to a lawsuit is the expense of your attorneys' fees. (This is an area I speak and write about a great deal. We'll also discuss lawyer costs in Chapter 15.) But many companies and managers underestimate the true costs, financial and otherwise, of employee lawsuits. I want to paint a picture of this for you here. It's not pretty.

Your Legal Fees

The first thing that happens when an employee sues you is that you have to start paying your lawyers to defend the lawsuit. Frankly, if this is the first time you're talking to your employment lawyer about this matter, you're already in big trouble.

Ideally, you've been working closely with your employment counsel from the moment that the issue with this employee turned into a "situation." Countless times in my career, I've wanted to ask a client—or have actually asked—"Why didn't you call me sooner?" Ironically, the answer is always the same: because the company wanted to save money on legal fees.

The problem is that it's almost always less expensive for your employment counsel to deal with an employee issue early on rather than after the employee lawyers up and files a claim. Once the employee has gone to the trouble to engage a lawyer and that lawyer does the work necessary to initiate a lawsuit, it's much harder to unring that bell. They're more committed to the fight than they may have been before all that. Early resolution of an employee dispute is nearly always much cheaper than after a case begins.

One of the biggest problems about legal fees is the uncertainty. Nearly all American lawyers and law firms bill their fees on an hourly basis. In other words, they painstakingly track how long they work on your project, then add up all the hours and fractions of hours they've expended at the end of a month, multiply by the appropriate hourly rate, and send you a bill for that amount.

It's a particularly ridiculous way of buying anything, if you think about it. How often do you buy something without knowing the price of it until after it's too late to change your mind? In the United States and around the world, the billable hour is under attack as an antiquated (law firms began using it in 1919) and anti-client business model.

At my own law firm, Shepherd Law Group, we abandoned the billable hour in 2006 and instead priced our services up front. As of this writing, there are very few law firms in the United States who will defend employee lawsuits for you on a priced (rather than hourly) basis. But firms are increasingly embracing this notion. If you can find a firm who will properly price your work, you can remove a substantial amount of uncertainty.

The most common question I get from employers is, naturally, "How much will this cost?" It's a completely reasonable and fair question, and one that lawyers who bill hourly have an exceedingly hard time answering. Lawyers' rates depend primarily on three factors: geography, firm size, and seniority.

Hourly Rates

The first factor is geography: where is the law firm located? If your law firm is in a major American city, its rates will be higher. The highest rates will generally be found in New York and Washington, DC. Then come major cities like Los Angeles, Chicago, Boston, Philadelphia, Atlanta, and San Francisco. The rates will continue to drop as you move farther away from the coasts, and farther away from the big cities. For example, where a lawyer at a small firm in Boston might charge $350 an hour, a similar lawyer at a similar firm in Newton, a city of 85,000 people ten miles west of Boston, might only charge $225 an hour.

The next factor is firm size. Unsurprisingly, the largest firms in the country can charge the highest rates. What is more, there tends to be very little variance in the rates at the largest firms, at least within the same city. While the large firms don't actually collude in setting their rates (American antitrust law forbids that), they do set their rates based on what their peer firms are billing. When rates at the largest firms change, they tend to change at all the largest firms in fairly short order.

Medium-sized firms do the same thing. They look at what their larger neighbors are charging, and then come up with rates that reflect what they feel is an appropriate discount for going to a somewhat smaller firm. (This is not to suggest that the quality of work at the medium-sized firms is any lower than at big firms.)

Then the smaller firms charge at a level below their midsize peers. Again, this has no basis in the quality of service or representation; it's just a generally accepted convention. As the owner of a small firm, I found it frustrating to try to position ourselves as just as good as our larger competitors, while charging fees that were sometimes half that of our BigLaw counterparts. (This frustration helped push me away from hourly billing.)

The third factor is the lawyer's seniority: the number of years that he or she has been practicing. Particularly at the larger firms, lawyers' rates will increase in lockstep as the years pass. Rarely will two lawyers in the same firm and practice area and with the same number of years charge different rates.

While it is true that there is often correlation between years of experience and quality of work, the notion that all lawyers advance at the same rate is ludicrous. Predictably, the lawyers' salaries also rise in lockstep at the largest firms. In fact, outside of government service and unionized workplaces, I can't think of any other occupation where pay increases purely on a seniority basis.

These three factors—geography, firm size, and seniority—account for nearly all of the variance in lawyers' billing rates. Tellingly, they don't really take into account other factors, like likelihood of success, urgency, or the needs of the client.

Hours Spent

The other part of the equation is the number of hours spent on your case. This is the hard part of the calculation. It's hard because you don't know ahead of time how many hours your lawyer is going to take. Even worse, neither does she. Lawyers, like most people, stink at estimating their time. There are two reasons for this.

First, we tend to be optimistic, and think that it *should* take a certain amount of time to do something. We tend to forget that things will go wrong, adding much more time to the process.

Second, lawyers don't want to scare away the client, so they have an incentive to underestimate the amount of time (and thus, amount of fees) needed to get a job done. This doesn't mean that the lawyers are necessarily being dishonest; it just means that they're incentivized to shade their estimates on the low side.

The bottom line is that the hours—and thus the fees—will end up being more than you and your lawyer anticipate.

But enough about how your attorneys' fees are calculated. You want to know how much it is going to cost you in dollars and cents.

Ballpark Estimate

As I've said, it's hard to say. But if you get yourself a decent employment lawyer with a reasonable amount of experience, how much you're going to spend on the employee lawsuit depends mainly on how far the case goes. If the fired employee gets a lawyer who only sends you a demand letter—"Pay us money or we'll take you to court"—then you might be able to get out of it for a few thousand dollars.

But if the employee goes ahead and files a discrimination claim (the most common type of claims) at a state or federal agency, you're looking at easily spending five to fifteen thousand dollars on your own legal fees to start. (Of course, this doesn't include any settlement amount you might end up paying.) That should get you through the initial response stage. If the case progresses into the discovery phase—where the agency or the parties start asking for documents, answers to written questions, and witness depositions—then you're going to be on the hook for tens of thousands of dollars; maybe between $30,000 and $70,000. (I'll describe this whole process in greater detail in Chapter 11.)

If the case is filed in state or federal court, those numbers go up. You can quickly approach $100,000 in legal fees. And if the case goes to a jury trial, $150,000 to $250,000 is not beyond the pale. The only good news here is that less than one percent of employment cases actually make their way to a jury trial. (We'll talk about court cases in Chapter 12.)

The Other Side's Fees

So far, I've only been talking about the costs of your own lawyers. Unfortunately, you might end up being responsible for the employee's attorneys' fees, also.

In the United States, legal fees are usually borne by the parties themselves; in fact, this is known as the "American rule." Contrast this with the United Kingdom, which uses a "loser pays" rule (also known as the "English rule"). Many commentators believe that this is why the United States is a more-litigious society than the United Kingdom is, despite the similarities in our common-law legal systems.

Under the British loser-pays rule, plaintiffs bear much more risk in bringing a lawsuit; they might end up being out of pocket for the defendants' attorneys' fees if they lose. In the United States, a plaintiff can often get a lawyer for free (working on contingency, receiving a fee only if they prevail) with no worries about paying for the defendant's legal fees.

In most employment lawsuits, the law allows for a modified version of the American rule on attorneys' fees: the loser pays both sides' fees, but only if the loser is the employer. In other words, there's even more incentive for an employee to sue.

There's virtually no chance that the plaintiff employee will have to pay the company's legal bills; and if the former employee wins, then the company will have to pay his lawyer's fees, as well as its own. This is true in employment-discrimination cases, wage-and-hour cases, and many whistleblower cases. Of course, to have this rule kick in, the employee has to actually win the case, either before a state or federal agency, or in front of a judge (or judge and jury) in state or federal court.

So when you're considering the possible costs of employment litigation, you need to take into account the possibility that you'll be responsible for the employee's legal fees on top of your own.

Other Costs

When adding up the costs of an employee lawsuit, don't forget to include four other big hits your company will take: time, distraction, morale, and possibly publicity.

Time

The legal costs are always a big deal when it comes to employee lawsuits. But what companies and managers almost always underestimate is the amount of time that they will need to spend defending the lawsuit. Time spent investigating. Time spent strategizing. Time spent talking to lawyers. Time spent talking with coworkers and supervisors.

All this time takes away from the true business of the company: the making of the widgets, or the providing of the services. Throughout my career as a management lawyer, the thing that my clients resented the most, even more than the money spent, was the time wasted dealing with the lawsuit.

And take my word for it: I'm a pretty nice guy. My clients liked me (especially when they weren't paying me by the hour). I don't come across as particularly "lawyerly" (which is never a good thing). And yet more often than not, I would catch the undertone of "Oh, it's you" in their voices when they answered my phone calls. Not because it was me, but because they didn't want to waste more time dealing with the litigation. In a perfect world, the firing of an employee is supposed to be the *end* of a problem. Dramatic, perhaps, but a definite end. But all too often, when litigation arises, it's just the *beginning* of the problem.

Distraction

Hand in hand with the time spent is the distraction that employee litigation causes. In the course of investigating the case and preparing the defense, members of my legal team would have to come to the client's offices and have meetings with various supervisors, executives, HR people, and coworkers. Sometimes, depending on the office layout, people would see us arrive with our briefcases and binders and think, "Here come the lawyers." You could see it on their faces. (In practice, we'd try not to look too much like lawyers, often leaving the suits and ties at home. But they'd know anyway.)

Then comes the scheduling dance, as complicated as a Virginia reel. The client would have to arrange to have the employees come meet with us, sometimes in a particular order that we'd require. We'd hole up in an obscure conference room and wait for the HR manager to deliver the next individual to us. Most of the time, the people would show up with trepidation plain in their expressions.

We'd then go through the same explanation that we'd given countless times before: nothing to worry about, sorry to take you away from your work, need to find out all the facts, we're counting on your discretion, please don't discuss this with your coworkers or anyone else, we'll have you back to breaking rocks in a jiff. But it's a major distraction, and it tends to mess them up for the entire day.

Put in a couple of days of interviews like that and the client never wants to see you again. By the time you're well into the litigation, the client is so tired of the time-wasting that it's far more motivated to settle the case. It's a war of attrition, and one that the employer often loses.

Morale

There's a morale element to all this, too, just like we talked about earlier with the actual firing. Knowing that one of their own is now the opponent in a lawsuit against the company is unsettling to employees, even if that former employee wasn't particularly well liked. The other side in a lawsuit is The Enemy, who needs to be defeated. It's human nature to imagine oneself in that position, and that's an uncomfortable feeling.

Combine this with the gossip issue we talked about earlier and you've got a major workplace-morale problem. It's natural for people to want to talk about the lawsuit; people find litigation interesting, which is why there are so many lawyer TV shows and movies.

This decreased morale and increased gossip has a real effect on workplace productivity, one you could conceivably measure in dollars and cents. For example, Gallup estimates that actively disengaged employees cost US companies $300 billion in lost productivity. When assessing the true costs of employment litigation, you need to account for its effects on productivity and morale.

Publicity

The last cost we'll talk about is that of publicity. Most of the time, this isn't much of an issue. Companies get sued all the time by disgruntled employees, so a lawsuit at your company is unlikely to be newsworthy. It might show up eventually in a lawyers' trade paper, like *Lawyers Weekly*, but no one reads those besides lawyers.

The exceptions are when you have a well-known company, a well-known individual, or an unusual and perhaps shocking set of facts. Only then do you need to worry about publicity from the litigation.

Employers tend to worry more about publicity than they need to. Publicity will usually have much less of an effect on your company than the other costs we've discussed. But in the right circumstances, it could be a factor.

If it does come up, make sure you're prepared. It's the natural reaction of companies and their lawyers to favor a bland "no comment" from an anonymous spokesperson. In my experience, reporters usually want to give a balanced story and would prefer to have the company give its side. Merely reciting that the company doesn't comment on personnel matters is often a wasted opportunity to stick up for the company.

Conclusion

To put it briefly, employment litigation sucks. It's expensive, time consuming, and morale busting. When deciding on your strategic approach to an employee lawsuit, make sure you pay attention to *all* the costs involved. Being aware of these costs is crucial to your understanding the risks of firing an employee.

Speaking of risks, next we'll talk about the 30 riskiest employees to fire. Letting go one of them has a greater chance of leading to the costs we've talked about here.

The 30 Riskiest Employees to Fire

Firing an employee is never without risk. But some firings are riskier than others. They're riskier because the employees have potential claims available to them that other employees don't have.

This is not to say that the employees on this list are more likely to sue than others. (Anyone claiming that women or blacks or gays or handicapped people are more likely to sue *because* they are women or blacks or gays or handicapped people is hopelessly misguided.) But if they choose to sue, they can create more problems than other fired employees can. That's why they're riskier.

The list, which I've developed over the years litigating employment cases for employers, is not a ranking; it's in no particular order.

Take special care in firing the following employees:

1. Female Employees

Let's be clear about one thing. Discrimination laws, for the most part, do not create special categories of people who are held in higher regard than their colleagues. Title VII of the Civil Rights Acts of 1964, which outlaws sex discrimination, does not say that you can or should treat women more favorably than men. Similarly, although you hear the phrase all too often, Title VII contains no reference to "reverse discrimination." If a man gets discriminated against in the workplace by women, it's not "reverse discrimination"; it's just "discrimination." Women have no more rights when it comes to discrimination than men have.

But that said, firing a woman is riskier than firing a man. Shouldn't be, perhaps, but it is. And the reason for that is that in the real world, guys don't win sex-discrimination lawsuits. Sure, every once in a while you'll hear of some outlier case where a man sought to become a Pilates instructor and was turned down in favor of, well, someone who *looked* like a Pilates instructor. But that's a rarity. Most of the time when a man brings a sex-discrimination lawsuit, it's a loser coming out of the gate.

So while legally, a woman has no more employment-discrimination rights than a man does, in the real world, she starts out with a better chance of succeeding in court than her male counterpart does. What is more, most plaintiff-side employment lawyers know this, so they'll be more encouraging of and more likely to bring a case on behalf of the female employee. Bottom line: firing a woman carries a greater risk than firing a man, all other things being equal.

2. Pregnant Employees

On my bookshelf in my office, I have an employment-law book written specifically for managers. It's not the greatest thing in the world, but it does have a chapter title that always amused me: "Never Fire a Pregnant Employee." Now while that's overstating things a bit, it's not a bad thought. Pregnant employees may very well be the riskiest of all employees to fire.

Pregnant employees are protected from employment discrimination by the same laws that protect against sex discrimination. When you think about it, this makes sense, since only women can actually get pregnant. Weirdly, it used to be that pregnancy was considered a disability, and the protections for pregnant women fell under the category of disability discrimination. Then it finally occurred to people that since pregnancy was necessary for the survival of the species, maybe it wasn't really a disability after all.

Pregnancy discrimination is different from all the other kinds of job discrimination in one important respect: the employee doesn't really need to show an actual bias to win. You see, at the heart of nearly all discrimination cases is the need to convince the agency, judge, or jury that the employer acted with bias (what lawyers call "animus") in his or her heart. In other words, to win a race case, an employee needs to convince the factfinder that the company fired him *because* of a prejudice against him on account of his race. (Obviously, since the court can't see inside the employer's heart, it needs to infer that bias from the employer's actions or statements.)

But pregnancy is different. First of all, no one's really *against* pregnant women. It's a safe bet that each of us has a pregnant woman to thank for our very existence. So proving antipregnancy bias is very difficult to do.

But the bigger factor is that pregnancy often causes employers to act differently, irrespective of any bias. For example, I once represented a small, family-run service business. During an economic downturn, they had to let go one of the two female clerks in a particular department. Both were equally qualified, but one of them was three months pregnant. The employer realized that if they laid off the nonpregnant employee, the pregnant one was going to go out on maternity leave six months later, and they'd be left with no one in that department. So they did what they thought was the sensible thing and fired the pregnant woman. And got sued for pregnancy discrimination, no surprise.

My client was very upset. They couldn't understand how anyone could accuse them of being biased against pregnant women. The CEO of the company was a woman and a mother, and several of her grown children worked there, too. The company was very pro-family and pro-women. They would never discriminate against a pregnant woman.

But under the law, they had done just that. They chose to fire the pregnant woman *because* she was pregnant—not because they had a bias, but because they knew that they'd be shorthanded later if they fired the nonpregnant one. That was enough to give the employee a winning case, and we settled on the eve of trial.

Firing a pregnant woman: very risky.

3. Recently Pregnant Employees

Same reasons apply as for pregnant employees. Also, maternity leaves are a major hassle for employers, especially smaller companies. Firing an employee right after she returns from leave has the danger of looking like a punishment for taking that time off. Plus, new mothers are often sleep deprived and frazzled. If you fire a new mother citing poor performance, it won't be hard for her to argue that her performance was related to her recent pregnancy.

So how long should you wait before firing a recently pregnant employee? There's no bright-line rule. The right answer is: however long it takes for a new mother not to be thought of as a "new" mother.

4. Employees on Family or Medical Leave

Related to pregnancy issues are maternity leaves and other family and medical leaves. For larger employers in the United States (with 50 or more employees within a 75-mile radius), rights to these leaves are protected by the federal Family and Medical Leave Act. The FMLA gives employees the right to take up to 12 weeks of (unpaid) leave a year for parental reasons (that is, the birth of a new child), medical reasons (to take care of your own health issues), and family medical issues (to take care of a close relative's health problems). The law requires you to reinstate the employee after the leave ends.

As luck would have it, economic or restructuring issues often arise at companies while an employee is on leave. When those issues result in the on-leave employee being let go, this raises a serious possibility of a lawsuit. It's not that you can never fire an employee who's on leave; it's just very risky.

5. Employees Just Back from Family or Medical Leave

This is analogous to recently pregnant employees. It's not uncommon for an employee returning from a family or medical leave to have performance or attitude issues upon returning to work. When these issues give rise to a decision to terminate, you're playing with fire. If you let go an employee who has recently returned from leave, it's not difficult to infer that the firing is a punishment for having gone out on leave in the first place. At best, it gives the fired employee another claim to bring.

How long must you wait then? It's the same as with recently pregnant employees: however long it takes before you stop thinking of them as having recently returned from leave. Six months maybe, or a year? Depends on the circumstances.

6. Employees Who Recently Asked for Family or Medical Leave

They don't have to be on leave or recently returned from leave to fall into the higher-risk category. Even an employee who recently asked for leave triggers the protections of the FMLA and state leave laws.

7. Older Employees

Unlike the other major discrimination types—race, sex, and national origin—age-discrimination rights do not apply to everyone equally. There is a cutoff; you acquire these rights on your fortieth birthday, and not a day before. If you're a 39-year-old web site designer in a company filled with 22-year-olds, and they fire you because you're so (relatively) freakin' old, and they even tell you that ... nothing you can do about it. Just as you can't vote before your eighteenth birthday, you can't bring an age-bias claim until you blow out 40 candles.

These rights aren't absolute, of course. For example, if you're a 42-year-old web site designer at the same company and you get fired while the 22-year-olds all keep their jobs, you might have a valid claim. But you'll probably lose, because 42-year-olds rarely win age-discrimination lawsuits, since no one really thinks of 42 as "old." (Of course, they can still bring the lawsuits, so firing anyone 40 or over carries that increased risk.)

On the flip side, just because you're older doesn't mean you've got a legitimate age claim. If you're 62 when you get fired in a reduction in force, but the other 60-somethings keep their jobs, and most of the other folks laid off are in their thirties and forties, you're probably going to lose your age-discrimination case.

But in terms of risk, firing someone who has seen 40 birthdays is more dangerous than firing someone who hasn't, all things being equal.

8. Employees Who Are a Different Race from Most

Race is the original protected category under Title VII. As with gender and women, it's important to remember that there's no such thing as "reverse" discrimination. Blacks and whites (and members of any other race) all enjoy the same protection against race discrimination under Title VII and the state-law analogues.

But as women are more likely to bring and prevail in a sex-discrimination lawsuit, minorities are more likely to raise a race-discrimination claim than whites are. Similarly, experienced plaintiffs' attorneys are likely to talk white would-be plaintiffs out of bringing a race claim. For this reason, firing an employee of a different race is riskier than firing a white employee.

9. Employees Who Are a Different National Origin Than Most

Title VII also protects against national-origin discrimination. That means you can't fire someone or make an employment decision based on the country that the employee or his or her ancestors came from. As with race and sex, it does not mean that employees with different national origins enjoy greater rights than other employees. But when you fire an employee whose national origin is different from that of other employees, that termination carries a greater risk.

10. Employees Who Are a Different Religion from Most

Another major protection that Title VII creates is against religious discrimina-tion. Hiring, firing, and other employment decisions cannot take into account an employee's religious beliefs. For example, you might run a bakery where all of your employees happen to be Catholic. You might like that because everyone belongs to the same church and has that in common. But if a Methodist applies for a job, you can't exclude her because of her religion. (There are limited exceptions, such as for religious organizations.)

What if an Orthodox Jew applies for the job, but says that he can't work on Saturdays? Although that restriction may prove to be an inconvenience for your bakery, you can't refuse to hire him because of that religious belief. Instead, you would have an obligation to reasonably accommodate his restriction. The exception would be if it was absolutely necessary for the person in that position to be able to work on Saturday. But it's a safe bet that an Orthodox Jew wouldn't apply in the first place for a job that required Saturday work.

While it's not common, some employees may profess to have religious beliefs that they really don't have. For example, an employee might claim to be a Wiccan to get out of work on Halloween, or claim to follow the beliefs of the Jedi to avoid working on May 4 ("May the fourth be with you"). But the law only protects employees with sincerely held beliefs.

When a client of mine was thinking about firing an employee, one of the questions I would ask is whether the employee had different religious beliefs from the other employees. If she had, that raises the possibility of a religious-discrimination claim, and makes the termination riskier.

11. Employees Who Are a Different Ethnicity from Most

Ethnicity is a vague term. Some people use it to refer to race, while others use it to refer to national origin. The US government doesn't consider "Hispanics" to be a race, and it isn't technically a national origin. But you can't fire somebody because he is Hispanic or because he is not Hispanic. This would be ethnic discrimination. Firing an employee with a different ethnicity qualifies as a riskier termination.

12. Employees Who Have a Disability

In 1991, Congress passed the Americans with Disabilities Act (ADA), drama-tically increasing protection from discrimination for workers with disabilities. The statute, which was revised and strengthened in 2009, makes it unlawful to make hiring and firing decisions because of a disability.

The law defines a "disability" as an impairment that substantially limits a major life activity. That mess of cumbersome legalese basically means any physical or mental limitation beyond a temporary minor condition, such as a strain or sprain. If an employee claims to have a disability, it's a decent bet that a court or agency will agree.

The key question is whether the disabled person can perform the essential functions of the job. The essential functions are the main activities that a person in this position absolutely has to be able to do. If there is a reason-able accommodation that the employer could make that would enable the employee to do the job, then the employer has to make that accommoda-tion and can't fire or refuse to hire the employee for that reason.

An accommodation is reasonable if it doesn't create an undue burden on the employer. For example, moving a desk from the second floor to the first floor to accommodate an employee in a wheelchair is a reasonable accommodation; installing an elevator is not.

Firing an employee with a disability creates a much higher risk of litigation, especially if the employee can make a credible argument that the disability had anything at all to do with the decision. While it doesn't mean that you should never fire a disabled employee, you need to know that it's a higher-risk termination.

13. Employees Who Have a Mental Disability

Nearly every workplace has an employee who everyone says is a little crazy. Sometimes, this can be an endearing quirk. Other times, this can be a drain on productivity and morale. Eventually, it may come time to fire the "whack-job employee." But if it turns out that his or her odd nature is the result of a genuine mental or emotional condition, the employee would likely qualify as disabled under the ADA.

Keep in mind that you can't fire an employee just because her coworkers fear that she might "go postal" one day. If the employee has never actually shown violent tendencies, then the employer is not free to fire her because of her condition.

Where this becomes a bigger problem for employers is when employees have (or claim to have) a less obvious condition. Examples include depression, post-traumatic stress disorder, and bipolar disorder. Sometimes, an employer may not even learn about the condition until after deciding to fire the employee.

A person with a mental disability is entitled to a reasonable accommodation in the same way that a person with a physical disability is. For example, a museum employee suffering from Tourette's syndrome who occasionally blurts out expletives might be assigned to a location where he would cause less disruption. But if one of the essential functions of his job was to interact with schoolchildren, an employer would not be required to keep him in that position.

When an employer has reason to think that an employee has a mental disability, firing that employee carries substantially greater risk.

14. Employees Who Are Thought to Have a Disability

To be a higher-risk termination, an employee doesn't actually have to have a disability. The law also protects employees who are *perceived* to have a disability. If you think that an employee "has something wrong with him," and that "something" if true would be a disability, then he enjoys the protection of the ADA even if it turns out that there's nothing wrong with him. This is more likely to come up with mental disabilities, where an employee might be perceived to be manic or bipolar (that is, "he seems crazy").

15. Employees Who Associate with Someone with a Disability

Less common is the protection against discrimination for employees who are associated with a disabled person. For example, if an employee has a son with a disability who might require care in the future, the employer can't fire or refuse to hire that person on that basis. Firing an employee who associates with a disabled person is a higher-risk termination.

16. Employees Who Are Alcoholics

Under the ADA, alcoholism is considered a disability. On the other hand, drinking alcohol and being drunk are not considered disabilities (with good reason). This duality can cause all sorts of problems for an employer. If a worker is caught drinking or being drunk on the job, it's completely appropriate to fire him. But if he then claims to be an alcoholic, you've got yourself a potential disability-discrimination claim. Make sure you document well the drinking or drunkenness.

17. Employees Who Are Gay or Lesbian

Sexual-orientation bias is not yet recognized under federal law. In the past fifteen years, the number of states protecting against it has risen from five to twenty-one states (plus the District of Columbia). Increasingly, firing a gay or lesbian employee—even in states that don't yet have sexual-orientation protection—is more likely to lead to litigation.

18. Employees Who Are Transsexual

Similarly, states are slowly changing their laws to protect transsexual employees (or employees with other gender-identity issues) from discrimination in the workplace. Even without statutory changes, experienced plaintiffs' lawyers may successfully be able to argue that gender-identity discrimination is a subset of sex discrimination. Firing a transsexual employee is a higher-risk proposition.

19. Employees Who Have Ever Complained About Discrimination

I call this the "irony" category. Over the years I've seen dozens of cases where the discrimination claims were marginal at best, but the employees were then able to bootstrap their lawsuits with decent retaliation claims. You see, once an employee complains about discrimination, the mere fact of complaining places them into a high-risk category. If that person then suffers some form of adverse job action, it isn't too difficult to infer that the original complaint had something to do with the job action.

The problem is, once an employee complains of discrimination, it is often very hard to salvage the employment relationship. No employer or manager appreciates being labeled as a racist (or sexist or whatever). A decent employee-side lawyer can easily tie together those resentful feelings to the adverse decision that was made after the complaint.

Too many lawyers like to show off their education by tossing out a little Latin. It's very annoying. But in this case, there's a well-known Latin phrase that applies better than any English counterpart: *Post hoc ergo propter hoc.* It means "After this, therefore because of this." (I actually learned it on *The West Wing*, not in law school.) It is usually a fallacy, but too often it carries the day in a retaliation lawsuit. Even when the underlying discrimination case was a loser.

Use extra caution in firing an employee who has already complained of discrimination.

20. Employees Who Were Sexual-Harassment Victims

In some states, sexual harassment has its own statute with protections for employees. In other states, and under federal law, sexual harassment is considered a subset of sex discrimination. As with discrimination claimants, employees who complain of sexual harassment are protected from retaliation. Firing someone who has complained of sexual harassment is a very dangerous proposition. We'll discuss this in much more detail in Chapter 14.

21. Employees Who Are Veterans or Active Service Members

While you don't generally see a lot of veteran-discrimination cases, it can be a risk factor if the employee served in the military. More common these days are cases involving active-duty servicemen and servicewomen returning to the workplace. The federal law USERRA (Uniformed Services Employment and Reemployment Rights Act) gives protection to members of the military. In general, you can't fire people because they've been serving in the armed forces, and you usually have to keep their jobs waiting for them when they get back. An exception is when you legitimately eliminate the job, such as for economic reasons. In any event, firing an active-duty service member is a high-risk termination.

22. Employees Who Didn't Get Paid for All Their Time Worked

The most common mistakes employers make involve employee pay. The states and the federal government take pay very seriously, and employers generally have very little wiggle room when it comes to pay issues. If you didn't properly pay an employee, and then you fire them, you pretty much guarantee that you're going to get a demand letter and maybe a lawsuit.

And the problem with pay cases is that if you actually owed the money, then there is no defense to not paying it. In fact, most states award multiple damages and attorneys' fees to employees with successful wage cases. So when you decide to fire an employee, first make absolutely sure that you have fully and correctly paid that employee. We'll talk more about these cases in Chapter 13.

23. Employees Who Didn't Receive All Their Overtime Pay

Overtime is governed by both state and federal law, and all employees who are not exempt are entitled to overtime pay if they work more than 40 hours in a single workweek. This law dates back to the 1938 passage of the federal Fair Labor Standards Act (FLSA). The Depression-era statute was originally designed to encourage employers to hire additional workers rather than pay overtime, as a way to combat high unemployment.

Over the past 70 years, though, it became so expensive to hire new employees that employers decided that it would be more cost-effective to pay overtime instead. But the statute is complicated and inflexible, and employers frequently commit technical violations. As with wage claims, an employee who hasn't been properly classified under the FLSA or who hasn't received all the overtime pay she was entitled to is a high-risk termination target. Similarly, any employee who has complained about overtime pay makes for a riskier firing.

24. Employees Who Are About to Receive a Bonus, Commission, or Option Grant

Sometimes employers will fire employees right before they were due to receive a particular payment, such as a year-end bonus. They will point to the bonus policy or plan that specifies that one must be employed on December 31 to qualify for the bonus, and then fire the employees on December 30. It's generally a bad idea. Those employees can bring claims for breach of the covenant of good faith and fair dealing, a jumble of legalese that basically means that the employer screwed them out of their bonuses. This makes their termination high risk.

25. Employees Who Ever Complained About an Illegal Practice

As with retaliation claims, it's dangerous to fire an employee who has complained about an illegal practice that the company may have committed. This employee will often enjoy whistleblower status, making it risky to fire him.

26. Employees Who Have Criminal Records

Many states have laws that protect criminals from being discriminated against because of their criminal past. Some states, such as Massachusetts, make it very difficult for an employer to even ask about a candidate's criminal record. If you fire an employee with a criminal record, you give them a possible claim to bring against you.

27. Employees Who Have Drug Problems

Employees with drug problems do not enjoy the same disability-discrimination protections as alcoholics do. But they can qualify for protection if they've stopped using illegal drugs and have entered a treatment program.

28. Employees Who Are Involved with Union Organizing

It's a fact of life that employers don't like union organizers, and quite frankly, they shouldn't. But if an employee is involved with union organizing and she then gets fired for poor performance, you can pretty much guarantee that she and the union will bring a grievance or an unfair-labor-practice claim against the employer. Union organizers are definitely high-risk terminations.

29. Employees Who Are Related to, Friendly with, or Live Near a Lawyer

This one is only a little bit facetious, and there's usually no way to know whether an employee has easy access to legal help. The real question an employer faces is whether the employee about to be fired is likely to lawyer up. With some people, you can tell that they're the type to run out and find an attorney. If so, that firing carries a greater risk of litigation.

30. Employees Who Are Fired with Less Retained Dignity Than They Could Have

Finally, any employee who is fired in a way that lessens the amount of dignity he or she retains afterward may end up suing you. It's usually avoidable. We discuss the concept of Retained Dignity, and how to maximize it, in Chapter 7.

Conclusion

These 30 employee types all carry a higher risk when you fire them. That doesn't mean that you shouldn't fire anyone on this list. But it does mean that you have to be even more careful when you do it. We'll cover how to do that in Part II of this book.

The Whys and Hows of Firing

Here's where we really get into it: the nitty, and the gritty. First we'll cover the specific reasons for firing employees, including those times when you absolutely have to let an employee go. Chapter 6 is the heart of the book: a step-by-step guide to performing the actual termination. Next I'll introduce you to a new and important concept: Retained Dignity. We'll talk about the value of creating a paper trail, and discuss what you should write down, and also what you shouldn't.

Sometimes employees deserve second chances; we'll discuss when it's a good idea and when it's a big mistake. Finally, we'll cover that unfortunate phenomenon of a poor economy: the layoff.

Why Me?

The Reasons for Firing

As I said before, I would never try to talk an employer out of a decision to fire an employee. For the employers I dealt with, this kind of decision was always very difficult. The notion that employers and managers actually enjoy firing people is absurd and found only in fiction. Any outliers who take pleasure in terminating their people don't last very long as employers.

Ending someone's employment is a major event in the life of that person, and even the least sensitive manager realizes that it needs to be handled carefully. Feelings of compassion (for the employee) and concern (for a possible lawsuit) mitigate the reasons for the termination. Once the employer decides to pull the trigger, it marks a determination that the reasons for firing were truly serious enough. The relationship between the employer and the worker is irreparably broken.

How does it get to this point, and how do you know when it's time to end the relationship? As always, it depends on the individual and the circumstances. But there are some things you should consider that can help you make the decision.

Performance Anxiety

Most often, when it's time to fire an employee, it has less to do with the individual committing a particular offense, and more to do with just generally sucking. Firing people for performance reasons is as old as employment itself. And by and large, it's a fair and understandable reason. Granted, often the lousy employee disagrees with the employer on the assessment of suckage. But that has more to do with how performance is measured.

In most jobs, performance is measured subjectively. If you're an overpaid starting pitcher who gives up two base runners every inning and six or seven runs every start, then your performance objectively stinks; those measurements are empirical and unchallengeable. Similarly, if you're a salesperson who always ends up at the bottom of the monthly revenue tables, there's not a lot of interpretation involved.

But most people today work in jobs where their performance is measured qualitatively rather than quantitatively. And qualitative measurement by definition involves subjective opinions. Where there are people's opinions, there are bound to be people disagreeing. Especially when an employee's livelihood is on the line.

It's important in those situations for the manager to be able to explain and justify her assessment of poor performance. Relying on facts (this customer complained, that shipment was late, this software was filled with bugs) is better than depending on adjectives and adverbs (he doesn't do good work, she's a lousy secretary, they don't work well together). Otherwise, these subjective judgments are prone to being challenged by the fired employee. And if the firing turns into litigation, those adjectives and adverbs might end up looking too subjective to support the termination.

How Bad Is Bad Enough?

The other problem with performance-based terminations is that performance measurements often span months or even years, rather than just depending on a particular incident. Of course, if the incident is so serious as to merit termination, that's different. The banker who makes a clerical error that results in thousands of dollars irretrievably leaving the bank is going to get fired. (That happened at the bank I used to manage before becoming a lawyer.) The sous-chef who forgets to close the freezer door, causing the restaurant to throw out a thousand dollars' worth of steaks, is going to lose his job.

But bad performance is more often a cumulative thing—a pattern of lousy work that builds up over time. None of the screwups alone would justify termination, but months of them in a row would.

This creates a problem for the employer: at what point do you decide to terminate? How much bad performance is too much? Again, you have the issue of subjective judgment. The answer is going to depend on a number of things: frequency of performance problems, their severity, the effects of the bad performance, the attitude of the employee, the morale of the employee's group, and so forth.

In Chapter 9, we'll talk about deciding when it makes sense to give the poor performer another chance, and when it's better to make a clean break.

Disloyalty Oath

Another major reason for termination is employee disloyalty. As with performance, this can arise in varying degrees. But in general, a disloyal employee is more dangerous than a poor-performing one, and you should usually be quicker to fire the disloyal one.

An age-old principle of common law is that employees owe a duty of loyalty to their employers during the course of their employment. Sometimes, you might hear this described as a fiduciary duty; but though the two concepts are related, they are not really the same thing.

A fiduciary duty is relationship of trust by the fiduciary to act on the beneficiary's behalf. A lawyer, a trustee, a corporate officer, a partner, a broker, and a doctor all have fiduciary relationships with the people who put their trust in them. The fiduciary has to put the beneficiary's interests ahead of his or her own interests.

An employee's duty of loyalty is similar, but not quite at that level. The employee has a more balanced relationship with the employer. Basically, a worker can't do something that benefits himself or herself at the expense of the company. For example, an employee can't self-deal, or divert a business opportunity away from the employer to his or her own benefit.

This issue comes up most often near the end of the employment relationship. The prudent employee will have a new job lined up before quitting the current job. That's fine, even though it generally involves some sneaking around and fake haircut and dentist's appointments (for interviews). (It's probably unavoidable, though. When an employer learns that an employee is thinking of leaving, the employer will just as likely show him the door right away. So some sneaking around is to be expected.)

Where people run into problems is when they try to serve two masters. In other words, the salesperson who discourages the prospect from buying from his current employer because he knows he'll get a better commission from his new employer. That's called diverting a corporate opportunity, and that's a classic violation of the employee's duty of loyalty. Of course, after the employee has left the current employer, that duty vanishes.

■ **Note** Keep in mind, though, that an increasing number of employers are effectively extending this duty by tying their employees up with noncompete and nonsolicitation agreements, preventing them from taking business with them to their new gigs.

The bottom line is that an employee shouldn't be doing something that harms the current employer. When an employer learns that an employee is being disloyal, termination is completely appropriate.

The duty of loyalty also arises in other circumstances, even before an employee is planning on leaving. For example, I once had a case where a female employee of one my clients had been having an affair with a married coworker. The guy ended up getting fired for an unrelated reason, and then got a new job at a competitor. Apparently, though, he was having a hard time making sales at his new job. So his girlfriend started sending him leads— diverting work away from her employer to her boyfriend's new company. Needless to say, she was very quickly terminated.

By the way, an employer can sue an employee for breaching the duty of loyalty. But it rarely makes financial or managerial sense to sue a former employee; it will almost never be worth it, and it's very hard to win damages. But employers would ask me all the time, "Can't we sue her?" My answer was typically, "Yes, but you don't really want to." It's a natural reaction for an employer to want to go after the disloyal employee. But it's a waste of time, effort, and money.

Seven Deadly Workplace Sins

Besides poor performance and disloyalty, there are seven deadly workplace sins—seven capital crimes—that in my book (which you're reading now) require the firing of an employee. They are:

1. Workplace violence

2. Dishonesty

3. Theft

4. Criminal activity

5. Insubordination

6. Sexual harassment, if it's serious or willful

7. Discrimination, if it's serious or willful

Let's examine each of these deadly sins in turn.

1. Workplace Violence

Employers need to have a zero-tolerance policy when it comes to workplace violence. This isn't a schoolyard or the streets. People will have their differences at work as in any other place. But they need to deal with those differences in a mature way.

If an employee physically assaults someone else at work—coworker, supervisor, vendor, or customer—they have to be immediately fired. No exceptions. That might seem like an overreaction if the actual fisticuffs were particularly minor. No matter. An employer has an obligation to keep its people safe, and permitting any type of physical violence in the workplace is completely unacceptable.

So too is the threat of violence. Again, people can have serious disagreements; that's fine. But as soon as an employee tells a coworker that he's going to kill him, or beat him up, or kick his ass, that employee has to be out of there, even if he "didn't really mean it." There is absolutely no room in the workplace for violence, and it's the employer's responsibility to enforce that. No second chances here.

2. Dishonesty

The next deadly sin is dishonesty. This one's a bit trickier than violence. It's also a lot more common.

Unfortunately, it's human nature to tell lies. But there are varying degrees of dishonesty. People do it all the time. "Do these pants make me look fat?" "No, honey." Or: "Oh, hi. So good to see you." Or: "Sure, I love beets." All lies.

But there are lies and then there are *lies*. The small white lies are a sort of social lubricant that enable us to avoid hurting people's feelings or causing bigger problems: "Yes, honey. Very fat." (*Dodges flying hairbrush.*) These small lies are usually borne out of a desire to be polite or avoid conflict.

But bigger lies about work are a different story altogether. Instead of avoiding conflict, they break down trust at the office. Trust is the lifeblood of the workplace; a good enterprise cannot operate without trust. Trust is what allows a manager to give employees the autonomy to do their jobs on their own without grown-up supervision. If a manager can't trust his employees, then he has to stoop to the level of supervision that is paternalistic and oppressive. This makes for bad management.

Lying—really lying—undermines that trust. Once the trust is gone, it's impossible to run a good business or be a good manager. So dishonesty needs to be dealt with in the strictest manner. If an employee lies about work—meaning a lie to the degree that it calls into question whether you can trust that employee in the future—it's time for that employee to go. Yes, maybe the employee made a mistake; an error of judgment in telling the lie. But if that lie causes you to doubt whether you can take the employee's word in the future, the relationship is irreparably broken. Time to show the employee the door.

I once had a client whose employee lied to one of its customers, ostensibly to keep the customer happy. The guy told the customer that it was paying a certain margin, which is exactly what it wanted to hear. Ironically, this didn't change the ultimate price the customer was paying; it just pleased the customer to know that it wasn't paying too much of a premium.

When my client found this out, it immediately fired the employee. Its trust in the employee was now in question. (He had also put the customer's trust of the company in question.) Without that trust, there was no way my client could supervise the employee without scrutinizing every last transaction. If the employer couldn't trust the employee and give him the autonomy necessary to do his job, there was no reason to keep him around.

Lies are rarely mistakes. You don't accidentally lie. A lie is intentional. There might be an understandable reason for the lie, such as to keep a customer happy or to cover up an actual mistake. But if trust in that employee is the casualty of the lie, then the employment relationship is permanently damaged.

There's another aspect of this as well: the "broken windows" theory. This is the notion developed by criminologists James Q. Wilson and George Kelling (and made famous in Malcolm Gladwell's *The Tipping Point*[1]) that says that people will take less care of an environment if it looks like the owners don't care. (For example, an abandoned building with broken windows is more likely to be vandalized than one whose windows are intact.) If coworkers

---

[1] (Little, Brown and Company, 2000).

see that an employee has lied and gotten away with it, they might get the message that the employer doesn't care about honesty. That doesn't mean that they'll start lying too, necessarily. But it becomes more likely that they won't take their jobs or their employer as seriously.

Lies at work kill trust. So you need to fire the liar. (Sounds a bit like a bumper sticker, I know. But it makes it easier to remember.)

3. Theft

While we're talking about liars, we should also look at their first cousins: thieves.

It's a related problem: someone who steals from the workplace is someone who can't be trusted. What is more, it means that they have no respect for the employer of the workplace, or that they put their own interests ahead of the team's.

First, let's be clear about what we're talking about. Taking some paper clips or a Post-It note or two is not stealing. I'm talking about real stealing, as in committing a crime. Most employees would never dream of stealing from their employers or anyone else. But unfortunately, some do. Why? Some people feel they are entitled to things they can't have. Others do it because they have some kind of a psychological problem. Some can't tell right from wrong. Some just need the money. All of them need to be fired.

As with lying, stealing is a problem for the employer because it destroys trust. (And you lose your money or stuff.)

Once you learn about the theft, you need to act quickly and decisively. There is never any legitimate justification for theft. The only question is whether it happened and who really did it. Of course, before you take any action, you need to get your ducks in a row.

First, you need to investigate, so that when you confront the accuser, you're sure of your facts. It won't do you any good to go making an accusation that turns out to be wrong. (This happens to me all the time at home. I accuse the cleaning service of stealing some minor possession of mine that's gone missing. Then I find it, right where I left it. Actually, it's a decent method for finding stuff. And I never actually say anything to the service.) So first make sure the thing you're missing is really missing.

Then make sure you know who did it. This might take some detective work on your part. But be quick and discreet about it. You shouldn't start a witch hunt over the missing strawberries like Captain Queeg in *The Caine Mutiny*.

Once you're certain about the theft and the thief, then it's time to confront the person. And fire him or her.

Unfortunately, I've had some experience in this. Not the stealing part; the firing-for-theft part. A while back, I ordered a thank-you gift for the family in Australia who had hosted me when I lectured there on advanced legal pricing. But I had some trouble confirming that it had shipped, and the company I bought it from was unhelpful and difficult to reach.

Late one night, I decided to go online and check my corporate American Express account, to see if the charge had ever been processed. Even though I owned the law firm, it wasn't my practice to review the charges on the Amex account; I had an office manager whose responsibility that was.

When I logged into the account, I quickly found the charge for the gift. (It was delivered soon after; that's not important to the story.) But I also noticed the charge next to it: a $30 taxi ride in New York City. At first I thought that this was odd, but then I remembered that one of my lawyers had been in New York City for a hearing around that time. But then I noticed that the charge hadn't been made on his card; instead, the office manager's card had been used. It also turned out that New York had been a red herring: the cab ride had been in Boston; the cab company was apparently headquartered in New York.

So now I'm thinking, "That's weird. I don't remember sending my office manager anywhere in a cab." So I pulled up all the charges on the office manager's card. Another cab ride. And another. And a bar tab. Plus supermarket charges. And pharmacy charges. The expression on my face went from curious to uncertain to utterly shocked. My office manager had been embezzling from me for the previous five months. Uncool.

It turned out that she'd worked there embezzlement-free for about a year and a half, all the while being entrusted with the finances of our small law firm. Then one day she used her Amex card for a cab ride. Three weeks passed, and she didn't get caught. (She had obviously realized she'd get away with it because she knew I didn't scrutinize the records.) Then the next cab ride. And so on.

Over the five months, her pattern of charging increased in frequency until she was using my firm's plastic as her daily method of buying groceries and personal items. She never made any large purchases; the most was for $75 at the supermarket. But it ended up totaling over $800. Not enough to cause serious damage, except to the trust I'd had in her.

I spent the rest of the night investigating. I went back two years on her charge card to make sure that there were no others. I also looked at the cards of my other employees: nothing. I checked our other accounts. Lastly, I checked to make sure that she hadn't made matching deposits in our checking account. I thought it was possible that she didn't have her own card and was using the firm card as a personal card, then repaying the firm. Then it wouldn't technically be stealing (if the firm didn't lose any money), but it would still be an unacceptable use of her card without permission. No dice. No deposits.

The next morning, I told one of my associates and asked her to join me when I confronted the office manager. (We'll talk more about how to do the actual termination in the next chapter.) When confronted, the office manager didn't deny it. She lamely contended that others had also done it (my research had already shown that to be false), and she seemed surprised by the total amount. She seemed even more surprised when I told her she was gone.

I watched her as she cleared out her desk and then sent her on her way. Before she left, I told her to think long and hard about whether she had taken anything else that I hadn't yet discovered, because if she had and didn't tell me, I would go to the police. She insisted (and I later confirmed) that she hadn't.

In the end, I was able to deduct the stolen funds from her final paycheck. (This can be tricky; we'll discuss this later.) So the firm didn't actually end up losing any money. But the cost to me of the betrayal of trust was high, not to mention the distraction and energy spent investigating.

But the decision to terminate was an easy one, even though my employee felt like a member of my family. (We were a very close firm.) Once I determined that she had stolen from me, I knew I could never trust her again. And this meant she could never work there again.

4. Other Criminal Activity

There are plenty of crimes besides theft that employees can commit. But if you learn that your employees are committing crimes, you need to make them ex-employees. Even if they're not committing the crime against the company or its workers. In fact, even if the crime has nothing to do with work.

This goes beyond the concept of "what you do on your own time is your own business." If your employee is engaged in criminal activity, you do not want that person working for you. The criminal behavior shows you the character of the person, and it calls into question whether you can trust him or her.

Of course, if the criminal activity is taking place in the workplace, that's a no-brainer. If someone's selling drugs in the mailroom, see you later. If an employee is running a child-porn ring on your company's servers, *hasta la vista*. If someone slashes the tires of a coworker's car in the employee parking lot, you fire the slasher without hesitation.

In this country, we are fortunate to have a system designed to protect people from being falsely convicted of crimes. There is a presumption of innocence, and a jury needs to be convinced beyond a reasonable doubt that the accused committed the crime. This is a good and important safeguard, but it does not apply to the workplace. To fire someone because they're committing crimes, you do not need to be certain beyond a reasonable doubt. You just need to be reasonably sure.

So what if an employee is arrested and accused of committing a crime that has nothing to do with work? What do you do? Do you fire him at that point, or do you wait until the criminal justice system has finished its process and found him guilty? The answer, unfortunately, is "it depends." It depends on the crime, it depends on the person, and it depends on the circumstances.

As the employer, you need to decide if the accusation and arrest of the employee make it impossible for you to accept having him in your work-place. Obviously, if it's a serious crime like murder or rape, you don't need to feel like you have to stand by him for the years it might take until the trial is over. But even if it's a lesser offense, like driving under the influence, you may decide that you don't want that type of employee representing you out in the world.

A caution, though: different states have different rules about making employ-ment decisions based on arrest or conviction records. Before you fire somebody because of a criminal matter, you need to talk it over with your employment counsel.

A final thought on crimes and misdemeanors: if the crime takes place at work, you will have a decision to make about reporting it to the police. With some crimes, especially those involving violence, you should report it. With others, like my office manager's embezzlement, it's going to be up to your best judgment. In my case, I got my money back, she lost her job, and she lost the ability to use our firm as any kind of a job reference. There was no need to get the police involved.

5. Insubordination

I mean insubordination in the real sense of the word. Flippancy is not insubordination. (If it were, I would be unemployable. On second thought, maybe that's why I run my own business.) *Insubordinate* means "defiant of authority" or "disobedient." If an employee acts insubordinately, she is undermining her manager and the company itself. No one needs that sort of person on their team. Basically, what she's telling you by her insubordination is that she doesn't want to be working there. Fortunately, you have the power to grant that wish.

Tolerating insubordination also sends the wrong message to the rest of the workplace. If you're willing to accept defiant behavior like that, they reason, then maybe you have doubts about your own authority. Pretty soon, they will too.

But true insubordination is actually fairly rare. Employees will have disagreements with their bosses from time to time. Mere disagreements or even arguments aren't necessarily insubordination. Refusing to do what a manager says is insubordination. As a manager, you shouldn't go looking for insubordination in every conflict with employees.

6. Sexual Harassment

Sexual harassment, in a nutshell, is unwelcome sexual conduct in the workplace. It is a very serious problem, and can lead to a lawsuit that can be very difficult to defeat. So how you deal with a harasser is very important. If you learn that an employee has been sexually harassing someone in the workplace (usually after a complaint and an investigation), you need to fire him (or her, but almost always him) right away. That won't necessarily avoid a lawsuit from the victim, but it's the right thing to do.

As with many things, there are varying degrees of severity and intent in the realm of sexual harassment. Technically, forwarding a dirty joke by e-mail can constitute sexual harassment, although that alone is not going to lead to a successful harassment lawsuit. Nor should it (on its own) lead to an employee's termination. Termination might be overkill for boorish behavior that lacks malice and that could be cured with training.

On the other hand, any sexual harassment that is serious or willful should be met with immediate termination. (We'll discuss sexual harassment in greater detail in Chapter 14.)

7. Discrimination

If you have an employee who is discriminating against someone else because of that person's race, sex, age, disability, or other protected category, you should fire him or her. But as with sexual harassment, there are varying degrees of severity and intent. If an employee does something discriminatory that isn't that serious and didn't appear willful, then training or some other discipline might be the better solution. But if the discrimination is serious or willful, then you don't want to keep around an employee like that. (We'll discuss discrimination in greater detail in Chapters 11 and 12.)

Conclusion

If your employees are performing badly enough, termination might be the only option. If you have employees showing signs of disloyalty, then it's time to show them the way out. And if you have employees who commit one of the seven deadly workplace sins, you need to fire them.

So now you know whom to fire. But how do you actually do it? That's the subject of Chapter 6.

How to Fire an Employee

It's brass-tacks time. This chapter covers all the details to help you plan and conduct a termination. How do you actually do the deed?

Don't Fire Angry!

You know the scene in *Groundhog Day*, when Bill Murray's character kidnaps the groundhog before committing suicide by driving a truck off a cliff? (Since the point of the movie is that he keeps reliving the same day, it's not really as dark as it sounds.) As he's driving, he holds up the groundhog in his lap with its paws on the wheel, making it look like the critter is steering. With the Punxsutawney police chasing them, Murray shouts to the groundhog, "Don't drive angry!"

It's good advice.

It's also good advice not to "fire angry." It's a fact of life that anger often plays a role in the final decision to fire an employee. Usually, the problem employee has done something (or *not* done something) to make you angry. OK, fine; that's what problem employees do. But you don't want your anger to be the thing that causes you to fire the employee. When we're angry, our judgment is impaired. It's harder to think straight and clearly. And straight and clear thought is essential to making a wise decision.

It is always a good idea to give yourself a chance to calm down. Firing an employee is a high-risk decision, and you want to make it in a levelheaded way. After you've calmed down and thought rationally about it, if it still seems like the right choice, then fire the employee.

Is There a Preferred Time or Day for Firing?

You might be surprised at how often I get asked this. People seem to think that there's a magic day or time (or both) that makes firing easier, or less risky. And some pundits have written articles suggesting one thing or another, with usually conflicting advice. Such as: *Better to fire on a Friday, so that the person has the weekend to calm down afterward.* Or: *Never fire on a Friday, because then the person will just stew over the weekend. Monday's better.*

Same with the time of day. Some people advocate first thing in the morning: get it out of the way early, then the fired employee can use the rest of the day to look for a new job. (Like that's going to happen.) Others suggest waiting till the end of the day, so that there are fewer people around to see her as she miserably clears out her desk.

It's a Bad Day No Matter What

I'm sorry to tell you that there's no black-letter rule here. You can make arguments for doing it on any day that ends in a y, and at nearly any time of day. Personally, I prefer whatever day makes the most sense. Once you've made the calm, coolheaded decision, it doesn't make sense to wait very long after that for the "perfect day."

I really don't buy into the Monday or Friday logic. The employee is going to be upset about the termination no matter what day of the week it is. He's not going to immediately jump back into the workforce and start trying to find a replacement job, so don't worry about that factor in making your decision. Whether he has the weekend coming up to think about it is irrelevant; he's going to be thinking about it no matter what day it is.

Not Miller Time

As for the time of day, I'm afraid I also don't have a hard-and-fast rule for you. I've done it myself early in the workday, and I've done it at the end of the day.

There's something to be said for getting it over with early, but that really only benefits you. It's not a fun feeling carrying on like everything's normal when you know that you're about to drop the hammer. Getting it done earlier in the day at least minimizes your stress. For the person getting fired, it's not going to hurt any more or less because of what number the hour hand is pointing to.

One reason for waiting till the end of the day is that there might be fewer people around when you do it. Perhaps you can arrange it so that the ex-employee-to-be is one of the last ones to leave, so that after the termination, there's no walk of shame for the fired employee. That makes sense.

But it's tricky. You don't want to have the person unexpectedly leave before you have a chance to have the termination meeting; that would unnecessarily prolong your stress. And if you set up a late-afternoon meeting for no good reason, the individual might suspect what the meeting's about. In the end, you might be better off doing it earlier in the day. Plus, the employee might want the opportunity to say goodbye to coworkers, depending on the circumstances.

A Lousy Christmas Present

One consideration that's worth keeping in mind is the broader time frame. For example, it's never a good idea to fire someone right before Christmas. That then becomes the story: "Those bastards fired me two days before Christmas." That never sounds good, and it may actually increase the risk of a lawsuit.

Other days to avoid: The employee's birthday. The day after her mother dies. The day after the Red Sox win the World Series. The basic rule here is this: be sensitive about the timing, but don't worry about the "rules" about times and days.

Where Do You Do It?

Depends on your workplace. If your office has a door that closes and gives you some privacy for a meeting, then that may well be the best place. A conference room that is similarly private is also a good bet. But a conference room with interior windows (and no shades) that is visible to the rest of the office is not a good choice. Nor is the employee's desk or cubicle, surrounded by his or her colleagues.

As I've said before, the firing of an employee is a private tragedy, not a public spectacle. The more public the setting, the more likely that the employee is going to be embarrassed (or at least *more* embarrassed). More embarrassment means less dignity (which we'll talk about next chapter), which means more chance of a lawsuit. So keep this in mind when you choose the locale.

Closing the Door

One thing about offices. Some companies have open-door practices, where people rarely close their office doors. My law firm always had this practice. I felt that it contributed to teamwork and collegiality if people felt free to stop by and discuss something. Yes, it perhaps got in the way of productivity from time to time. For that reason, there are plenty of law firms (and other companies) who maintain a practice of closing their internal doors. But who would want to work there?

At my firm, we only closed our doors for two reasons. One was much less ominous: when we had a deadline approaching and needed to buckle down and work without interruption. But you always made a big deal about it, telling everyone (this was a small office, mind you) what you were doing and why your door was going to be closed. This let people know not to bother you, and also kept them from worrying about the door closing.

But the second reason for closing the door was a more stressful one: because I was going to have a serious and private conversation behind that door. Generally, one could assume that it had to do with discipline, performance problems, someone quitting, or someone getting fired.

If someone came to my office and asked to close the door, I knew right away that he or she was giving notice. (I'm not saying that this happened all the time, but over a 13-year period, this occurred a few times.) But if I invited someone in and then closed the door, the message was already delivered. In that case, the door closing was the equivalent to the "we need to talk" line in a romantic relationship. Whatever is said after that line is bound to be bad.

So closing your door, especially in a small office used to having doors open, could send a message about the termination as clear as posting a sign. I'm not saying keep your door open—the privacy aspect is too important for that—but be sensitive about the messages you're sending.

Can I Get This to Go, Please?

What about outside the office? In the movie *Jerry Maguire*, the title character's boss takes him out to lunch to fire him. Jerry comments on this as soon as he realizes he's being let go, noting the assumption that he'd be less likely to make a scene in a public place. This is silly. You shouldn't be worried about a scene. In fact, the employee (like Jerry Maguire) will likely be more offended by that notion. No—better to do it at the office, but make a real attempt to do it in private.

Should You Have Witnesses?

This is an important consideration. As with so many things, it depends. In my own personal experience, I've done it both ways. It all comes down to trust. How much do you trust the employee you're about to fire?

Flying Solo

I once had a bookkeeper at my law firm. She was a lovely person, very pleasant to deal with, always responsive and on time. Unfortunately, she kept making errors in her arithmetic. (And for some reason, the error always revealed that we had *less* money in the bank than I'd previously thought. You'd think that statistically, in the long run, we'd sometimes have *more*.) It finally got to the point where I just couldn't rely on the reports she gave me, so it was time to let her go.

But I had no reason to not trust her as a person. There was absolutely no animosity between us. When I brought her into my office and closed the door, it was clear from the look on her face that she knew what was about to happen. She was accepting of her fate, and didn't put up any defense. She teared up a bit, thanked me (believe it or not), and then quickly left the office without a word to anyone else. Having that particular meeting alone was perfectly fine, because I trusted that she wasn't going to make a scene or get into a fight.

Having a Wingman

On the other hand, with the office manager I had to fire for embezzlement (see Chapter 5), a witness was imperative. Given what she had done, I had no reason to trust her anymore. I had no idea how she would react to her termination, which (unlike the bookkeeper) was going to come as a surprise. Better to have some company.

The main reason to have another person in the room with you is to protect you from allegations that you conducted yourself inappropriately during the termination meeting. A firing is a highly charged emotional event, and the person being fired might grasp at any weapon available to fight back with.

This is especially a concern if the employee is female and you're male. It's very easy for a distraught and irrational former employee to claim that you made an inappropriate sexual advance or remark while you were alone in the room. This isn't being paranoid; these things happen in the real world (although not too often). Having a witness helps remove the possibility of a bogus claim like that.

Same thing applies if you're a woman and the fired employee is a man. Although harassment claims of this variety are much less common, they are not unheard of.

And it's not just about gender and sexual harassment. In any situation where the fired employee could make a claim of discrimination, it's a good idea to have a witness to back you up. That way, if the employee suddenly fights back with allegations that you made a racially or ethnically insensitive remark, it's not just "he said, she said."

Safety First

The other reason for having a witness is to minimize the chance of physical violence. If the person about to be fired has a temper, it's a good idea to have someone with a relatively imposing stature on hand to keep the employee from getting any ideas.

Workplace violence is an incredibly important issue. According to the Bureau of Labor Statistics, one in ten workplace deaths are homicides. I'm not an expert in workplace-violence issues, and the subject warrants its own book, rather than a couple of paragraphs. I will say that you should always be aware of the possibility of violence, use common sense, and do what you can to avoid riling up the fired employee.

Don't Gang Up

The downside to having company in the meeting is that the other person's presence can make the terminated employee feel like he's being ganged up on. There is a different dynamic in a room where it's two on one. That said, I feel that most of the time, it's still better to have another person with you. But you can do things to mitigate the employee's feeling of being ganged up on.

Not to get too touchy-feely here, but body language and seating arrangements can actually make some difference. If possible, have your witness sit in a neutral space, maybe off to the side (but not behind the employee). This may not work in your office, so don't worry too much about it. In a conference room, all three of you might sit at one end of the table, with the employee on one side of you and the witness on the other.

Again, to be clear: you don't need to obsess about these details. Just be conscious of appearances.

What Do You Say?

In many ways, this is the hardest part: how do I tell someone that I'm firing her? I've had employers and managers ask me to draw up an actual script for them, something I always refused to do.

Instead, I'd advise them on things they should say and things they shouldn't say. Over the phone, I'd hear them scratching down notes and I'd worry that they would turn it into a script anyway. I can't hear you scratching notes now, but please: don't use a script. If you find it helpful to write down some words or phrases ahead of time, fine. But for heaven's sake don't use any kind of script during the actual termination. That will appear disrespectful and weak.

Picking Your Verb

Some people get all worked up about the word *fire* and worry about finding the right euphemisms. Forget about all that. In the history of Earth no one has ever felt one iota better because they were "terminated" instead of "fired." *Termination* always struck me as a lawyerly, jargony word anyway.

Personally, I've favored the phrase "let go." It doesn't have the loaded power of *fire* but it leaves no doubt about what just happened. "Lay off" can be misleading because it connotes a reduction in force; that is, firing someone because there isn't enough work or the company has too many employees.

Another way you can go is to say, "It's time for us to go our separate ways." I find this appropriate when the reason for termination is to remedy a recent bad hire—when it never really worked out. There's no rule that requires you to actually say "You're fired," or some variant. When you tell an employee that it's time to go our separate ways, he'll understand that he's just been fired.

Don't Leave the Door Ajar

We talked about the office door; now I'm talking about the metaphorical door. And this is one of the most important pieces of advice I can give on the termination conversation. It is imperative that you don't conduct the meeting in such a way that the employee believes that the door's still open for you to change your mind. For this reason, I always recommend that managers use the past tense. It's a done deal, a fait accompli. "We've made the decision to let you go."

What you never want to do is use the future tense: "We're *going to* let you go." If you do that, the employee might think that there's a way to get you to change your mind, and might infer a lack of resolve on your part. If the employee thinks the door's been left open just a crack, he might try to stick his foot into it. He'll start trying to convince you to change your mind, usually with some promise to do better. Then, when you slam that door fully closed, it can hurt even more. It's much better to leave no doubt that this is a final decision, and that it has already been made.

Don't Get into a Debate

You need to remember what the purpose of this meeting is: to tell the employee she's fired. It is not to have a mini-trial about all the things she did wrong. This is not the time for you to justify your actions or your decision. You did your justification work beforehand when you made the actual firing decision. And if it all goes wrong, you'll have a chance to justify yourself later, during the lawsuit. The termination meeting is not the place for it.

If you start going on and on about the reasons for termination, you will be inviting a debate. It's human nature for the employee to defend herself when she feels she's been unfairly judged. A debate is the last thing you want here.

This kind of debate leads to greater hurt feelings, and a greater sense of unfairness. This increases the risk of a lawsuit. Instead, your brief monologue is more along the lines of "We've decided to let you go. The reason is _____. We wish you the best of luck with your future."

Is Honesty the Best Policy Here?

This might sound obvious, but when you're firing an employee, you need to tell the truth.

Actually, that's only half right. Well, closer to two-thirds.

Anyone who's ever watched *Law and Order* or been in a courtroom knows by heart the oath that witnesses take before testifying:

> Do you swear to tell the truth, the whole truth, and nothing but the truth?
>
> I do.

Makes sense. It really breaks down this way:

1. You'll tell the truth

2. You won't leave anything out, and

3. You won't add any lies.

For a witness in a court proceeding where the goal is to get justice, this three-part standard for testimony is the best way to do it. But the workplace is not a court of law. The goal isn't necessarily justice. Instead, the goal is to run a workplace the right way and to avoid unnecessary and costly litigation.

Firing an employee is a high-risk situation. When you do it, you should follow only the first and third prongs of the testimonial oath:

1. You'll tell the truth

3. You won't add any lies.

What you say could come back to haunt you and the company in a lawsuit, so make sure that everything you say is the truth. Otherwise, if it can be shown that you lied at this point, it's not hard for a judge or jury to think that you or the company lied at other points. Cases are won and lost on credibility more than they are on laws and lawyering.

But forget about the "whole truth" part (the "you won't leave anything out" part). You have no obligation to tell the fired employee absolutely everything, and you almost certainly shouldn't. For example, you might fire somebody because their performance is bad and because, frankly, you just don't like them. In the termination meeting, you should leave out the "frankly, I just don't like you" part.

Managers and HR professionals understandably want to take the edge off these high-stress meetings. There is a desire to sugarcoat the termination a bit, to relieve the tension and perhaps allow the employee to save some face on the way out. That's fine.

But resist the temptation to say anything that's not true. It's not worth it. Instead, sugarcoat the termination by leaving out the part of the truth that might be incendiary and hurtful. A terminated employee is entitled to know why he or she is being fired, but not every single reason.

Keep the whole truth to yourself.

Do I Have to Give the Employee Something in Writing?

Ideally, no. Many employers are under the impression that they're required to give fired employees a written termination letter. Worse, they often think that this is the place where they write up all the bad things about the person and justify the termination.

That's a terrible idea.

Letters like this are very dangerous. First, because the words are written, they tend to sting more. I'm not sure I know why this is; I just know that it's true. Probably because the written word has more of an air of permanence; it's there in black and white, rather than something that's spoken and more easily forgotten. Plus, the recipient has the opportunity (often taken) of rereading it over and over; no good can come of that.

What is more, the letter is destined to be Exhibit A if the employee ends up filing a lawsuit. And if the letter isn't perfect, a decent plaintiff's lawyer can wrap that thing around your neck (metaphorically, of course) during the litigation.

Don't give the employee extra reasons to be upset with you; stick with the spoken word.

One point: some states do require an employee to give fired employees something in writing. For example, Missouri requires employers to issue a "dismissal letter" to a fired employee who requests one. The letter, which has to be given within 45 days of the request, must state what service the employee performed and what the reason was for the dismissal. This is a ridiculous law that helps no one; certainly not the fired employee. But if you're an employer in one of the states that requires something in writing, comply. But the less said the better.

Is It Ever Appropriate to Fire Someone by Phone, Letter, or E-mail?

No.

It amazes me how often you hear of people doing this. For example, in the movie *Up in the Air,* George Clooney starred as a roving corporate terminator (non-cyborg division). His job was to go to companies' offices and fire people. But during the movie, his own job became jeopardized by a desire to conduct terminations "more efficiently" by videoconference.

Even though this was a fictional story, companies are increasingly looking for ways to streamline the termination process. But this is not an area where efficiency is an important goal. You might spend less time conducting the actual terminations, but you'll end up with unhappier fired employees, which will mean more lawsuits. And lawsuits are never efficient.

Leave Your Layoff Message After the Beep

A few years ago, Freshfields, a gigantic London law firm, laid off 14 trainee solicitors. Like most major law firms in 2009, Freshfields had to trim its staff in response to the worldwide economic crisis. What makes them different is the way they did it: by leaving the unlucky 14 employees a voicemail. Not only that, but instead of partners doing the deed, they staffed it out to HR.

Apparently, English firms respond to bad press the same way their American cousins do: by defending the indefensible. A *Daily Mail* story quoted a firm flack:

> It was not ideal from our perspective but we were trying to get the information out as soon as possible. We did not want to take the chance of them hearing first from someone else.

How thoughtful. To be fair, Freshfields gave the laid-off lawyers a severance to soften the blow. How much? you might ask. Well, the firm spokesperson wanted to be discreet:

> Those people that we have not retained received an ex gratia payment. We feel it would not be appropriate to confirm the exact amount.

Of course, of course. And it's not like that word would get out. A secret's a secret, old chap. Oh, wait. What's this? The internet? Bloody hell!

Turns out the firm gave severance payments of a whopping £700.

Apparently, "ex gratia" is British for cheap.

This cowardly method for firing people is in danger of becoming a trend. In 2008, the *Chicago Sun-Times* fired people over the phone. The following year, the *Boston Globe* reported on a local social-media-software company revealing layoffs via Twitter and blogs.

Getting the Sack at the Shack

Back in 2006, RadioShack Corp. fired about 400 employees by e-mail. The good news is that it saved the price of a ream of paper, and maybe some postage. Apparently, no one thought about the bad news—the terrible press it received for its Internet Age management gaffe. The story was all over the media, and the blogs had a field day with it.

According to news reports, the e-mail waiting for the unlucky employees that Tuesday morning read: "The workforce reduction notification is currently in progress. Unfortunately, your position is one that has been eliminated." You can imagine the number of committee meetings that went into drafting that abomination.

In its defense, the company noted that it had warned employees that the "workforce reduction notifications" would be delivered electronically, and that employees were invited to ask questions on a company intranet.

Maybe it was more efficient to fire 400 people this way. But this is an example of losing sight of the obvious consequences of callous behavior in favor of increased efficiency. Yes, it's a lot of work to do a reduction in force. (We'll discuss these in Chapter 10). Yes, RadioShack paid severance to these employees. Fine. But it's a big deal to lose your job. And when employees feel they were treated without respect or dignity, they are much more likely to sue. And that will cost a whole lot more than a ream of paper.

The company defended the reduction in workforce (RIF) as necessary to "improve its long-term competitive position in the marketplace." But improving its "competitive position in the marketplace" requires attracting the best talent. Who would want to work at RadioShack after seeing how they handled this RIF?

CompUSA Didn't "Get It"

In 2007, struggling computer retailer CompUSA decided to close its remaining stores. The way it informed its employees that they were all losing their jobs was through a soulless form letter. A copy of the letter quickly made its way around the blogosphere. (It was in fact a government-required WARN letter. We'll discuss those in Chapter 10.)

The letter opened "Dear Team Member." I appreciate that CompUSA had a lot of employees to fire, but couldn't they have bothered to insert the unlucky recipient's name in each letter? (You know, guys, they have computers that can do that now.) The letter said:

> This letter will serve as formal notification under the Federal Worker Adjustment and Retraining Act, 29 U.S.C. § 2101, et seq. ("WARN") that CompUSA, Inc. ("the Company") will permanently discontinue all operations located at [redacted]

> As a result, the Company expects Store number [redacted] to close permanently between March 1, 2008 and March 14, 2008. Your last day of employment with the company will occur sometime between February 8, 2008 and February 22, 2008. This layoff is expected to be permanent. There are no applicable bumping rights related to these layoffs.

> We thank you for your service to CompUSA, Inc. If you would like additional information regarding the closing of CompUSA, Inc. stores and operations or how it affects you, please contact [redacted]

It was "signed" by printing an HR official's name in boldface italics.

Did they need to keep reminding the fired worker that CompUSA was incorporated—four times in a three-paragraph letter? And couldn't they get a human being to actually sign the letter?

CompUSA's tagline when it shut down was "We got it. We get it." Obviously they didn't get it. They didn't get it at all.

You're firing people. Have the decency to act like it means something to you. It certainly means something to the employees. A personalized letter, or even a seemingly personalized mail-merged one, with a real human being's signature makes a difference. It might not seem like a lot—it might even seem like a waste of time—but people notice these things.

Getting fired sucks. But getting fired suckily (by e-mail, by form letter, by voicemail) sucks even more. Worse, it makes the fired employees more disgruntled, and thus more likely to sue.

Be a person. And fire in person.

Telling Coworkers

How do you quell the gossip? We talked about this earlier. But it's worth repeating: don't be overly concerned about workplace gossip. Most of the time, you're going to be powerless to stop it.

The bottom line is that an employee's termination is no one else's business. So many managers feel the need to defend their actions or quell rumors. Don't worry about it. The risk of having a few people chat about an employee's departure for an hour or two is nothing compared to the risk of embarrassing that employee with an unnecessary announcement.

Letting the Person Resign

Some people think it makes a difference whether you fire an employee or let that employee "resign." Most of the time, this notion is misguided.

It usually makes no legal difference whether an employee resigns or is fired. There are two basic situations where it does matter. One is when the employee is under contract rather than at will. In most employee contracts, how a resigning employee is treated is different from how a terminated one is.

The other exception is for unemployment purposes. In general, an employee is entitled to unemployment benefits if she is fired, but is not if she quits. There are exceptions to this: if an employee is fired for something very serious, like workplace violence or burning down the factory, then the termination will not trigger eligibility for unemployment benefits. On the other hand, if an employee quits because of an unreasonably bad situation (such as being the victim of sexual harassment), then the resignation will not preclude eligibility for unemployment benefits.

But calling an employee into your office and telling him that he has to resign is not the same as having that employee give you his notice. Forced quitting equals firing, no matter how you slice it.

Now there can be a situation where you may want to give the employee an opportunity to save face by resigning. This is much less common than you might imagine. For example, if a senior executive ran his division into the ground and needs to be replaced, but he's well-liked and has been at the company for a long time, you might consider giving him the opportunity to say that he left to pursue other opportunities. Just don't say too much; you don't want people to figure out that it's not really true.

How Much Notice Should You Give?

This can cut both ways. On the one hand, you don't want to have a situation where an employee knows she's already on the way out. On the other hand, you'd ideally like to avoid having the termination be a complete surprise.

If the firing is related to performance or discipline issues, the employee ought to already know that you're unhappy with her. When it comes time to have the actual termination meeting, she should have some sense that it's coming. Surprises are bad because they add an additional layer of emotion to the firing.

Any termination is automatically going to lead to feelings of anger, hurt, disloyalty, betrayal, defensiveness, and sadness in the employee. But the element of surprise has a multiplier effect. If the person has some sense that the hammer's going to drop, he or she can at least partially prepare for that on an emotional level. But if it comes as the proverbial bolt from the blue, and he or she is emotionally unprepared for it, the reaction is apt to be stronger.

Transition Time

How much time should you let the fired employee remain at work? This question comes up with surprising frequency. Many employers worry that the company will suffer during the transition from the fired employee to the replacement employee. To avoid this, managers sometimes ask the employee to stay on for a week or two and help with that transition.

Bad idea.

Let me put it to you this way: the employee you just fired wasn't a very good employee or you wouldn't have done it. So now that you've told him that he stinks and he's fired, you expect him to suddenly be motivated enough to help you? That's crazy. Even if you give a significant financial incentive for that transition help, the employee's loyalty is going to be pretty much nil.

Once an employee knows he has no more future at a company, it's human nature for him to check out. If he stays, even for a little while, he's barely going to mail it in.

I've seen this happen with employees of mine who have given their notice. As a professional courtesy, they will tell me that they've gotten a new job and that they'll stay on for two or three weeks to help transition their cases to other attorneys. But in most instances, that period of two or three weeks ends up being too long. It's not really their fault. It's perfectly natural not to care as much when there's no more future. Even more so with employees who quit rather than who got fired.

No, the better course of action is to make a clean break. After you tell the employee that she's fired, then it's time for her to go. She should gather up her stuff, say her goodbyes (if she wants), and hit the road. Staying any longer is superfluous.

It can also be dangerous. If the employee is unhappy about the termination (and that's usually the case), there is the danger that the lingering fired employee will sabotage things. Most people won't do something serious, but many fired employees may be more inclined to photocopy some files or lift some supplies on the way out. The less-ethical ones might try to take secrets or divert customers. It's just not worth the risk.

Of course, this means that you need to be sure you have all your ducks in a row before you conduct the termination. If there are things you need that employee to do before she leaves, you better make sure they're done *before* the termination.

In addition, if the employee works on sensitive matters, you should make sure that the employee's computer and e-mail access are shut down, ideally during the termination meeting. If it's done before the meeting, you'll tip her off; afterwards, and she might be able to do some damage.

After the Termination Meeting

Another frequently asked question has to do with monitoring the employee after the termination and before he leaves. Do you have security frogmarch him to the door? Do you watch him gather his stuff at his desk, or do you send it to him after he leaves?

Depends. I know: that's your least favorite answer. It's a lawyer's answer, which is why I hate giving it. But it's the right answer.

It depends on the circumstances of the employee. If you fired him for, say, theft, then hell yeah you keep a close watch on him while packs up his desk. Better yet, you'll send him his stuff. Similarly, if the person has a temper and you're concerned about damage or violence, don't let him walk around un-attended after the meeting.

On the other hand, if it's a performance-based termination and you have no particular reason to think he's going boost something on his way out, then you don't need to hover over him while he packs his cardboard box. Too many employers think they need to closely monitor the fired employee even if there's no reason to think that he's going to do something bad.

Safety has to be the primary concern. If you think the fired employee is going to freak out afterward, then it's a good idea to have security involved. But if there isn't a substantial risk, then don't unnecessarily humiliate the fired worker by treating him like a criminal after he just lost his job.

What About the Final Paycheck?

Most states require that you pay the fired employee all the wages she's earned up to that point on the day of termination. This can be a bit of a hassle when you use an outside payroll service. In those cases, it's not good enough to send out the final paycheck on the next regularly scheduled pay date.

Instead, what you need to do is call up your payroll provider and ask them for the correct withholding amounts for a terminal paycheck. Then write the check manually for the proper amount. Obviously, you need to be discreet about this, and you need to make sure that your payroll company will be equally discreet (most will be). The last thing you want is for your payroll service to call the employee to check on something before you've had a chance to do the termination meeting.

Sometimes the employee might owe you money, particularly if the firing is because of theft. You may be able to reduce the employee's final paycheck to cover the debt, as I did with the embezzling office manager. But if you do this, you have to make sure that the deduction doesn't bring the employee's wages below minimum wage. Moreover, your state's laws might have specific restrictions about deductions like this. Check with your employment counsel beforehand.

Managers have often asked me about pay for that final day, especially if the termination meeting takes place in the morning. I always tell them that this is not the time to get cheap. People hate to be nickel-and-dimed. Unless your employee is Alex Rodriguez and a partial day's pay is a sizable amount of money, don't screw the employee out of that day's pay. Give her pay for the whole day, and tell her you're doing it. It's a nice gesture that might slightly soften the blow.

Vacation: All I Ever Wanted

Another thing to keep in mind is that final wages owed might also include accrued, but unused, vacation time. Most state wage laws mandate that you pay out this unused accrued vacation time along with the final paycheck. This is because the states treat vacation as another form of wages, and they take wages very seriously. (Wage violations can be considered a crime in some states. We'll cover wage lawsuits in Chapter 13.)

Whether the employee is entitled to vacation pay depends on what kind of vacation policy you have. If employees "earn" their vacation all at once at the beginning of the year, then an employee fired on June 30 is going to be entitled to half her year's vacation time (less what she's already taken). On the other hand, if employees' vacation accrues over the course of the year (usually on a monthly basis), then you need to take out the slide rule and figure out if you owe her anything. Many payroll companies will take care of this for you.

Release Me

The best way to make sure that a fired employee won't sue you is to have her promise not to. But you're going to need to get that promise in writing, and you're going to have to give something to her in exchange. That something is severance pay.

An offer of severance pay can accomplish important things. First, it can help soften the blow of getting fired. If the severance pay is high enough to make a difference to that particular employee, it could go a long way to ameliorating the anger and hurt feelings of getting fired.

Second, severance pay can buy you a release from a future lawsuit. In exchange for the severance, the employee promises not to sue you over the termination. Different laws require that a release contain specific language, so you'll need to work with your employment counsel on this. I've included in Appendix C a sample severance agreement that we used many times. This can give you some ideas about tone and content, but don't use it as your own; the laws of your state might have different requirements.

When you look at my sample, you'll notice that it looks like a letter to the employee from the boss rather than an agreement that a lawyer drafted. That's intentional. You want your severance agreement to be readable and understandable by the employee. Although the law requires the agreement to advise the employee to consult with a lawyer, you don't actually want the employee to do that. An accessible agreement lowers the chances of the employee's needing a lawyer.

I often get asked questions about how much severance you should give. There are no rules of thumb, though. It depends on several things: the circumstances of the termination, the employee's salary, the employee's longevity with the company, history of other severance packages, market conditions, and so on. When considering a severance amount, ask yourself if it would seem fair to you. Maybe ask (discreetly) other people you trust. Remember: you're trying to make the employee sign the agreement and be less hurt and angry.

You can give the fired employee severance without asking for a release in return, but I rarely recommend it. Otherwise, the severance money you give might go toward financing the lawsuit against your company. No good deed goes unpunished, and so forth. Only give a gratuitous severance if you're certain that the employee would never sue.

Conclusion

As I've said throughout, firing an employee is a hard task—the hardest task an employer or manager has to do. Paying attention to the different issues we've discussed in this chapter will lessen the risk that the termination goes wrong. Also, Appendix A has a checklist to help you make sure you don't miss anything.

Next, we turn to a new concept that can dramatically improve your chances of avoiding a termination-related lawsuit.

Retained Dignity

In this chapter, I'm going to introduce you to a powerful new concept: *Retained Dignity*. Your ability to improve this vital factor is critical. Keeping this in mind when you go through the process of firing an employee will help you reduce the chance of being sued.

Employees Are Individuals

One of the fundamental principles of management and human resources is that all employees are different individuals, and they cannot be reduced to numbers on a financial chart. In fact, this is why some people in business fail to take human resources seriously. They write off the field as too touchy-feely, in contrast to the dollars-and-cents world of finance and operations.

And they're right, to a degree. HR and management need to be human-oriented rather than number-oriented. You can't manage people as if they are numbers or assets. The term "human capital" has become increasingly popular recently. But this carries the danger that managers will start to see people as items on a balance sheet, right next to plant and equipment. Numbers have a tendency to dehumanize our thinking, and that it is a terrible—and risky—way to manage people.

Convert to a Metrics System?

That said, there is some value in trying to quantify certain aspects of the management and HR processes. Some forward-thinking companies are starting to use HR metrics to quantify their return on investment (ROI) for various human-capital operations and initiatives. While many things in the HR world cannot be quantified, I learned in my practice that many employers and managers respond well to the notion that how they handle employee firings can have a direct impact on the company's bottom line.

Some people take great comfort in being able to calculate the return on an investment. If a company buys a new piece of equipment for a million dollars, and the new machine will enable them to make $1.5 million more in its first year of use, then the ROI of that purchase was 50 percent in that first year. (That's some machine.) Obviously, it's a lot easier to calculate ROIs on financial investments and the like. Calculating a return on investment in the management and HR world is considerably more difficult. But it's not impossible.

Measuring the Wrong Things

Like many things, though, this can be taken to an extreme. While it can be useful to recognize the effect that the management of employees has on a company's income, you don't want to create a business model where everyone's value is reduced to some number. What is more, there are many elements of a particular employee's worth that simply cannot be quantified.

In fact, overquantification is a problem in many industries. In law, especially in larger law firms, an associate's worth is primarily measured by the number of billable hours that she bills in the course of a year. But this single number (which, when multiplied by her hourly rate, gives the total revenue she generates) fails to recognize the unique qualities that makes this particular associate who she is: her specific knowledge, experience, level of care, attention to detail, client-service skills, charisma, persuasiveness, writing ability, speaking ability, and so forth.

This is a major problem with quantification: measuring the wrong things just because they're easily measurable. (It's not very hard to track hours.) This leads to focusing on oversimplified numbers, which ends up as a substitute for actual management.

The ROI of Employees

Nevertheless, for some managers—especially the left-brain types who prefer to focus on numbers and facts instead of the right-brain "soft" factors—using some human-capital metrics can help them pay attention to the fact that how you treat employees has a major effect on your company's financial performance.

In his book, *The ROI of Human Capital: Measuring the Economic Value of Employee Performance* (AMACOM, 2000), consultant Jac Fitz-enz describes numerous ways to quantify the value of employees and their contributions to an enterprise. Here are just a few examples of measurements that Fitz-enz describes:

- *human capital return on investment* =
  revenue − (expense − total labor cost) ÷ total labor cost
- *human capital market value* =
  (market value − book value) ÷ full-time equivalents (FTEs)
- *human capital value added* =
  revenue − (expense − total labor cost) ÷ FTEs

I'm not advocating a blind reliance on these or other values. In fact, Fitz-enz's background is in the area of benchmarking, which I have little use for. (Benchmarking focuses too much on what other companies are doing, rather than paying attention to what *your* company should be doing.)

But I do believe that it can be helpful to think about the concepts in *Firing at Will* in terms of the financial consequences of your actions. First, let's look at risk.

Minding Your Ps

One of the major themes throughout this book, and one of the most important concepts I used in my practice as a management lawyer, is the notion that every management decision contributes to a risk of employment litigation. I describe this risk as P, which stands for the probability that the employee in question files a claim.

P is never equal to 0.0 (or zero percent); there's always at least a metaphysical chance that any employee will file. And P is never equal to 1.0 (a 100 percent chance), even with the employee who dramatically shouts, "I'll see you in court!" on the way out of the workplace. There's at least some small chance that this employee will fall down and bump his head and get amnesia. ("Hmmm. I feel like there was something I was supposed to be doing in this courthouse... Oh well.")

I have always found it helpful for employers and managers to see their role as doing what they can to lower P to an acceptable level, and to avoid doing things that tend to raise P. Too often, people want guarantees; they want certainty. They want to know for sure that a lawsuit's not going to happen. But that's not realistic. Lawyers tend to get themselves into trouble casting about for the mythical perfect solution—one that reduces *P* to zero. Instead, you should focus on reducing the risk as much as you reasonably can.

Before we look at what you can do to lower *P*, let's first look at how the employees and their lawyers decide whether to sue.

"How Much Can I Win?"

When would-be plaintiffs (the people who sue other people) go visit their lawyers for the first time, this is the question they most want to ask. Don't get me wrong: I'm not suggesting that all plaintiffs sue their employers solely to make money. But it's a big factor for many of them. And right from the start, they're calculating dollar amounts and probabilities.

I'm going to tell you a secret, but you have to promise to keep it between us: for about a year after I hung out my own shingle, I represented employment-law plaintiffs. Not because I wanted to, mind you. I didn't feel I had a lot of choice.

Working on the Dark Side

After graduating from law school, I ended up in a five-person, management-side boutique in Boston. Even though I hadn't originally considered becoming an employment lawyer (they were hiring, and I needed a job), I found that I really enjoyed the field. When I decided to open my own firm four years later, I knew I wanted to continue doing the same work: representing employers. But I didn't take any clients with me, and management clients are hard to come by.

So for the first year in my new firm, I also accepted employee clients. In fact, I primarily took employee clients. (In my experience, it's fairly unusual for employment lawyers to do work for both kinds of clients at the same time.) It wasn't too difficult to make the switch to the other side, since the law was the same. In fact, knowing the strategies from the other side of the table helped me be a more-effective plaintiffs' lawyer. And employee clients are much easier to get than employer clients; everyone knows employees who are having job problems.

But I didn't like it. Philosophically, I tended to agree more with management. And I preferred the ongoing relationship that comes with representing employers. With employee clients, they hire you for the single matter—usually after they've been fired—and then it's over, and you never see them again.

Another difference is that with management clients, you feel like you can make a difference helping them improve their workplaces. But with employee clients, all you can do is help them with their one-time problem. And since no one ever wants their job back (I've never seen it happen in my entire career), all you can do for them is try to get them money.

Never Really Enough

And here's where the real problem occurred. The money was never enough. I'm not saying that all employee plaintiffs are greedy, although many are. Instead, what I'm saying is that the money quickly gets spent in their minds, and they often forget to do some basic math.

For example (and this is from one of my actual employee cases), I represented a young woman who was retaliated against after claiming that she had been sexually harassed by a supervisor at a huge international company. Turns out that the sexual-harassment claim itself was pretty weak, because even though the incident in question actually took place, she admitted to me that she had incited it to some degree.

But the retaliation part of the claim was solid: after she complained to HR about the harassment, she got reassigned to another division and taken off the high-profile project she had been working on. This significantly impacted her career.

Knowing this, I threatened the company with litigation, and then set about trying to get a favorable settlement from their lawyers. It soon became clear to me that we were going to be able to get $50,000 from the company. This is an excellent settlement, especially without having filed an actual claim. (I'd only threatened the claim.) But in my client's mind, she was already spending the fifty large.

Problem was, she had sort of forgotten that my fee was the traditional one-third contingency, meaning that $16,667 would go to me. Uncle Sam and the Commonwealth of Massachusetts were poised to take another forty percent or so of the fifty grand, or about $20,000. That left her with a total net take of about $13,300—which is just not the same as $50,000. So despite what I would call an unequivocal victory—a $50,000 settlement after writing a letter and a few settlement phone calls—she ended up being very disappointed.

Thus, employees who better understand fees, taxes, and basic math recognize that they need to seek even more money to get to their desired levels of happiness. So employers will face even higher demands from plaintiffs' lawyers.

Playing the Odds

Besides getting a sense of how much they could stand to win (and "winning" usually means "settling for"), the employee and his or her lawyer need to get an idea of their probability of winning. "What are the odds?" is probably the second-most common question for lawyers.

It's also the most common question that I heard from employers, and the question I least liked to answer. Trying to guess the odds—usually in the form of a percent chance—is next to impossible.

Instead, what I'd tell my clients is this: in employment litigation, there are no sure things. There is no 100 percent chance of winning, and there is no 100 percent chance of losing. A slam-dunk case, or the closest thing to it, has maybe a 75 percent chance of winning. There are too many variables among judges, juries, and administrative agencies to have a comfort level greater than that.

Even if I felt certain that we could win, I still wouldn't give us more than a 75 percent chance. More often, I would place us somewhere in a range of 40 to 60 percent; that is, from somewhat more likely to lose to somewhat more likely to win. Any lawyer who tells a client that there's a 90 percent chance of winning is selling something.

If the employee and the plaintiff's lawyer do some basic decision analysis, they will multiply the hoped-for monetary take by the estimated chance of winning. So a lawsuit that has a 50 percent chance of winning an award of $100,000 has an expectation value of $50,000—which is probably enough for most plaintiffs' lawyers to go forward.

So that's the calculus of the case's value. But in many ways, the more important equation revolves around the employee's emotions. Because that's where the decision to sue really comes from. Fortunately, it's also the area where you as a manager can make a difference.

Natural Anger

It goes almost without saying that most fired employees are going to feel some degree of anger at getting fired. Yes, they're likely to feel sad. Maybe hurt, too. But hurt feelings and sadness, in my experience, don't tend to push fired employees into action (that is, into bringing an action). Anger, on the other hand, does. At the risk of paraphrasing Yoda, anger leads to hate, hate leads to the Dark Side ... or the plaintiff's side. Anger can drive the employee to strike back at the company or the manager. And the best way of striking back is by lawyering up.

Different employees will feel different levels of anger. Likewise, different firing situations will lead to different amounts of anger. But my sense is that there is a baseline level of anger to be felt by a particular employee in a particular circumstance. I call this level the Natural Anger (NA) factor.

Firing an employee who has a calm, Zen-like demeanor and who doesn't really need his job and is basically just phoning it in will likely lead to a low Natural Anger score. Firing a hothead employee with anger-management issues who beat up the mailroom guy who looked at her funny will probably lead to a high Natural Anger amount.

I find it helpful to think of this number in a range from zero to ten on a ten-point scale. So an employee who's only prone to a medium level of anger who's fired for a moderately serious reason might have a Natural Anger score of five. (Don't get freaked out by the actual numbers. These are just different ways of looking at low, medium, and high levels of anger. It's all subjective, of course.)

One thing you want to do is avoid increasing that NA score by acting in a way that makes the employee angrier than she otherwise would be.

Feeling Screwed

There's probably a nicer way to describe this component, but it probably wouldn't be as apt. In an episode of *The West Wing*, President Bartlet (Martin Sheen) concedes to a voter that because of a decision he had made as the governor of New Hampshire, dairy farmers "got rogered but good." I kind of like that expression, which is apparently a British synonym for "getting screwed." But I don't want to offend any Rogers (too late?), so we'll stick with "Feeling Screwed" (FS).

Just as with anger, there is a natural tendency for fired employees to feel like they got screwed to some degree. In politer terms, they feel like they weren't treated as fairly as they could have been.

In my experience, nearly all of the fired employees who end up suing their employers score high on this factor. They feel like they got the raw end of the deal, and that their termination was a form of injustice perpetrated on them. The greater the injustice, the greater the likelihood of going to court.

It's similar to the Natural Anger component, but it's not identical. A person can be angry that she was fired, but deep down will recognize that the decision was basically sound, or that the manager treated her fairly.

But an employee with a high Feeling Screwed score is going to have a considerably higher level of resentment toward the company, and the probability of a lawsuit will increase substantially.

V for Vindictiveness

So now we come to our first formula. For all you liberal-arts types, fear not. You won't be called upon to do any differential calculus. Keep in mind that most people who go to law school tend not to be quantitative types. On the other hand, those of you who are natural mathematical geniuses will have to be patient with me here: the math we're going to do is pretty simplified.

With that said, here it is:

$$NA + FS = V$$

where V stands for Vindictiveness. It is Vindictiveness that causes fired employees to stand up and fight back against the employer who wronged them. That combination of Natural Anger and Feeling Screwed impels them to talk to a lawyer and give serious thought to filing a claim. Whether they go forward with it will depend on how high they score on the Vindictiveness scale.

But the employer can help lessen the chance of a lawsuit by increasing a different factor.

The Concept of Retained Dignity

Over the years, I saw firsthand the effect of firing people without protecting their dignity. It is, in my experience, the number-one leading indicator of employee lawsuits. It is one thing to lose your job; it's another to lose face. Employees who feel like they lost more than their job—who feel like they were screwed over—are much, much more likely to sue.

On the other hand, the more dignity an employee is left with after the termination—the level of Retained Dignity—the less likely a lawsuit is.

So how do you measure this concept of Retained Dignity? In my experience, I've found that Retained Dignity is the inverse of Vindictiveness. Now don't be alarmed, but I think that a chart or two might help you conceptualize this.

The more Natural Anger and Feeling Screwed an employee has, the less Retained Dignity (see Figure 7-1).

Low Retained Dignity

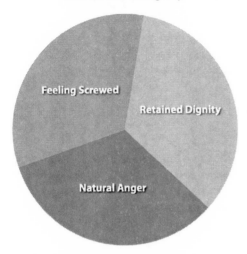

Figure 7-1. Higher Vindictiveness means lower Retained Dignity.

On the other hand, if the Natural Anger and Feeling Screwed factors are kept lower, the Retained Dignity will be higher (see Figure 7-2).

High Retained Dignity

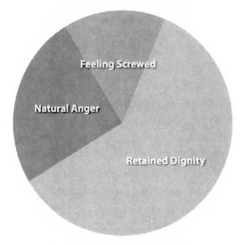

Figure 7-2. Lower Vindictiveness means higher Retained Dignity.

Ideally, you want to keep the Retained Dignity greater than the Vindictiveness (Natural Anger plus Feeling Screwed). But don't get caught up in numbers and scores and pie charts. This is just to help illustrate that the more you focus on reducing the fired employee's feelings of anger and of being screwed, the more dignity the employee will retain.

If the employee's Vindictiveness is greater than his or her Retained Dignity, you're in serious danger of facing an employee lawsuit. Whether the employee files will depend on that low Retained Dignity combined with the expected value of the lawsuit.

So What Can You Do?

The way your actions and decisions can have the greatest effect is in lowering the Natural Anger and Feeling Screwed scores, and thus increasing the Retained Dignity. By thinking this through and acting accordingly, you can lower your risk of a lawsuit—which should be your main goal.

Lowering Natural Anger

There's nothing you can do about the personality of the worker you're firing. If she is a hothead who's prone to anger and easily set off, that's going to be a problem. But Natural Anger includes both the employee's personality and the circumstances of the situation, and it's the latter part where you might be able to make a difference.

Planning ahead to the actual termination meeting, you can consider ways of delivering the news that lessen the likelihood of antagonizing the employee. (Remember: the employee's going to be upset no matter what. We're talking about to what degree.) These are some of the things we discussed in the last chapter.

Taking care to deliver the news respectfully and compassionately can go a long way to lowering the Natural Anger factor. Picking the right time and the right place can make a difference. And avoiding a debate about who was right and who was wrong, or about the merits of the worker as a person or even as an employee, are good ways to avoid a spike in the Natural Anger score.

Ideally, you want the fired employee to remain calm during and after the termination meeting. That means you need to remain calm, too. Getting into an argument is a guaranteed way of inciting anger, which lowers the Retained Dignity score.

Lowering Feeling Screwed

Similarly, you want to minimize the amount that the employee feels like he or she is getting a raw deal. The best way to do that is to try to make the employee feel like the termination is understandable and justifiable. This is easy to say and difficult to do.

As I said in Chapter 6, you don't want to use the termination meeting to lay out your case for why you're firing the employee. Doing that will make the employee defensive, which is exactly what you don't want. So you need to try to have the employee understand (but not necessarily agree with) the decision—*without* going through a bill of particulars.

The last thing you want is to make the employee feel like the firing is arbitrary and capricious, to use a legal standard. A decision that is arbitrary and capricious always feels unfair to the person affected by it, and will translate into a high Feeling Screwed score.

As I mentioned before, the bookkeeper I had to fire recognized that she had made too many arithmetic mistakes for me to trust her work anymore. Her termination wasn't a surprise to her, and she seemed to feel that it was justified (even if she didn't agree with it).

But there was no need for me to chronicle her missteps during the termination meeting, and there was no reason for me to do anything to put her on the defensive. Similarly, because I presented the decision as a done deal, there was no fleeting feeling of getting one more chance—which would have increased her Feeling Screwed factor once that particular hope was dashed.

One more thing: nickel-and-diming the fired employee over the final paycheck or vacation calculation will increase both the Natural Anger and the Feeling Screwed factors. Don't do that. By contrast, giving the employee a little extra or doing something to ease the effects of the decision might actually lower both scores.

Conclusion

The Retained Dignity factor takes this concept out of the fuzzy, touchy-feely world of HR and puts it squarely into the analytical world of operations and finance. There have always been ethical reasons for firing employees in a way that preserves their dignity. Now there are financial reasons, too. Higher Retained Dignity scores mean lower employee-lawsuit costs. And focusing on keeping Natural Anger and Feeling Screwed scores low will go a long way to keeping you and your company out of court.

Now that we've covered the magic of Retained Dignity, it's time to turn to something else that contains magical properties: paper.

The Paper Trail

We've talked about the magic of Retained Dignity, and how the proper attention to keeping that factor as high as possible will lower the risk of an employee lawsuit. Now we're going to discuss something that seems so ordinary, so prosaic, and so routine that it can't possibly have magical powers. But it does.

I'm talking about paper.

Paper Beats Rock ... and Scissors

Paper—and specifically the words written down on paper—carries enormous power that employers often underestimate. How you use this power, whether for good or for evil, is up to you.

Let me explain: when you talk to an employee about something he did wrong, or something he failed to do, the words tend to exist only in the time and space of that conversation. You might remember saying them for a while, although memories fade over time. The employee might remember your saying them, assuming he understood them in the first place. But again, memories fade.

Later on, maybe the employee has remembered to do what you talked about. Or maybe he hasn't. Maybe he didn't understand what you meant. So when he does it wrong again, you're going to be even more irritated and angry. Lather, rinse, repeat.

Finally, you get to the point where you can't take it anymore, and you go all Chapter 6 on him. (Yes, I just invented that saying. Feel free to use it. When people don't understand you, tell them to buy this book. Thanks.) So you fire him.

Trial and Error

Flash forward a couple of years (no exaggeration) and the fired employee's lawsuit is now going to trial in state court. Turns out he claims that you fired him not because of his pattern of bad behavior, but because of his age (let's say he's 54). He claims that he was a really good employee, or at least an adequate employee, and that you made up these "disciplinary events" so that you could exercise your deep-seated bias against AARP-eligible employees.

Today is Day Two of the trial, and as the manager who fired the guy, you're the key witness of the day. After some boring, rote questions about your education, work history, and managerial duties, the employee's slick lawyer goes in for the kill:

SLICK LAWYER

So you *claim* [he makes finger quotes here] that you spoke to Mr. Jones about his performance problems, is that right?

YOU

I don't *claim* it. I *did* speak to him.

SLICK

When, exactly?

YOU

Uh, well ... must have been about three years ago. I remember that it was warm out.

SLICK

You "remember that it was warm out"? You don't know what date?

YOU

Uh, not exactly. But I spoke to him several times.

SLICK

Give me the dates of those conversations.

YOU
(blushing now)

I'm not sure of the dates.

SLICK

Of course not. [sarcastically] Was it "warm out"? Strike that.

What exactly did you say to Mr. Jones? What were your exact words?

YOU
(looking down at your shoes so that you don't
see the jury members shaking their heads)

I don't remember.

SLICK
(triumphantly)

No further questions.

Not good. Now, in this version, look at the difference if you used the magic power of paper:

SLICK LAWYER

So you *claim* [he makes finger quotes here] that you spoke to Mr. Jones about his performance problems, is that right?

YOU

I don't *claim* it. I *did* speak to him.

SLICK

When, exactly?

YOU

I spoke to him at 9:30 in the morning on June 24, 2009, right after our daily sales meeting. We met in Conference Room B.

SLICK
(taken aback)

Uh, how can you be so certain? That was almost three years ago.

> YOU
> (confidently)
>
> Because I wrote it down immediately after the meeting.
>
> SLICK
>
> And do you remember what you said? Exactly?
>
> YOU
> (triumphantly)
>
> I do indeed. I said, "Biff, if you photocopy your butt one more time, I'm going to have to fire it."
>
> SLICK
> (dejectedly)
>
> No further questions.

Now the jury members are shaking their heads at the plaintiff and his slick lawyer.

By the way, those two Oscar-worthy scenes were examples of cross-examinations, where a lawyer asks adversarial questions of a witness who is friendly to the other side.

On Direct

The other way this could go down is where your company's lawyer could put you on the stand and ask you questions herself. That's called direct examination.

Your lawyer would ask you if you spoke to Jones about the butt-copying incident and you'd say yes. She'd ask you if you remember when it was and you'd say yes and give her the date and time. She'd ask you how you can be so certain and you'd say because you wrote it down. Then she'd reach back to counsel's table and her associate would magically produce *the actual sheet of paper you wrote on.* She would pause to let the jury admire this bit of leger-demain.

She'd ask the judge's permission to approach you and show you your own notepaper. Then she'd hand it to you and ask you if you recognize it. Of course. How do you recognize it? Because it's in my own handwriting. Is it dated? she'd ask. And you'd say, of course, and you'd announce the date and time. And then she'd ask you to read the critical sentence that you wrote in your own handwriting. And in a clear, steady voice, you'd read, "Biff, if you photocopy your butt one more time, I'm going to have to fire it."

And you know what?

The jury would absolutely believe that it happened the way you said it did. Because a jury is never going to think that you later fabricated the documentation. Yeah, sure, it's possible that you could have. There's no way to carbon-date the notepaper and perform sophisticated spectrographic analysis on the ink. This isn't *CSI: Dubuque*, or whatever. This is the real world.

We make assumptions in the real world, and one of the assumptions we make is that people wouldn't bother to go to the trouble to fabricate documentary evidence. It's just not worth the effort. So if you can produce a piece of paper that backs up your testimony, you've got yourself a powerful weapon in defending against the lawsuit.

Reality Check

One thing you should know about employee-lawsuit trials: they almost never actually take place. In Massachusetts, where I practiced, only about 2 percent of all civil cases filed in the state's superior courts actually went to a jury trial. And that proportion is pretty consistent around the country. In employment cases, the percentage is even less, because most employee lawsuits have a fee-shifting component that makes trials even more unpalatable (see Chapter 3).

Instead, cases either get settled (sometimes literally on the eve of trial) or the employer successfully gets the claims thrown out on legal grounds. So these courtroom scenarios I've just described are by no means common. So what's the big deal? you might ask.

The Real Job of Management Lawyers

I would often explain to my manager clients that my job as their employment counsel was to imagine the worst-case scenario and then plan accordingly. The worst-case scenario was always an employee lawsuit, and the *worst* worst-case scenario was one that went to a jury trial.

But knowing that we had this type of documentary evidence in our arsenal would give us confidence about our ability to win the case, and would also help guide us during settlement negotiations.

If It Isn't Written Down, Then It Probably Didn't Happen

So we would tell our managers about the value of writing things down. Because from the point of view of a judge or jury (or administrative agency), if it wasn't written down, it's hard to truly believe that it happened that way. It's much easier for us lawyers to attack the spotty recollections of witnesses years after the fact when there isn't any documentary evidence backing up their stories.

As a manager, it's good to get into a habit of writing everything down. I actually learned this lesson the hard way, long before I became a lawyer.

After college, I went to work for a Boston retail bank in its management-training program. As I worked my way up the ladder, I would get assigned to different downtown branches. After I'd been there a couple of years, I was an assistant manager in a branch that had no current manager. So for a couple of months, I was the acting branch manager.

Then the bank hired a guy from outside the company to become the branch manager of my branch. He didn't know the branch as I did, and he didn't know the bank's operations or methods as I did. The other employees liked me and respected me, since I knew what I was doing. And this guy wasn't naturally likable. I'll call him "Carl," because that was his name.

Right off the bat, Carl didn't like me. Since I'm naturally charming (ahem), it must have been because he felt threatened by my greater experience and stronger relationships with the staff and customers. Whatever. Despite the lack of warmth from the guy, I thought we worked out a professional relationship with him as the boss and me as the number two.

I thought wrong.

Turns out the guy really had it in for me, and wanted to get me fired. So he went to senior management with a memo listing my faults and transgressions, and he included dates and times. What I hadn't appreciated was that Carl had taken many detailed notes, day in and day out. So even the most minor incident was captured in black and white along with the date and time.

It was an impressive performance on Carl's part. The only way I was able to save my fledgling banking career was by relying on my own fairly decent memory. But it was a struggle, since I was going up against what appeared to be an official record. In the end, I had enough people in the bank's management who liked me and didn't care for Carl. A year later, I was promoted to manager (ironically, right as I was being accepted into law school). Carl, on the other hand, didn't last very long at the bank.

It was an important lesson to learn as a manager, and one I carried with me as a management lawyer. I'm not saying that you should be like Carl. But his practice of taking notes was an effective one, and it almost cost me my job.

The Best Method of Documentation

Clients would often ask me how they should go about keeping managerial records like this. I would tell them what I'm telling you now:

The best method of documentation is the one that works for you personally.

Some managers worry that notes scribbled in their messy handwriting on burrito wrappers won't look "formal" enough. Who cares? Quite frankly, I'd find your burrito notes even more compelling than some fancy computerized database.

Some people prefer to use their computers to type up notes. Some make entries in a paper-based calendar. Others write in a notebook or on index cards. It doesn't matter. As long as you can find a method that allows you to consistently capture and record the events you care to remember, who was involved, and the time, date, and location of the incident or conversation. That's all that matters. Just watch out for guacamole stains.

The Downside of Documentation

There is a downside to all this note-taking, though, and we should discuss that for a bit. This isn't to dissuade you from documenting managerial decisions and workplace incidents. It's just to raise your awareness of some of the potential pitfalls.

As I mentioned before, one of the magical properties of words on paper is that they seem to take on greater significance than spoken words. That means that when you write something bad about an employee, those written words carry more force than if you just orally admonish him. Part of the reason is what we just talked about: that the written words will be more believable in a future court case.

But another part of the reason is that people naturally place greater importance on something that's in writing. Written statements tend to be more formal than oral statements, in part because many people think they're supposed to write more formally than they speak. (I, for one, don't believe that, and try very hard not to write "like a lawyer." Maybe that's why you're still reading this.)

When we receive news by letter, it tends to carry more weight than when we hear the same news by telephone. So it's natural that a write-up of an employee's transgression will seem more important—and ominous—than a face-to-face discussion of the same incident.

This problem then gets maximized by the laws of most states. Just as people place greater importance on written statements, so too do people become more concerned about their written personnel files. Employees often worry about written statements being placed in their "permanent record."

On the Record

And many managers have used personnel files as a sort of weapon to keep employees in line. That's why many progressive-discipline policies contain different levels of warnings: verbal (meaning "oral") warnings and written warnings, with the latter being more serious. (Some companies have the nonsensical intermediate step of "written verbal warning," which is some-how less serious than the *written* "written warning." I have yet to under-stand the difference. I'll have more to say on progressive-discipline policies in Chapter 16. Spoiler alert: I hate them.)

In response to this managerial tool, states have enacted laws that give em-ployees broad rights to review their personnel files, or even get a copy. Some state laws also allow the employees to challenge documents that have been placed in their file, letting them tell their side of the story (as if that mattered). Many of these laws put a deadline on when the employer must turn over the file after the employee's request.

Mass. Hysteria

The worst of these personnel-records laws was just passed in, not surpris-ingly, Massachusetts. You won't be surprised to know that my home state has long been one of the most pro-employee jurisdictions in the US (along with California). Employers have long had to reveal employees' personnel records upon request. But in 2010, the law was modified to require em-ployers to proactively inform employees whenever something bad was placed in their files.

The rationale for this law is beyond me. In fact, it was tucked away in an "economic development" bill that was laden with higher-profile items like a sales-tax holiday. Absolutely no good can come from this new notification law. In fact, I believe that the new law is very likely to lead to more employee lawsuits.

Massachusetts employers now face a dilemma about documentation. On the one hand, I always warned clients to document employee issues as much as possible, just in case the issues go to litigation. On the other hand, the new law makes putting relatively innocuous information into a personnel file a much more-provocative event. Now a quiet, low-level note in a file carries the risk of unnecessarily agitating the employee. Agitated employees become disgruntled employees, and disgruntled employees sue. Under the new law, employers are damned if they do and damned if they don't.

The law doesn't benefit anyone (except lawyers). The amendment snuck in below the radar, without any discussion in the employment-law community. It's anti-employer, in that it places companies at increased risk for employee lawsuits. While advocates could possibly argue that workers benefit from increased "transparency," I disagree. There are times when a prudent employer should make a minor note in a file without escalating it to a human-resources event. Employees shouldn't need to be stressed out by every less-than-positive note made in a file. But the new law makes that unavoidable.

As of this writing, Massachusetts is the only state that has this new level of required notification. But other states have a tendency to follow Massachusetts where employment laws are concerned. (For example, Massachusetts was the first state to enact an employment-discrimination statute and set up an antidiscrimination agency.) So you need to keep an eye on whether your state makes a similar change. If it does, adding something in writing to an employee's personnel file could end up backfiring and causing a larger problem.

Ideally, you could keep your informal notes and burrito-wrapper scribblings in a separate management file. That way you have the backup you need without adding it to the personnel file and stressing out the employee. This option has largely been taken away from employers in Massachusetts. But if your state allows it, it's a good practice to follow.

A Red Flag

One final note on personnel-file requests: they almost always signal that the employee has lawyered up. Even though many employees realize that they have a legal right to see their files, very few avail themselves of that right without their lawyers' instructing them to do it. It is always one of the first things that an employee-side lawyer tells her client to do. If you suddenly get a request by an employee for a copy of his file, you should assume that he has hired a lawyer and is considering litigation against you.

A Warning on Warnings

Many employers get too hung up on written warnings. They see them as an intermediate tool for disciplining employees and correcting bad behavior that falls short of the need for termination. And that's fine, to a point. As I've said throughout this book, firing an employee is a serious and risky act. If you can avoid it and still accomplish your managerial goals through lesser means, that's great.

But when you find yourself in a situation where you're inclined to issue a written warning, first ask yourself what the document's actual purpose is. Not the warning's purpose; that's easy—it's to tell the employee not to do it again, or face termination. I mean, what's the *document's* purpose? Is it to convey a greater level of seriousness to the employee than a mere verbal warning would do? OK, I get that. But why don't you feel that you're able to convey seriousness in a face-to-face conversation? Some managers use these written warnings to avoid difficult conversations.

In my experience, both as a manager and as a management lawyer, employees usually obtain a greater and clearer understanding from a personal conversation than from a formal written document. So I'm not sure that the written format is as effective as many employers believe.

Is the document's purpose to be able to prove that the warning took place in a future litigation scenario? Also a valid reason. But you can accomplish that simply by making a note, as discussed above. Filling out a formal "written warning" form isn't necessary to prove that the warning happened.

Sign on the Dotted Line

And there's another thing about these forms. They often have a line for the employee to sign in acknowledgment of the warning. I understand the sentiment behind this acknowledgment line: you want to be able to establish that you warned the employee about the bad behavior and that the employee acknowledged the warning. But this creates more problems than it's worth.

When an employee is asked to sign a written warning, it takes a stressful situation and makes it worse. It's one thing to receive a formal warning. But to be asked to sign the form suggests that the employee is *agreeing* to what's written on the form—something that most warned employees are unlikely to want to do. Even if you tell the employee that signing it doesn't mean that she agrees with what's written there, she will still be uncomfortable with doing it. Signing it *seems* like an implicit agreement.

I can't tell you how many times I've looked through personnel files rife with written warnings that have "Employee refused to sign" scrawled over the signature line. To which my reaction was always: "Duh."

Don't bother with the silly employee-acknowledgment line on written warnings. They add nothing to strengthen the document, and they only cause greater stress and anger in the employee. And think long and hard about whether the written warning form is really the way you want to go. (Again, we'll talk more about this in the discussion of progressive discipline in Chapter 16.)

The Dumbest Managerial Tool

As little as I like written warning forms, I like annual performance appraisals even less. In fact, I find them to be utterly useless. Most companies use them because they think they're supposed to. I get that. In fact, I made that mistake for the first couple of years that I ran my law firm. Doing annual performance evaluations seemed like the managerial thing to do. (And mine were pretty damned good, if I do say so myself.)

But they're a stupid tool. Why? Let me count the ways.

Same Time Next Year

First of all, emphasizing that employees' performance should be measured on an annual basis suggests that there's less reason to measure it on a more-frequent basis. That's insane. First of all, who can possibly remember how a particular employee was performing ten or eleven months ago? So what ends up happening is that the past month or two get undue weight in the "annual" evaluation.

Second, if the purpose is to correct poor performance or behavior, why would you wait till the end of a year to do that? Performance and behavior issues need to be dealt with when they arise, not saved up till the end of an arbitrary twelve-month period. Similarly, if the appraisal is intended to reward good behavior or performance, why in the world would you wait?

"Hey, Alice. That thing you did back in March was terrific. Way to go."
Alice: "Huh?"

Third, if the purpose is to tie the evaluation to a decision about a possible pay increase, that's also foolish. In a well-run and well-managed company, pay decisions should be made on the basis of the employees' individual contributions on an ongoing basis, not based on the mere fact that they avoided attrition for another calendar year.

My fourth problem with annual basis is that managers tend to blow it on the timing. I always did. An evaluation that was intended to go out in early January would just as likely get finished in late March. That's normal, because managers usually have more-important managerial tasks to accomplish, like running the actual business.

The problem is, if you tell your employees that you're going to do annual performance appraisals in January, they're going to expect to receive them in January, along with some sort of a pay raise. When January slips into February and then March finally comes around, those employees are going to be unhappy with you, even if they know you've been busy doing real work.

Nature Abhors a Vacuum

Another problem with annual performance appraisals is that they can end up taking on undue importance sitting in an otherwise sparse personnel file. Many managers are diligent about completing their team members' performance appraisals on time every year, but beyond that, they don't add a lot of written documentation to the employees' files.

I've seen this scenario happen more times than I can count:

A company fires an employee for poor performance. The employee, unhappy with that decision, comes up with a reason to sue the company (usually some form of employment discrimination). In its defense, the company insists that the employee's performance sucked and that the firing was legitimate.

Then in the discovery process of the lawsuit (where the sides exchange documents and answer lawyers' questions), the company turns over the employee's personnel file (if it wasn't previously requested by the employee before the litigation began). And this is what the file looks like: A résumé. A cover letter. An employee information sheet. A W-4. And three annual performance appraisals filled with "satisfactory" and "meets expectations" entries. In other words, *not* the sort of file that screams out "lousy employee."

Now your documentation routine is actually hurting your chances in court.

If You Can't Say Something Nice...

Here's my biggest problem with APAs (I got sick of typing "annual perform-ance appraisals"): it's hard for managers to get the right level of negativity. Yes, I meant that. Negativity. You see, if an employee is really lousy, the per-formance appraisal is pretty easy. It almost writes itself. All you have to do is chronicle all the things that employee has done wrong over the past year. In fact, employees that bad are often fired before you ever need set pen to paper on an APA.

No, the bigger problem is with your average-to-good employees. People have a sense that if they check off "Exceeds Expectations" on all the evaluation factors and only write nice platitudes in the comment sections, that someone will think that they really didn't "evaluate." In other words, there's a bias against uniformly glowing performance reviews, and an expectation that there needs to be *something* negative to write about.

In a 2008 article entitled "Performance Appraisals: Paper Shuffling," Vera-Sage Institute cofounder Ron Baker criticized the practice of annual per-formance evaluations as outdated and overly focused on the negative. Baker is the world's leading guru on value pricing, and his books and ideas formed the foundation for much of my law firm's no-hourly-billing business model and for Prefix, LLC, my current pricing consultancy. In the post, Baker ques-tioned employers' slavish devotion to appraisals:

> Firms have an irrational faith in the effectiveness of performance appraisals. Most firms and employees are dissatisfied with the per-formance appraisal process, so it remains a curiosity why this methodology continues to exist.

Instead, he believes that the goal of firms should be to

> strive to create a meritocratic environment that rewards risk tak-ing and innovation, rather than rigid, stultifying union-type jobs that reward seniority, mediocrity, and complacency.[1]

In a similar vein, HR guru Frank Roche wrote an article about appraisals on his KnowHR web site called "Focusing on the Negative Never Works." In it, he explains why he believes performance appraisals are broken:

> In total, it's because I've never seen negative reinforcement work for long. Anyone who has taken Psych 101 knows it doesn't. So

---

[1] VeraSage Institute, "Performance Appraisals: Paper Shuffling," www.verasage.com/index.php/community/comments/performance_appraisals_paper_shuffling/, December 27, 2008.

here's what I'm asking companies to do: Dump documenting the bad stuff.

It would be really simple. If you're serious about performance management being a way to get the most out of people, what good can come from the "7 Good Things and 3 Bad Things" approach to performance management? Here's an idea: Write down 10 good things. And have your managers tell people daily what they've done right.[2]

In other words, break the managerial habit of trying to find something bad to say in a performance evaluation.

Baker, Roche, and others advocate more-frequent and more-proactive communications between managers and staff about performance. For example, Baker strongly advocates that managers take a page from the US Army's handbook and conduct after-action reviews after every project or job. These informal but immensely useful exercises document what people did, what went right, and what went wrong. They become a much more-effective teaching tool for both managers and staff than any annual performance appraisal could ever be.

In our litigation-obsessed society, many managers are afraid that if they put too many good things in a performance appraisal, it will make any future employee lawsuit that much more difficult to defend against. While there is logic in that sentiment, I think it ends up being an example of throwing the baby out with the bathwater. Just manage your people, and don't worry so much about the performance appraisals.

Conclusion

Paper is an important tool in a manager's toolbox, and words on paper can take on almost-magical significance. Use this tool wisely. Get into the habit of documenting things. Rethink whether written warning forms are a useful managerial device. And try to get your company away from annual performance appraisals and into more-effective tools for improving employee performance.

We've spent a lot of time talking about firing employees. (Which makes sense, given that it's the subject of the book.) But when does it make sense *not* to fire an employee? That's what we cover next.

---

[2] KnowHR, "Focusing on the Negative Never Works," www.knowhr.com/blog/2008/12/14/focusing-on-the-negative-never-works/, December 14, 2008.

Second Chances & PIPs

In case you haven't noticed, this book is about firing employees. (And if you haven't noticed, one of us isn't doing our job very well. Probably me.) But you could call this the "opposite" chapter, because it's all about *not* firing employees. Turns out, not firing employees the wrong way can cause just as many problems as firing employees the wrong way.

I've said it before, but it's worth repeating: one of my rules as a management lawyer was that I would never tell an employer not to fire someone after she made that decision. And the corollary to that rule was that I would never tell an employer *to* fire an employee if she didn't want to. But this corollary had an important exception that arose surprisingly often.

The exception is when I realize that the manager knows that the employee needs to be fired, but seems afraid to actually do it.

Be Not Afraid

As I've said, firing is a very stressful thing for a manager to do. (Yes, it's more stressful for the employee.) It's an extremely unpleasant task, and you're not going to relish performing that job. So naturally, you're going to be inclined to put it off. You might even be afraid to do it, knowing that you're going to hurt the employee in the process.

That's OK. It's normal to worry about it. You're supposed to be reluctant to do it.

But you have to rip the bandage off. It's going to sting for a bit, but it's got to be done.

"I Wish I Knew How to Quit You"

A lot of people, when faced with a stressful choice to make, will end up doing nothing and hoping that the problem will resolve itself. I've seen this happen countless times with problem employees.

Problem employees are usually unhappy with their jobs; in fact, that's often the root of what makes them problem employees. But managers who are reluctant to fire them will work to convince themselves that the problem employees will eventually quit. In other words, the problem will end up solving itself.

But in real life, problems rarely solve themselves. Maybe it's Murphy's Law (in which I majored in law school), but the employees you want to quit rarely do. That's part of why we call them "problem employees"—they're going to remain your problem until you solve it.

Waiting for the Other Shoe to Drop

A related phenomenon is when you give the problem employee enough rope to hang himself—and instead he uses it to hang on to his job. In other words, you decide that an employee is bound to do something even worse than he's done before—something so bad that his termination after that would be basically automatic. It's just a matter of time, you tell yourself, for him to mess up one last time. You're waiting for the other shoe to drop.

Sadly, though, problem employees rarely cooperate with your termination-by-default plan. Whether they know that you're watching their every move and they're just being more careful, or whether they just end up with a run of good luck that keeps them out of trouble—either way, it will suddenly be six months later and you still have the same problem employee.

This is not a valid management approach. Hoping your problems will go away is not the same as acting decisively. And the repercussions can be serious.

First, you have to put up with the problem employee whom you otherwise would have fired. This adds to your own stress and makes your job more difficult. In turn, that alone can harm the company.

Second, it can send a dangerous message to the other members of your workplace team. They might view your management-by-default approach as being a sign of weakness, and having a weak manager is very troubling to employees. Next thing you know, your better employees might be looking for employment elsewhere. Then you have the worst-case scenario: your good employees flee what they think is a sinking ship, and you're meanwhile stuck with your problem employee. Not good.

Third, with the hoping-it-goes-away strategy, you might miss your best opportunity to fire the problem employee. We can call this the Rick Paradox.

The Rick Paradox

Rick was an inside salesperson at a client of mine. "Rick," of course, isn't his real name. Rick's primary job was to get on the phone and sell computer components like hard drives and surge protectors to other companies. He worked primarily on commission, and although he was usually in the third or fourth quartile among inside salespeople at this company, he generally made a decent amount of money.

But Rick was a jerk.

He was pleasant enough on the phone to his prospects and customers, although if you knew him personally you would recognize that he was being fake. But in his dealings with coworkers, he was especially unpleasant.

He had an answer for everything. He constantly criticized just about everything, but nothing was ever his own fault. If a sale didn't go through, it was because someone else in the department blew the order fulfillment, or there was a problem with the component, or the customer was wishy-washy. It wasn't him. It never was.

He'd complain loudly and freely about not getting enough sales support, or enough vacation time, or enough sick days, or enough healthcare benefits. He was also something of a jailhouse lawyer, always pointing out when a company policy wasn't being followed to the absolute letter.

No one really liked Rick.

After a while, Rick started having discipline problems. He was downright insubordinate to his supervisor, sometimes refusing to make certain calls. He constantly neglected to turn in his call logs on time, bitching and moaning that a "real company" would have an administrative assistant do the paperwork so that he could focus on sales. His supervisor gave him two different written warnings because of late or incomplete call logs.

Going Too Far

His boss had warned him several times that he needed to call back a particular customer. To be fair, the customer was a difficult one, and you couldn't really blame Rick for not wanting to return the call. But that was part of his job; it was Rick's responsibility. And Rick put it off and put it off. Finally, when his supervisor had gotten angry, Rick said that he had made the call, and then he turned in a call log to back it up.

But Rick's supervisor wasn't so sure, so after Rick left for the day, he checked Rick's computer. (All the inside sales were made through a computerized phone system that tracked everything.) He pulled up the call tracking for the time that Rick said he'd called the difficult client, but there was no such call. Giving him the benefit of the doubt, the supervisor reviewed the tracking system for the hour before Rick's log entry. Then the hour after. Then for the entire day.

No call to the client. Rick had lied, and then falsified his log.

Last Chance. And Then Another Last Chance

So now Rick's supervisor had a solution to his problem. Rick had insubordinately refused to follow repeated instructions, lied about having completed the task, and falsified records to back up his lie. Pretty clear what the supervisor should do next, right? If he had read Chapter 5, he would have known that the lying and the falsification fit under the Second Deadly Sin of dishonesty, and that insubordination is the Fifth. Time to fire Rick, right?

The problem was that Rick's supervisor disliked conflict. He was a nice guy; too nice, really. He tolerated Rick's bad attitude in part because Rick made the company money from his sales, and in part because he was reluctant to fire him. Having Rick and his difficult personality around was stressful, but actually firing Rick would have been more stressful.

So the next day, Rick's boss confronted him with the discovery of the falsified customer log. Once he realized that he was caught, Rick confessed that he hadn't made the call. He meant to, but other things came up, and he didn't get around to it. He said that he didn't want to disappoint his supervisor by again saying that he hadn't done the call, so he said that he had. Then he needed to have the log reflect that. His plan was to make the call the very next morning. He was very sorry.

Instead of firing Rick, the supervisor went to human resources and worked out a "performance-improvement plan" (PIP) for Rick. The PIP spelled out the different areas where Rick was falling short in his performance, including his attitude, his paperwork, his insubordination, and the dishonesty he showed over the customer call.

The PIP then defined specific goals that Rick would need to achieve to remain employed at the company. The plan would go into effect immediately and would last for 90 days. If at the end of the 90-day period Rick had met the standards of the performance-improvement plan, he would be able to remain employed at the company. If not, his employment would automatically terminate.

Rick's supervisor and an HR official formally met with Rick to go through the terms of the PIP and make sure he understood. He said that he did. Then they asked Rick to sign the formal acknowledgment at the end of the plan document, and the supervisor and the HR person also signed it. Each kept a copy of the plan.

Murphy's Law Again

Rick's boss was actually pretty pleased with the outcome. During the meeting, Rick had acted appropriately contrite. He repeatedly promised that it wouldn't happen again, and he expressed gratitude for the second chance.

The supervisor wasn't so sure. He'd seen Rick say the right things in a tight spot before. But he also believed that Rick would have a hard time fulfilling the detailed standards and goals of the PIP over a three-month period. He had given Rick just enough rope to hang himself with, and now all he had to do was sit back and wait for Rick to mess up one final time.

Of course, that's not what happened. Instead, Rick followed the PIP to the letter. He met every single standard set out in the plan. Some of the things he did better than others; for example, his sales numbers actually improved a bit, and he behaved more civilly with his coworkers. He finished his paperwork on time—barely—and although it was far from perfect, it was adequate, and it complied with the terms of the plan. He never came in late, and didn't miss a day.

And on the ninety-first day after the PIP meeting, Rick's boss had no choice but to unhappily sign off on Rick's successful completion of the performance-improvement plan.

And Then What Happened?

You can well imagine. Rick's performance improvements tapered off the further away he got from the end of the 90-day period. A few months later, he was back to his old unpleasant self. Soon after, he started missing his deadlines for turning in his logs, and his disrespect toward his supervisor returned.

And now it was much harder to fire him.

Why? Because Rick's more recent transgressions were minor compared to the time he lied and falsified his paperwork. And he had successfully navigated his PIP. If he gets fired now, the case against him is weaker. If he gets fired and he claims some form of discrimination (he was over 40), his case will be that much stronger.

The best opportunity for getting rid of this problem employee happened months before, and the timid supervisor missed his chance. In the meantime, the department's morale suffered as coworkers watched the kid-gloves treatment that Rick received. The supervisor took a bad situation and made it worse by not being decisive.

Don't Be a Pipsqueak

It should come as no surprise that I'm not a fan of performance-improvement plans, at least not in the way they're typically used. Most of the time, when managers and human-resources professionals set up performance-improvement plans, it's under a scenario similar to Rick's. Sometimes, a company might actually have the need for a PIP written into a rigid progressive-discipline policy (see Chapter 16), or included in a collective-bargaining agreement with a union. Bad news. But usually a PIP is the result of management that is reluctant to do the stressful and risky work of conducting a termination.

In my opinion, there are several serious problems with PIPs.

The Paternalism Problem

One problem with performance-improvement plans is that they tend to come off seeming paternalistic. Now wait, you cry. Wasn't Rick's behavior childish? Of course. So doesn't he need some paternalistic guidance to get him back on track? My answer is: usually not.

In my experience, few employees appreciate being treated like children. In fact, a corporate culture that relies on rules and regulations and personnel policies up the wazoo tends to foster a disconnect between management and employees. Treating employees like wayward children rarely leads them to suddenly start behaving more responsibly. If anything, it brings about derision and rebellion.

So when you have an employee who's already giving you serious trouble, hitting her over the head with the equivalent of a trip to the principal's office in junior high school and a pedantic list of standards for improvement is unlikely to suddenly turn her into a model worker.

The Template Problem

Fire up the Google and type in "performance improvement plan template" (without the quotes). As of this writing (September 2011), there are more than 1.6 million hits. What's with all the PIP templates?

Actually, it makes perfect sense. As someone who writes for a living, I appreciate that there are few things more difficult than staring at a blank screen and having to create a document from scratch. As a practicing litigator, faced with having to write a brief or a motion, I always found it helpful to have some form of template to get the writing started. So I'd pull out a similar brief or motion I'd written before and start there, using the old one as a template.

But templates lead to a problem. A detailed template for something like a performance-improvement plan naturally leads to a sort of fill-in-the-blank mentality. It leads the manager or HR person to effectively cut and paste in things to say from previous PIPs, or to type in rote answers to the questions presented in the template. And that's a problem.

Employees are individuals with individualized problems. They need to be treated as individuals. Using a template to help manage an employee's performance has the opposite effect. A template tends to standardize the performance-improvement plans of different employees. If your company has a PIP template, you're doing something wrong. You're probably doing too many plans, and you're probably making them too similar.

Void for Vagueness

Even with a template, performance-improvement plans are still difficult to write. Often, you feel like you need to put more things into the document, just to give it some appropriate heft and seriousness. A one-paragraph PIP seems almost frivolous. More commonly, there's some pressure to come up with at least a two- or three-page masterpiece.

But this need to reach a certain length can lead managers to add vague language, such as:

- The Employee will maintain a job-performance level that meets or exceeds all defined standards for performance during the Plan Period.
- The Employee will at no time violate any of the Standards of Conduct outlined in the Company Employee Handbook or the Company Code of Conduct.
- The Employee will at all times conduct himself/herself in a manner that is respectful to his/her coworkers and Supervisor.

This is the sort of banal language that bogs down many performance-improvement plans. The jargony corporatespeak, the clumsy attempts to be gender neutral ("himself/herself"), and the goofy overcapitalization are all hallmarks of lawyerly documents.

More importantly, these admonitions are too vague to be of any use. All they really say is that the employee needs to do a good job, follow the rules, and not be a jerk. You need a performance-improvement plan to tell someone that? More importantly, if that's actually something the employee doesn't already know, do you want to waste a "Plan Period" letting the person catch up on the most basic concepts of employment and social interaction? Probably not.

Lawyerly Language

Plan documents tend to be either written by lawyers or written by HR folks attempting to sound lawyerly. Neither is a good thing. But don't take my word for it. Go back to our Google search for a second. Click through and take a look at the templates, many of which were written by lawyers or HR consultants. They all basically read the same way.

They're filled with formal, overwrought language, such as "It is your responsibility to access resources and carry out these and/or other strategies to improve your performance in the identified Quality Standard." Yikes. Who talks like that?

Just as we discussed in the last chapter, managers tend to sound different when they get in front of a keyboard and try to compose what they think is supposed to be a "formal" document. It's human nature, and it's why so much business writing (and for that matter, legal writing) is so bad. Scrolling through the Google hits, you'll see far worse examples.

But consider the person reading the plan document. Anyone reading this kind of obtuse prose is going to have his or her eyes glaze over. Formalistic writing loses its power to effect change. I've read thousands of these documents, and I still have trouble getting through them. An employee with no experience wading through these documents hasn't got a chance.

Don't be tempted by the easy way out that performance-improvement plans provide. PIPs, especially those generated from a company template, can turn into a crutch for managers looking to avoid the more difficult decision of terminating problem employees.

When to Give Another Chance

So are performance-improvement plans always a bad idea? Often, but not always. Sometimes it is the right decision to give an employee a second (or third, or whatever) chance.

Forgiveness is an important quality in a manager. So is recognizing that employees are human beings, and thus fallible. And as we've talked about, you don't want to make a decision in anger to fire an employee.

But there are second chances and there are second chances. As we discussed in Chapter 5, I believe that employees who commit one of the Seven Deadly Sins do not deserve a second chance. Rick's lying about having made the client call, and falsifying the call log to reinforce the lie, called for his immediate termination. My employee who embezzled with the firm credit card likewise did not deserve a second chance.

On the other hand, my bookkeeper with the math mistakes deserved and got a second chance. She hadn't committed any of the deadly sins, and she wasn't a problem employee in the sense of being difficult to deal with. She just had performance issues. So I gave her second chance, and then another one. And when the mistakes continued and it became clear to me that I could no longer trust her work, it became time to let her go.

Who Deserves It?

As I said before, you never want to give an employee a second chance when the truth is that you actually want or expect the employee to fail. If that's the case, then it's time to fire the employee. Only give another chance to employees who you want to succeed and you expect (or at least hope) to succeed.

For example, you could be dealing with an employee whose declining performance stems from some personal or family issues. Maybe she's just going through a tough time right now and needs some compassion and some prodding. If you're confident that the employee has the potential to get past whatever's keeping her down, a second chance might be exactly what she needs.

So do you give her a written performance-improvement plan? I still say no, but others may disagree. I certainly wouldn't give her one of those template-based plans we talked about. I see no good coming from one of those.

Instead, you need to sit down with the employee and work out together exactly what she needs to do to save her job. If you think it's useful for both of you to write this down in a list or a set of notes, fine: do just that. But it's more effective if you do it together in your meeting, rather than firing up the PIP generator and spewing out one of these vague, meaningless, lawyerly documents.

Some lawyers will tell you that the value of the PIP here is to prove that you had this discussion and set out these performance standards. That way, if things go awry and a termination and lawsuit ensue, you have evidence that you gave her these performance standards and that she signed the PIP. But I don't really care about that; it's not a serious risk.

Just as I said in discussing written warnings in the previous chapter, I'm not concerned about proving that the employee read, understood, and signed her performance-improvement plan. It's enough that you as the manager took some notes about what you discussed. That way, if you ever make it to the witness stand, you can testify with certainty that at ten in the morning on April 16, 2009, you and she sat down and discussed these three standards that she would have to meet to keep her job. The jury will believe you, because you have your notes. Even if she denies it.

Conclusion

If your company is handing out a lot of performance-improvement plans, you're doing something wrong. While the people who draft these plans often mean well, the plans tend to be counterproductive. (On second thought, they might *not* mean well, if they actually don't want the problem employee to successfully complete the plan.) Either way, PIPs tend to be a poor substitute for hands-on, individualized management.

If an employee should be fired, don't go the PIP route. Fire that employee now; you might not get a better chance. On the other hand, if the employee shows promise and deserves a second chance, then sit down with him and work out together how to save his job. You don't need to download a template to do that.

In the next section, we'll talk about what can happen when a termination goes wrong.

Sign of the Times
Layoffs

One of the most difficult types of termination a company can face is the mass layoff. Employment lawyers call them reductions in force, or RIFs. In a down economy, layoffs become increasingly common. Obviously, they are devastating for the employees who lose their jobs. But they are also miserable for the managers and HR professionals who have to make the decisions.

Monday, Bloody Monday

A few years ago, on a single Monday—January 26, 2009—America's largest companies laid off about 70,000 employees. This happened in a month when 200,000 American workers had their jobs cut. Granted, many of these workers had been at a handful of huge companies: 20,000 at Pfizer; 8,000 at Sprint; 7,000 at Home Depot. But that single Monday was an incredibly unhappy day around the country.

Note A language note: The verb—to *lay off* someone—is two words. The noun—*layoff*—is one, without a hyphen. The adjective—a *laid-off* worker—is hyphenated because it's a phrasal (or compound) adjective that precedes the noun. But the worker was *laid off*—no hyphen. It's hard enough to do a layoff. It shouldn't be so hard to write about it.

Over at the *KnowHR* blog that week, Frank Roche's post, "How in the Hell Do You Lose 71,400 Jobs in One Day?" had terrific advice for the so-called layoff survivors:

> I wish I had some really great HR advice today. I'm a little shell-shocked, but here's what I'd say: For those of you who are still there . . . kick ass. Do your best work. Stop going to meetings. Start doing things. Make money.
>
> Now's the time to do our best work.

On my own workplace blog, *Gruntled Employees*, I echoed Frank's advice:

> I completely agree. I would add that HR professionals, managers, and executives need to get in the trenches and rally the troops (feel free to add any other militaristic metaphors you like). Fear is driving the economy, and fearful employees are not gruntled employees. Thus, fear diminishes profits.
>
> Talk to your employees. Tell them that it's going to be all right, that we'll make it through this OK. Live together, die alone. . . .
>
> Tell them to do one extra thing today that will help make the company more profitable. Make one extra call to get a sales appointment. Perform one extra quality check of a component. Think of one extra idea for innovation.
>
> And then do it again tomorrow. And the next day.

Of course, this advice was for the managers at companies trying to avoid further layoffs. But what if the layoffs become inevitable? How should your company handle it?

Sending the Wrong Message

During this terrible layoff run in early 2009, I noticed a trend in press releases and internal memos about the layoffs. In announcing the RIFs, whether publicly or "internally and confidentially" (which these days just means publicly with a slight delay—these memos and e-mails never remain confidential anymore), the companies explained the layoffs, cited the recession, but then talked about how *well* their company is doing.

Which made me wonder: did they ask the workers they were laying off, "Do you want the good news first or the bad news?"

Examples abounded. A *CNET* article entitled "IBM quietly lays off North American staff" came right after Big Blue announced a 12 percent increase in earnings. Cellphone maker Ericsson issued a release entitled "Ericsson Reports Strong Fourth Quarter," but then laid off 5,000 workers worldwide. *Internet News* had this headline: "EMC Trims Staff Levels Despite Record Revenues." According to the popular law blog *Above the Law,* a sizable regional law firm issued an internal e-mail talking about its "strong 2008" while announcing that it was laying off 6 percent of its lawyers.

Perhaps some of this was Churchillian stiff-upper-lip talk to rally the remaining troops (and investors). But it's a safe bet that many of the laid-off workers (as well as a lot of those still left on board) were left wondering if the layoffs were truly necessary. More likely it was tone-deaf corporate marketing trying to minimize the PR impact of the reductions.

To be sure, job cuts may help prop up profit margins in the short run. But companies need to remember that recessions end. And on the other side, these companies might wonder why they stopped being employers of choice in the eyes of the talent they will then need to hire. People remember how they were treated on the way out, and they tend to tell other people.

Bottom line: make sure your messages are consistent. If you're laying people off, don't brag about how well things are going.

Of Layoffs and Leaks

One of the concerns we heard over and over from our corporate clients facing imminent RIFs was how to avoid the gossiping and rumormongering that can surround layoffs like circling vultures. Oftentimes, ahead of a planned layoff, companies will go all Jack Bauer–style need-to-know on their employees. The thinking there is that layoffs should be kept secret until they're rolled out at H-hour. This keeps the rumors to a minimum, and keeps employees productive until the embargo lifts and the layoffs actually occur.

That's dumb.

Well-intentioned, but dumb. You see, one of the main principles of this book is that any given employee at any given time has a certain probability—P—of suing the employer. Certain events, such as firing the employee, tend to raise P. While it is impossible to reduce P to zero, it is the role of managers, HR pros, and employment lawyers to help lower P.

In my experience, surprising employees with bad news tends to increase P. For that reason, we would always tell clients that an employee who is about to be disciplined or fired should not be surprised by it. Otherwise, the surprise acts as a multiplier of the bad feelings that come with the bad news, and it raises P even more.

The same is true in a layoff situation. To be sure, no one wants the workplace grinding to a halt because everyone's too busy gossiping and spreading rumors before an expected layoff. But carefully leaking some information about the upcoming layoff, maybe a week beforehand, gives people a chance to come to grips with their possible fate.

Those whose departments are underperforming, or whose own work performance is weak, may come to realize that their departure is inevitable. I'm not saying that they're going to be happy about it. But without the element of surprise to exacerbate the hurt feelings and other emotions that come with a layoff, their personal P may be low enough to avoid lawsuits.

Are the Layoffs Really Necessary?

Don't assume that they are, if you have any say in the decision. Sometimes companies get themselves into a mindset that their circumstances are so dire that only a reduction in force will stop the bleeding. And they might be correct. But before making that drastic choice, you should consider every other possible solution.

Looking at other ways to lower workforce costs is a good idea. Cutting back on hiring or even implementing a hiring freeze are potentially useful ways to lower these costs and possibly forestall a RIF. Even if the layoff then becomes necessary, the fact that the company first cut back or froze hiring might make the layoff go down easier. Conversely, if laid-off employees know that the company is still hiring other employees, it may be seen as adding insult to injury. This could increase the risk of litigation.

Other possibilities include voluntary-severance plans and early-retirement plans. (Obviously, these are only viable options in larger companies.) This involves creating a "package" of severance and improved benefits to induce employees to voluntarily leave the company. One of the nice things about an early-retirement program is that it's unlikely to trigger age-discrimination claims. Federal age-discrimination law excludes most voluntary early-retirement plans from being evidence of age bias.

Many voluntary plans include formulas for calculating severance benefits, often taking into account both age and years of service. The problem with this is that it takes away the company's discretion in how to deal with those employees. Formulas often prevent individualized decisions. And another concern is that the "wrong" employees will take the plan; in other words, you may end up losing your better employees instead of your lesser ones.

Having a Plan

If you do conclude that layoffs are necessary, you then need to make sure you have a plan. A haphazard reduction in force is a short path to disaster.

A reduction in force is a big-picture event for a company, so the top executives should be involved, working hand in hand with human resources. What you don't want is lower-level managers making their own idiosyncratic decisions so that different departments end up with very different results.

First off, you need to make sure that the rationale for the layoff is clear. Sometimes when this isn't so, decisions can be made that are at odds with the real reason for the layoff. For example, if the reason for the RIF is to move the business away from underperforming divisions, it wouldn't make sense to also cut people from the stronger areas.

Next, you need to decide what criteria you're going to use in determining whom to let go. Some of the criteria will have more to do with the positions than with the individuals. For example, certain jobs might be deemed nonessential and more likely to face cuts regardless of the people in those jobs.

Other factors will depend more on the individuals. Some of these criteria might be objective: performance scores, job level, seniority, particular skill sets. Others might be more subjective, such as depending on past performance or future potential. It should go without saying, but what you absolutely have to stay away from are the kind of demographic factors that are the basis for the protected categories we discussed in Chapter 4 (and will discuss more in the next two chapters): race, age, sex, disability, and so forth.

Who actually makes the individual decisions is also important, particularly at a larger company. On the one hand, there's some risk involved if lower-level managers have too much say over such an important decision. On the other hand, senior management and HR might not have enough familiarity with the individuals to be able to make the right decisions.

Assessing the Risks

The biggest risk that comes with a reduction in force is the claim that the layoffs were done in a discriminatory manner, or at least that they ended up having a discriminatory effect (also known as "disparate impact.") For this reason, many employment lawyers will advise you to perform some statistical analysis after you make the cuts but before you announce them. But this is fraught with problems.

Say you decide that you need to cut 100 jobs to save your financially struggling company. You go through the process and come up with your cuts. Then your HR department or your employment counsel conducts some statistical analysis on the layoffs. The point of this analysis is to determine whether the layoffs will leave the company at risk for a discrimination lawsuit.

Let's say that your analysis shows that 40 percent of the people (or 40 employees; I did that in my head) selected for layoff are over 40 years old. Not necessarily a problem on its own. But then you notice that only 20 percent of your total workforce is over 40. Now it looks like a problem, because older employees are getting laid off at double the expected rate. And this means there's an increased risk of an age-discrimination lawsuit.

Note I use age as the example here because it's the protected category most likely to come up in a reduction in force. But you can substitute any other category and face the same problem.

But how do you fix this? Are you supposed to go back and "massage" the numbers, changing who gets let go so that you end up with a proportional result? In other words, deselect 20 of the older employees and replace them on the layoff list with 20 younger employees? Of course, then you're *actually* discriminating—using age as a factor (or even *the* factor) in deciding whom to fire.

Technically, employees under 40 don't have any age-discrimination rights, but it's still morally wrong if not legally wrong. And if the protected category at issue is one of others, like race or sex, making these "corrective" changes is both morally *and* legally wrong.

So what do you do when your statistics look bad? You need to resist the temptation to "correct" your numbers so that they don't "look" discriminatory. Just because your statistics for the layoffs are disproportional compared to your workforce demographics doesn't mean that there was discrimination involved in the decisions. Instead, your HR people and your employment counsel need to review the individual decisions to make certain that there was no *actual* discrimination involved.

Obviously, if you find that there was discriminatory selection, then corrections are absolutely necessary. But if they're not, then you need to focus on backing up the rationale and criteria for your decisions. Yes, the disparate statistics probably increases the risk of a discrimination lawsuit. But the better you can support your selection criteria, the better you'll be able to defeat any future lawsuits.

A Written Warning

We talked before about layoffs and leaks, but there are certain situations where the law *requires* a company to give specific notice about a RIF. If a company employs at least 100 employees and conducts a "plant closing" or a "mass layoff," then the federal Worker Adjustment and Retraining Notification Act (better known by its hopelessly forced acronym, the "WARN Act") requires the company to give at least 60 days' written notice.

The terms "plant closing" and "mass layoff" have very technical definitions that your employment counsel can explain to you. The Act also specifies what the notice must contain, including the date of the action, whether it's expected to be permanent, whether there will be "bumping" rights (that is, whether senior employees can pull rank and get junior employees laid off in their places), and whom to contact for further information.

There are a few exceptions to the WARN Act requirements, which like the rest of the law are hypertechnical and confusing. These exceptions have to do with "unforeseen business circumstances," natural disasters, or status as a "faltering company" (meaning that it has sought and been turned down for capital).

In addition to the federal law, most states have their own "mini-WARN Acts" with very different definitions and employer obligations. In some states, a "mass layoff" can involve as few as 25 employees. Make sure your employment counsel explains to you the laws that cover your company.

Release Me

When you do go forward with the layoffs, if you are giving some sort of severance package (whether it's voluntary or involuntary), you want to make sure you get something very valuable in return: a release from future lawsuits. In other words, the severance benefits become part of an exchange, and the employees only receive them if they agree in return to forgo any right to sue the company over the termination.

The most important component of the release is the surrendering of any discrimination or wrongful-termination claims. (Wage claims, on the other hand, usually cannot be waived.) But it's not enough just to have the employees agree to waive their potential lawsuits. The releases have to include certain specific things to be enforceable. Otherwise, you could find yourself in the unfortunate situation of having paid out severance to someone who can still sue you despite having promised not to.

The release requirements vary based on the state and federal laws that govern the claims being waived. For example, releases must be written in a way to allow them to be understood by the employee, or else the waiver won't be found "knowing and voluntary." The release needs to explicitly inform the employee that he or she has the right to consult an attorney before signing, and may take a certain amount of time to consider it. And the employee has to receive something of value that he or she would not have received without signing the waiver.

If the employee affected is 40 or older and is being asked to waive the right to sue for age discrimination, this triggers additional requirements under the federal Older Workers Benefit Protection Act (employment lawyers pronounce this like "Oprah" without the *R;* if your lawyer insists on pronouncing it "O-W-B-P-A," you've hired yourself a boring pedant).

There are a bunch of important technical requirements under OWBPA. For example, the laid-off employees have to be given 45 days to consider signing the release. (It's only 21 days in an individual termination.) Even after they sign it, they have another seven days to change their minds and revoke it. And they have to be given disclosures about the ages and job titles of the people who were selected for the severance plan, and the people who weren't. This information is designed to help them determine whether they've been discriminated against on the basis of age. No other protected category gets these additional rights. But then again, "over 40" is the only protected category that nearly every US senator and representative is a member of.

Conclusion

Layoffs are an unfortunate and highly stressful action of last resort for companies facing hard times. Failing to manage this carefully will cause the company to experience even harder times. Layoffs are difficult enough without litigation.

Speaking of litigation, it's time now to learn about just what happens when firings go wrong.

The Worst-Case Scenario

Part III is all about what you want to avoid: employee lawsuits. This section takes you through the unpleasant process of having an angry fired employee suing your company. We'll go step by step through the most common type of litigation—the discrimination case—both in court and before administrative agencies. We'll also cover wage cases and sexual-harassment claims: two types of litigation that are very difficult for an employer to win. Knowing what you could face will help you try harder to avoid it.

Discrimination Cases Part I

Agency Charges

I've been using the terms *lawsuit, claim,* and *case* interchangeably, but they're not technically the same. A discrimination claim is an allegation by the fired employee that you have committed employment discrimination. It consists of a set of alleged facts that, taken together in the context of the governing statute, leads to the conclusion that you violated that statute. The case is the mechanism by which the employee seeks to make you pay for this violation. It's a lawsuit when the case is brought in a court, either state or federal.

This chapter will take you through a discrimination case from start to finish at an administrative agency. The following chapter will deal with discrimination lawsuits filed in court. As a manager, you have to hope that these two chapters are the only places you experience them.

Vocabulary Lesson: A Tort

As fired employees storm out of the workplace for the last time, it's common to hear them threaten a nasty and expensive "wrongful-termination lawsuit." Oftentimes, they say that because they don't know any better—they've heard the term on TV or in a movie, and they think that's what it's called. And technically, they're right: a fired employee *can* file a wrongful-termination (or wrongful-discharge) claim.

But as soon as they get in front of a lawyer who actually handles employee cases, they quickly learn that a wrongful-discharge case is usually a loser. As we discussed back in Chapter 1, most employees are at-will employees, and an employer is generally able to fire at-will employees. What is more, a wrongful-discharge claim is a type of tort claim. *Tort* isn't legalese or jargon; it's a legitimate term of art that describes the legal theory under which the claim is brought. The word *tort* comes from the Latin word *torquere*, which means "to twist" or—I kid you not—"to screw." In other words, a person who commits a tort against you has in fact screwed you over.

Tort claims are based on the *common law*, which is the part of English law that comes from court decisions and longtime custom. This is contrasted with *statutory law*, which are laws enacted by a state legislature or by the US Congress. In the employment-law setting, there is a very important difference between common-law claims (such as tort or contract claims) and statutory claims. Common-law claims don't provide for attorneys' fees.

Under the so-called "American rule," each side bears the cost of its own lawyer bills, regardless of who wins the case. But in many statutory employment claims, the law provides for the losing employer to pay the winning employee's attorneys' fees—but not the other way around. This can make a huge difference, as fees can easily reach well into the six-figure range.

The Best Kind of Claims for Employees

So even though the fired employee might shout threats about a wrongful-discharge lawsuit on his way out, his lawyer will quickly explain to him that his best available claim is probably an employment-discrimination claim.

One note: the employee may also have some form of wage claim, such as failure to pay proper wages or a failure to pay overtime. These are also good claims for employees, in that the relevant statutes usually provide for multiple damages and attorneys' fees. But they don't tend to have the high possible payoffs that winning discrimination claims can have. That's why discrimination lawsuits are often a disgruntled employee's weapon of last resort.

What Is a Discrimination Claim?

In a nutshell, an employee bringing a discrimination claim is accusing your company of having made a workplace decision based on an illegal reason. That illegal reason has to do with the employee's membership in a protected group, usually involving personal factors that can't be changed (or at least, can't *easily* be changed). To win the claim, the employee has to prove that the decision stemmed from the employer's bias against members of that protected group.

We talked about the different protected groups in Chapter 4. Most of the 30 riskiest employees to fire are members of protected groups. Because antidiscrimination laws are statutory, the actual laws that apply to your company depend on where your company is located. There are federal protections that apply to companies nationwide. In addition, each state has its own list of discrimination protections. And the list is always changing (and increasing).

You'll need to check with your employment lawyer to make sure you know which laws cover your company. But here's a basic list:

- race
- sex
- age (40 and over)
- religion
- national origin
- ethnicity
- sexual orientation (some states)
- sexual identity (a few states)
- genetics
- disability
- veteran status
- pregnancy
- employees who have complained about discrimination
- criminal-record status

So to bring a discrimination claim against you, the employee has to allege being harmed by a workplace decision that was based on one of these categories.

Who Can Bring a Claim?

As we discussed in Chapter 4, it's not only the employee's membership in one of these categories that matters. Instead, what really matters is that the basis of the decision had to do with these categories. For that reason, a male employee can bring a sex-discrimination claim if he's alleging that he was adversely affected by a workplace decision that was made *because* of his gender.

At least that's the legal answer. The real-world answer is that a man is going to have a very hard time bringing a successful sex-discrimination case. Sure, there are the notable exceptions, like a male dance instructor getting turned down for a job at a dance studio for women. But for the most part, a guy's not likely to win a sex-discrimination claim.

Most discrimination claims arise from terminations, which is why they get two whole chapters in this book (three if you include most of Chapter 4). But a discrimination claim can also arise from other managerial decisions or actions. An individual can claim discrimination over things like failing to hire, failing to promote, paying less, unfairly disciplining, and so on. These claims have their own particular problems. Most importantly, they're made by current employees instead of former employees. Defending a discrimination claim brought by a current employee is a decidedly not-fun situation.

But in this book, we're concerned with claims brought by fired employees, which are much more common. So what do they have to do to win?

How an Employee Wins

To win an employment-discrimination lawsuit, the fired employee has to prove that the employer made the harmful decision based on an unlawful bias against one of the categories mentioned above. That means that the employee has to convince the factfinder in the case that this unlawful prejudice existed in the heart of the manager. But that's hard to do, since we haven't yet perfected any scientific method of mindreading.

Without the ability to see inside a person's mind or heart and determine for certain if that person has discriminatory bias and used that bias in making the decision that harmed the employee, the factfinder in the case must rely on the evidence presented. But unlike in *CSI: Saskatoon* or whatever, evidence in discrimination cases tends to be harder to come by.

Direct and Circumstantial Evidence

In any court case, there are two basic kinds of evidence: direct and circumstantial. Direct evidence is evidence that directly supports the notion that something happened, without the need to rely on any sort of inference. Direct evidence can be spoken testimony, where a witness testifies that she saw the thing happen.

For example, a witness could testify that she heard the manager say, "I fired Tony because I hate people over 40." It can be written evidence, like a note in the manager's handwriting or an e-mail sent from the manager's computer saying, "We should get rid of Louise because this company has too many women working here." As you can imagine, this sort of evidence doesn't come up too often in employment-discrimination cases.

By contrast, circumstantial evidence depends upon inference to support the truth of the assertion made. This sort of evidence suggests a connection between it and the assertion, although that connection may be wrong. Because an inference may be wrong, it is often more difficult to prove something with circumstantial evidence than with direct evidence.

When judges give their instructions to juries at the close of a trial, they always explain the difference between direct and circumstantial evidence. The most common way I've heard it explained is with this wintry scenario:

You wake up one morning and there's snow on the ground in your front yard. If you looked out the window during the night and saw that it was snowing, you've created direct evidence. Later, on the witness stand, a lawyer can ask you how you know that it snowed on the night in question. Your testimony "I looked out the window that night and saw that it was snowing" is direct evidence that it snowed that night.

On the other hand, if you hadn't looked out the window during the night, you would not be able to provide direct evidence of snow falling on the night in question. Your testimony about this mysterious meteorological occurrence would go like this:

LAWYER

How do you know it snowed on the night of January 11, 2009?

YOU

Well, just before I went to bed that night, I looked out the window and saw no snow on the ground. When I woke up the next morning, I looked outside and saw snow on my front lawn. About two inches' worth. So I concluded that it snowed, you idiot.

This fascinating testimony of yours is circumstantial evidence. (Don't say the "you idiot" part.) You didn't see it actually snowing that night, so you can't offer direct evidence of the frigid precipitation. But because there was no snow when you went to bed and there *was* snow on the ground when you awoke, you can *infer* that it snowed during the night. Your testimony to that effect is circumstantial evidence. Yes, it could be wrong. Maybe some of your friends brought in a one-ton dump truck from the mountains to deposit a huge pile on your front lawn as an elaborate prank. That's possible. Not likely, but possible. Much more likely that the judge or jury will buy your inference and accept that it snowed on the night of the 11th.

Just how hard you need to convince the judge or jury depends on the burden of proof.

Burden of Proof

If you watch any TV or movies, then you probably feel like you know about burden of proof. The judge in the TV show will explain to the jury that they need to be sure "beyond a reasonable doubt" that the defendant is guilty. In other words, the jury needs to be sure that the defendant did what he was accused of, and that any doubts they might have are unreasonable ones.

But the reasonable-doubt standard only applies to criminal cases, where the jury has to determine whether the defendant is guilty or not guilty. In civil cases—that is, in lawsuits over disputes between two or more parties—there is a different standard to follow. Civil cases aren't about guilt; they're about winning.

In a civil case, the judge or jury's job is to figure out which side wins. So the standard of proof that applies in most civil cases is "a preponderance of the evidence." In other words, the plaintiff—the party bringing the lawsuit—must convince the judge or jury that the evidence is more likely to support her side than it is to support the defendant's position. Sometimes you'll hear people describe this as "51 percent," though that's a slight exaggeration; "more likely than not" works out to be a hair over 50 percent.

Of course, it can be a little misleading when you talk about 51 percent or 50.000001 percent or whatever. Obviously, there are no objective measurements involved. Instead, the jurors have to ask themselves whether they think that the plaintiff has proved that her claim is at least slightly more likely to be correct than the other side's defense. "Preponderance of evidence" is just a fancy way of saying "slightly more likely."

By the way, I often hear people talking about "guilty" or "not guilty" in the context of employment cases. Those words don't apply in a civil case; they apply only in a criminal case. In a civil case, it's all about who wins. The court either finds "for the plaintiff" (that is, the employee wins) or finds "for the defendant" (the company wins). Although in a sense, everyone loses when an employee lawsuit goes to trial (except, of course, the lawyers).

Getting Inside the Employer's Head

So now we've talked about evidence and standards of proof. But how does a plaintiff actually prove that the manager who fired her had a discriminatory motive? Let's assume that the manager wasn't dumb enough to speak or write down his biased intent. So how can the court get inside the manager's head and determine if there was discrimination?

Obviously, it can't. There's no method of mind-reading that can be used in a court of law to prove discriminatory intent. But over time, the courts have come up with a method to prove discrimination without having direct evidence. This order of proof is called "the *McDonnell Douglas* test," or more cumbersomely, "the *McDonnell Douglas* burden-shifting framework," but you don't need to know that.

It's called that because of a 1973 US Supreme Court case called *McDonnell Douglas v. Green*, where Green had been a mechanic at the aerospace company before being laid off in a 1964 reduction in force. He claimed, among other things, that his termination was motivated by his being black. The case litigated all the way up to the Supreme Court. The facts and outcome of the case aren't important to our discussion.

What *is* important is that the Court in its decision set up a framework for shifting the burden of who needs to offer up evidence in a discrimination case. Lawyers call that the "burden of production," as in who has to "produce" the evidence. This doesn't mean that the burden of *proof* shifts. The plaintiff always has the burden of proving her case under the preponderance-of-evidence standard. Instead, it means that there is an order to proving these cases, and the order has three basic steps.

Uh-oh: Latin Ahead

First, the employee has to offer evidence that she has a prima facie case of discrimination. I know, I promised you no Latin in this book. But this isn't an example of lawyers trying to sound all fancy. This is simply the term of art. It means "at first impression." The employee has to provide evidence that she has the basic makings of a case. Usually, this involves four things:

1. She is a member of one of the protected categories we listed above (such as, she's a woman);

2. She performed her job "adequately" (and the courts have set the bar really low on this requirement);

3. Something bad happened to her at work (as in, she got fired, or some other adverse job action); and

4. Similarly situated employees with similar qualifications who were outside her protected category were treated more favorably.

Once the plaintiff has offered evidence making out a prima facie case, there is now a presumption that the employment decision was discriminatory. Now the burden of producing evidence shifts to the employer to dispel this presumption.

But It Was Legit

The second step is for the employer to provide evidence that it had a legitimate and nondiscriminatory reason for making the decision. It's not a particularly high threshold either. The employer merely needs to provide some evidence that there was a decent reason for firing the employee, such as lousy performance or insubordination or any of the Seven Deadly Sins. Almost anything, really. By producing evidence to support a legitimate, nondiscriminatory reason for firing the employee, the employer manages to dispel the presumption created by the prima facie case.

Then the burden of providing evidence shifts *back* to the employee.

Yeah, but That Was a Lie

This third step is where the rubber meets the road. Almost every plaintiff can make out a prima facie case. And almost any sentient employer can come up with a legitimate, nondiscriminatory reason for the decision. So now the burden of production returns to the employee. She now needs to put forward evidence that the employer's stated reason was a lie, or else come up with something else to show that bias motivated the decision. If she can't produce this evidence, the employer wins. Otherwise, the case continues.

This concept of the employer's stated reason being a lie is usually described as "pretext" evidence. In other words, the plaintiff is claiming that the employer's ostensible reason for firing her was a pretext for the real reason, which was discrimination. The pretext itself suggests the discrimination.

This is why you never want to give any kind of false reason to an employee you're firing. I'm not suggesting that managers have a tendency to be dishonest. Usually, I see well-meaning employers try to sugarcoat a termination with a so-called white lie. The most common one is "we're eliminating the position." Then they go and run an ad for the same job. I've seen that happen many times. These managers might believe that the well-intended lie will soften the blow at termination and make the employee not feel as bad about being fired. While that's a noble sentiment, it's way too risky.

This framework has been modified over the years since the 1973 *McDonnell Douglas* decision, and these changes are beyond the scope of this book. Also, courts in different states sometimes use different versions that only apply within their jurisdictions. But the basic premise remains the same. If you use a lie when firing an employee—even if it's only a white lie—you are giving that employee a stronger chance at beating you in a discrimination case.

So what does that discrimination case look like?

Anatomy of a Discrimination Case

Unlike with other employment claims, an employee cannot go to court immediately to seek relief. He first needs to make a claim of employment discrimination with the appropriate state or federal agency.

Nearly every state has an administrative agency empowered by statute to investigate and adjudicate discrimination claims. There is also the federal Equal Employment Opportunity Commission, which operates nationwide. In some states, it is more common for cases to be brought in the state agency; in others, the EEOC gets the majority of the cases. When there's a choice, the savvy employee lawyer may make a strategic decision about which agency to file at.

Filing a Charge

Regardless of which agency is chosen, the first step in the employment-discrimination case is to file a charge. Usually, this involves the employee's physically going to the office of the agency and speaking with an intake clerk. The clerk will take down the employee's identifying information, as well as that of the employer. Then the clerk will ask the employee to describe what happened that made him believe he was discriminated against. A competent clerk will invite the employee to tell his story from beginning to end, then go back and ask appropriate questions. Unfortunately, underfunded agencies have a hard time hiring enough competent clerks.

The result is that a typical charge often contains an unreadable mash of alle-gations that is then signed by the employee. When you see this mess, don't get your hopes up. Just because the charge is poorly written doesn't mean that the case will be any easier to win. The decision-makers will know that the intake clerk wrote the thing, not the employee.

Some employees' lawyers will write up their own statement to turn in to the agency and have it appended to the standard charge form. This usually (but not always) leads to a more professional and more understandable (and thus more convincing) charge.

Who's Who?

The charge forms have boxes to check off the protected categories. It will also include room for additional defendants besides the employer, such as supervisors or other coworkers. Unfortunately, it's becoming increasingly common to add individual defendants.

By the way, the terms *plaintiff* and *defendant* are usually reserved for court cases. Most agencies will call the employee the *complainant*, or sometimes the *petitioner* or *charging party*. I always get a kick out of it when inexperienced plaintiffs' lawyers pronounce *complainant* with an extra *T* in it ("complaint-ant"); that tends to tell me a lot about them.

The employer is usually known as the *respondent*.

First Look at the Charge

The agency will then process the charge. This could take days, weeks, or months, depending on the agency. Most agencies have rules or at least guidelines for the timely processing of charges. Unfortunately, most agencies are also saddled with huge backlogs of cases, and these timing rules tend to go by the wayside.

Sometimes, the agency will review the charge at the outset to make sure that it actually has the makings of a claim. For example, it might check whether the employer and the employment site were located in the state that the agency covers. It might also check whether the employer has enough employees to be covered by the appropriate laws. For example, the main federal laws, Title VII and the Americans with Disabilities Act, require an employer to have 15 employees to be covered. If the company has 14 or fewer employees, those statutes don't apply. Different state laws have different minimum numbers; some minimums are as low as one.

But most of the time, the agency will process the charge without looking into these things. If the location or employee complement is wrong, the agency assumes that the employer will bring that up in its defense.

Tick, Tock

Employees have a time limit to file their charges, usually 300 days from the most recent discriminatory act (again, depending on the statute). If there were multiple discriminatory acts, the employee might be able to bootstrap the untimely acts (those more than 300 days old) into the charge by connecting them to an act inside the timeliness window.

The rationale for the time limitation is that the further away from the incident you get, the more difficult it becomes to investigate. Witnesses leave, or simply forget. Companies relocate. Life moves on. It's also true that as time passes, would-be plaintiffs become less angry, and thus less inclined to sue. Ironically, though, an approaching filing deadline tends to spur employees to action. In my experience, the most common time for a charge to be filed—if not immediately after the termination—is in the days just before the deadline.

The Employer's Position Statement

After the agency initially processes the charge, it mails the charge along with some other paperwork and instructions to the employer, as well as any individually named respondents. As soon as you receive it, and before you do anything else, you need to call your employment lawyer. If you don't yet have an employment lawyer, perhaps because you haven't needed one yet, good for you. Call your business lawyer and ask her to find you an employment attorney. (We'll talk more about lawyers in Chapter 15.)

A Brief Rant About Employment Lawyers

At most agencies, neither side is required to have an attorney represent them in the proceedings. Some companies will decide to have their HR people handle the charge. They say to themselves, "How hard can it be? It's not exactly rocket science." And they're right. It isn't exactly rocket science. Neither is pulling teeth, but you wouldn't have your HR department handle that. Or maybe you would. Obviously, I have a bias here. But if you want to increase your chances of losing an employment-discrimination case, then by all means have someone other than an employment litigator handle it. Maybe the mail-room guy is free. End of rant.

More Tick, Tock

After receiving the charge, the employer will have a short time to file a response: usually between two and three weeks. That's not a lot of time. That's why it's imperative to get your employment lawyer working on the case right away. Setting up meetings and interviews and document reviews take time, and your lawyer is going to need time to actually draft the response and run it by you. Often the lawyer can get an extension, especially if there's a good reason. But using an extension here might prevent you from using one down the road in the case, so spend your time wisely.

The employer's response to the charge usually comes in the form of a *position statement*, which sets out the employer's reasons why the claim should fail. What the position statement looks like depends on the rules of that particular agency and the preferred style of your employment lawyer. There are three basic types.

Answer Style

The first is the answer style. This kind of position statement mimics the answer filed in a court case. In it, the lawyer uses numbered paragraphs that either admit or deny the corresponding allegations in the charge. This is usually followed by a cursory list of legal theories under which the employee's claim should fail. Answer-style position statements tend to be dry and boring. They are also much easier to write than the other two styles. If your agency requires this style, then so be it. But if there's a choice, using this style misses an opportunity to persuade the decision-maker that you should win.

Brief Style

The second is the brief style. Not "brief" as in short, necessarily, though it should be; "brief" as in "legal brief." This form is similar to the kind of brief that a lawyer in court will file to argue for summary judgment (we'll talk about that process in the next chapter). A well-written position statement in this format is a persuasive document that explains why the employee's legal claim should be thrown out.

Letter Style

The third style is the letter style. It's very similar to the brief style, in that it's a detailed document designed to persuade the agency that the claim should fail. But because it's written in the form of a letter, there's a tendency for it to sound somewhat less formal than a brief. That doesn't need to be the case: a lawyer who writes well can certainly create a highly readable brief-style position statement, while a less-skilled writer can turn a letter-style response into a stiff, turgid, *lawyerly* document.

My preferred style over the years was the letter format. I found that it gave me the ability to make my client's case in as persuasive a way as possible. It enabled me to make a better-defined, more polished argument than the answer style, and it appeared less lawyerly and boring than the brief style. I've included an example of a letter-style position statement with the sample documents in Appendix C.

Depending on the agency, once you file your position statement, the case can go into a black hole of bureaucracy, where the power to not get things done is so strong that not even light can escape from it, or something like that. I've had agencies take two years or more from the filing of the position statement to finish processing the charge. Some agencies are better than others, and will move the case to the next step in 90 or 180 days. Your employment lawyer should be able to give you an idea of how long to expect to wait.

Agency Investigation and Discovery

When the agency finally gets around to processing your charge, one of two things will generally happen. The first is that it might simply decide to issue a ruling based on the papers it has before it: the charge and your position statement. In other words, the agency might conclude that it doesn't need to do any further investigating and that it has reached a decision based on the parties' submissions alone—generally in the employer's favor. This is more likely to happen if the charge has some fatal flaw in it, such as having missed the filing deadline or the employer's not having enough employees to be covered by the statute.

The second and more likely next step is that the agency will begin an investigation. Often this is little more than an investigator (who is usually not a lawyer) making phone calls to the employee and the company, or their lawyers. If your company starts getting those calls, you need to alert your employment lawyer right away. The investigator may wish to talk to specific company officials or other witnesses. Ideally, your lawyer will be involved in those conversations.

Another part of the investigation may involve discovery, where the agency will ask one or both sides to provide certain documents or written answers to questions, or both. This is analogous to the discovery process in a court case, where the parties themselves make the requests. Sometimes in an agency proceeding, the parties will get to take discovery from the other side, but that more commonly happens later on in the process.

Depending on the agency where your case is, there may be an investigative conference of some kind during this phase. Usually, this is kind of a mini-hearing, where the investigator gets the chance to hear from both sides and maybe ask a few questions. These conferences rarely last more than 15 or 20 minutes and usually don't involve witness testimony. Remarkably, many complainants fail to even show up. (This should end their cases right then and there, but it usually doesn't.)

Probable-Cause Determination

Once the investigation is completed, it's time for the agency to issue its ruling. Usually, the ruling comes in the form of a probable-cause determination. (Some agencies, including the federal EEOC, refer to it as "reasonable cause.") This is a ruling about whether the case has enough merit to go forward. If the agency finds that there is probable cause, it means that it believes that the employee has established enough evidence that could allow him to win his case. It doesn't mean that he will win, or even that he's likely to win; it just means that he has a chance. If the agency finds a lack of probable cause, it means that the employee hasn't established evidence to support a claim that has a chance of winning.

If the agency rules against the employee here, the case is over at the agency unless he appeals. And unlike in court, where winning on appeal is rare, appeals here actually have a fighting chance of succeeding. Either way, the employee also has the option of moving the case to court, assuming that the statute of limitations (usually three years) hasn't run.

If the agency finds probable cause, then the case can continue at the agency. Some agencies, including the EEOC, don't have an adjudicative function, so the agency's involvement ends at the cause stage. Then it's up to the employee to move the case to court.

Conciliation

If the case remains alive at the agency, the next step is often some type of conciliation meeting. This is a sort of mediation session between the parties (and their lawyers), facilitated by a neutral person from the agency. Unlike private mediation, the conciliation doesn't usually cost anything. How effective the process is will depend on the skills and level of commitment of the conciliator. I've had excellent results when the conciliator made a sincere effort to bring the sides to a resolution. And I've wasted countless hours when the conciliator was basically mailing it in.

If conciliation doesn't lead to a settlement, then the case proceeds to litigation. This is when the two sides usually get the opportunity to take discovery (ask for documents and written answers to questions) and conduct witness depositions. And then comes the public hearing.

Public Hearing

This is very similar to a trial in a court. But there are some important differences. First of all, there's no jury. Instead, the case is presided over and decided by a hearing officer. This is usually a senior agency official who acts like a judge. Many people like this because they believe that a jury is unpredictable. On the other hand, if your hearing officer doesn't like your side from the start, you're going to have trouble winning. That's less of a problem with a jury of six or twelve.

Another major difference between agency hearings and court trials is that agencies usually don't care as much about the rules of evidence. The hearings tend to be considerably less formal than court trials, and the hearing officers are less likely to be concerned about hearsay or lack of foundation. Some lawyers may tell you that they prefer this; that's probably because they didn't do too well in their law-school evidence course.

The rules of evidence are difficult and tricky, but they serve an important purpose: they prevent unskilled or unethical lawyers from putting forward bad evidence. I don't mean "bad" as "bad for your side"; I mean "bad" as in "being of questionable merit." The rules weed out evidence that lacks proper support, such as hearsay testimony.

The hearing begins with opening statements from the employee's lawyer and the company's lawyer, and then the employee's side begins calling witnesses. The company's lawyer has the opportunity to cross-examine them.

When the employee is done submitting his case, then it's the employer's turn to put on witnesses.

The case will usually take a few days. A court reporter (or increasingly, a digital recording system) will make the official record of what's said and done. Often, the hearing officer will dispense with any closing arguments, preferring instead to receive written briefs from the lawyers.

After a week, a few weeks, or even a few months, the agency will render its decision. If the employee wins, then the agency will determine whether he's entitled to compensatory damages, and how much. Agencies often aren't allowed to issue punitive damages, the purpose of which is to punish the employer instead of just making the employee whole. In addition to damages, the agency will award the employee his attorneys' fees.

If the employer wins, there are no damages and attorneys'-fee awards. The case simply ends. Either side can appeal, either to a larger body within the agency (like the full commission), or to a court.

Conclusion

And that's what an agency discrimination claim looks like. Court cases are somewhat different. We'll cover them in the next chapter.

Discrimination Cases Part 2

Court Cases

An employee does not have the right to go directly to court without first stopping off at the appropriate state or federal agency. So on either track, agency or court, the employee must first file an administrative charge. After that, the employee has a choice. The first option is to follow the agency track that I laid out in Chapter 11. The second is to withdraw the case from the agency (we call it "pulling" the case), and then file a lawsuit in court.

Pulling the Case

Different agencies have different rules for when and how this happens, and these rules are set out by the applicable statutes. At some agencies, the employee gets the ability to go to court as a matter of right after a certain period, such as 90 days. That doesn't mean he necessarily has to wait, though. He can usually request to expedite the withdrawal and get an immediate right-to-sue letter (which is exactly what it sounds like: a letter that says he has the right to sue in court). Sometimes the employee may need to state a reason for this; other times it's just a matter of asking.

Once the employee has the right to sue in court, either by permission or because of the passage of time, the next decision for the employee and his counsel is which court to file in.

Forum Shopping

The employee and his lawyer often have a choice, because most of the time, both federal and state courts have jurisdiction over discrimination claims. (The exception is usually when a state law recognizes a protected category that federal law doesn't, such as sexual orientation.) There are pluses and minuses to the different courts, although these are often exaggerated.

For example, the conventional wisdom is that federal courts are more employer-friendly than state courts are, and that federal juries are more sophisticated than their state-court peers. I'm not certain that either of those statements is true, but many experienced litigators swear by them. They may be truer in some states than in others.

One thing is true in most states: the federal courts usually have greater resources. Their budgets are usually greater, their judges are more highly paid and often more experienced, and they have greater access to top law clerks.

Federal judges are often culled from the state bench, and they are appointed by the president and confirmed by the US Senate to lifetime appointments. State judges, on the other hand, sometimes have shorter terms; in some states, judges are popularly elected.

One big difference is the judges' law clerks. Many state courts don't have the budget to hire top new law-school graduates to serve as judicial law clerks for a year, while federal judges usually get two each. To obtain those federal clerkships, the candidates generally have to graduate at the top of the class from the more-prestigious law schools. Their job is to research the legal issues involved in the cases and help the judges write their rulings and opinions. As a result, a litigator may have more confidence that a federal judge will have a better and more detailed understanding of the particular laws governing the case. If the lawyer thinks the law favors their side, that may be reason enough to choose federal court.

Another factor might be docket backlog and speed. In many jurisdictions, the state court may be much slower at turning around cases than the federal court. That can cut both ways.

And in some states, judges rotate through different sessions every three or six months (this is called "riding circuit"). It's an anachronism, and it leads to many inefficiencies. Over the course of a two- or three-year-long case, the parties may appear before four or five different judges, each of whom has to be brought up to speed. In federal court, you generally get the same judge for the life of the lawsuit.

One more thing: while the choice of court (this is called "choice of forum" or "venue") is the plaintiff's prerogative, the defendant can sometimes trump it. If an employee brings only state claims in state court, that's where the case will stay. But if the employee brings *both* state and federal claims in state court, which happens frequently, the defendant has the right to get the case transferred to federal court. This is called "removal," and it doesn't even require the filing of a motion; the defendant simply has to give notice to both courts and the employee, and the case gets moved.

Other than these details, and things like jury size and civil-procedure and evidence rules, the lawsuit will proceed roughly the same way in either state or federal court.

Always Complaining About Something

The first step is for the plaintiff employee to file a complaint with the court and "serve" it upon (that is, deliver it by process server to) the defendant employer. This document consists of a long set of numbered paragraphs, each one containing a factual allegation. These allegations, taken together in the context of the controlling law, add up to the reasons why the plaintiff thinks he should win his lawsuit.

The allegations are followed by one or more numbered claims, or *counts*, which define the legal theories under which he claims he's entitled to prevail. It ends with a *prayer for relief*, which is generally a request for damages and attorneys' fees. Depending on the court, those damages may or may not be quantified; usually they're not.

Is That Your Final Answer?

The defendant then has a short time (usually 20 days) to file and serve its answer to the complaint. The answer tracks the complaint, numbered paragraph by numbered paragraph. For each allegation, there are only three possible responses:

1. admit the allegation,

2. deny the allegation, or

3. state that you don't know the answer, which has the effect of a denial.

This makes for hopelessly boring reading, and judges have told me that they don't pay much attention to the answer. It's kind of a silly document, because there's no real room to advocate for your side.

At the end of the admissions and denials, the defendant includes *affirmative defenses*. These are legal theories that, if proven, would defeat the plaintiff's claims. Examples include a failure to state a claim in the complaint or missing the statute of limitations (that is, filing the claim too late).

The employer has an alternative to the answer. It can file a motion to dismiss, asking the court to throw out the case on purely legal grounds. But this has a very high threshold for winning. You need to convince the court that even if it accepted as true every single factual allegation made by the employee, he still has almost no chance of winning his case. If the court grants your motion, the case is over. (Unless the employee appeals.) This really only succeeds if the plaintiff basically filed the wrong case. Some defense lawyers will file this as a matter of course, but it's almost always a waste of time and legal fees.

Once the defendant employer has answered (or has lost on a motion to dismiss), the pleading stage ends and the case moves into the discovery phase.

Written Discovery and Depositions

The purpose of discovery is ostensibly to "discover" the truth. This has developed over the years into a mechanism for the parties in a lawsuit to gather evidence from each other before a trial, without the direct supervision of the court.

But lawyers often turn this process into a series of snarling mini-battles over minutiae. When the lawyers can't resolve their discovery issues among themselves, one side or the other (or both) file motions to compel (to force the other side to respond) or motions for protective orders (to limit what the other side can get).

Most lawyers will tell you that they hate discovery disputes; I certainly did. On the other hand, the lawyers' overwhelming desire to win (and quite frankly, to bill hours) makes it difficult to give in on discovery arguments. And judges absolutely loathe discovery disputes, and often show a pox-on-both-your-houses mentality in ruling on them.

There are four basic types of discovery: written interrogatories, requests for admissions, document requests, and depositions.

Written Interrogatories

Lawyers, being lawyers, prefer to describe something as simple as written questions with a fancy name like "interrogatories." That's all they are. Usually, the court's rules have limits on how many "ints" each side can take. The problem with interrogatories is that the clients don't actually answer them; the lawyers do.

And by "answer," I mean "not really answer." Lawyers can object to the questions on various legal grounds, such as the question calls for information protected by the attorney-client privilege. Unfortunately, many lawyers play fast and loose with the discovery and evidentiary rules, and so they end up dodging more questions than they answer. In my experience, I found interrogatories to be of limited usefulness.

Document Requests

This is exactly what it sounds like: your lawyer drafts requests for the other side to produce written documents that could have some bearing on the case, and the employee's lawyer does the same. Unlike with interrogatories, there is less that the lawyers can do to prevent these requests from being responded to, other than to assert privileges.

In a discrimination case, the employer usually has all the documents related to the actual employment, so the employee's counsel asks for those. But the employer can also ask for documents that might prove helpful in defending the case: financial records, medical records, phone records, e-mails, computer files, text messages, Facebook entries, and so forth. Of course, the employee's lawyer can ask for these things also.

One important thing to keep in mind here: the threshold for whether something has to be turned over to the other side is pretty low. The lawyer requesting the documents doesn't have to first prove that they're relevant to the case. Relevance is something that the judge will determine later on if necessary. Instead, the lawyer can ask for almost anything that might lead to admissible evidence. So you should be prepared to turn over more than you want.

Requests for Admissions

The third type of discovery is the least commonly used: requests for admissions. Again, these are exactly what they sound like. Your lawyer gives the employee's lawyer very carefully drafted questions—basically a true-or-false test. The only appropriate answers are admissions, denials, or statements that the party doesn't know the answer. Used carefully, requests for admissions can do a fairly effective job of locking a party in to its story. But for some reason, most lawyers neglect this tool.

Depositions

The final type of discovery is the deposition. This is often the most effective method. A deposition is where a party calls a witness from the other side to testify under oath in front of a court reporter who makes a transcript of the session. The primary witnesses are usually the employee and the manager. Other witnesses can be asked to attend their own depositions. If there's any doubt about whether they'll come voluntarily, the lawyer can subpoena the witness to attend—essentially ordering them to appear under penalty of law.

The deposition usually takes place in the conference room of the lawyer who's conducting it. Present in the room are the court reporter, the lawyers for both sides, the witnesses, the employee, and a representative of the company. The lawyer asks the witness a series of questions that the witness must answer without consulting with her lawyer. If a question violates an evidentiary rule, the opposing lawyer can object on the record. But since there's no judge present, those objections are noted and then otherwise ignored for the time being. The witness still needs to answer, in all but a few limited circumstances.

A skilled lawyer taking a deposition has two jobs: discovering facts and locking the witness into her story. A "depo" is effective at fact discovery because the witness can't hide behind her lawyer and has to answer the questions in her own words. And a depo is effective at locking a witness into a story because if that story were to change at trial, the opposing lawyer can read back the transcript in front of the jury (or better yet, have her read it back) and then ask that most precious of questions: "Are you lying now or were you lying then?"

Depositions also give the lawyers a chance to preview witnesses and see how well they'll perform under pressure at trial. And there's a lot of gamesmanship between the lawyers at depositions, with both sides performing in front of their clients. Depos are time-consuming: major witnesses can take an entire day or even multiple days. And they can be very boring.

But sometimes, they can be filled with high drama and surprises. I once asked a former employee about a string of obscure but seemingly innocent e-mails, knowing full well that the e-mails related to a secret affair he'd been having with a coworker. After his face turned deep purple, his entire tone changed. That deposition directly led to a favorable settlement of the case.

Summary Judgment

Once the discovery phase (which can last many months or even years) is over, the employer's counsel will need to decide whether it makes sense to file a motion for summary judgment. This is similar to a motion to dismiss, but with a slightly easier standard.

Now that all the evidence has been gathered, the employer filing this motion would argue that even if the facts were viewed in the light most favorable to the employee, he still wouldn't win. In other words, there would be no reason to try this case in front of a jury, because even if the jury drew every inference in the employee's favor, it would still rule against him.

This argument is made in the form of a written brief, and then the employee's counsel writes an opposing brief. Then a hearing is typically held where the lawyers on each side present their arguments and answer questions from the judge. Afterward, the judge will "take it under advisement" and issue a ruling sometime (usually a week or two) later.

Despite the easier standard, it is still difficult to win summary judgment in a discrimination case because these cases often turn on intent. That's usually considered to be an issue that a jury, not a judge, must consider. If the employer manages to win at this stage, it's usually because there was some fatal flaw in the employee's case. It's also possible that the judge will grant partial summary judgment, dismissing some of the claims but keeping others (usually the critical one) alive for trial.

Most Cases Settle

If the case does not get dismissed at the summary-judgment stage, all that's left is for it to go to trial. Well, that's not strictly true. It can still settle. In fact, nothing spurs settlement better than an imminent trial date. Only about one percent of discrimination lawsuits filed in court actually make it to a jury trial.

You often hear the expression "settling on the courthouse steps." It's an expression for a reason: it happens all the time. Heck, I once had a case settle *in* the courtroom, while the judge waited in his chambers, 20 minutes before he was going to begin empanelling the jury. So the odds are good that the case will get resolved before trial.

The problem is that the lawyers need to prepare as if they're going to trial, no matter what. It would be malpractice to play the odds, assume that the case will settle, and not do the trial-prep work. This makes for a very wasteful situation, where employers have to spend tens of thousands of dollars—often more than a hundred thousand dollars—to have their case prepared to go to trial, only to have it settle the weekend before.

Negotiations

A good employment lawyer is skilled at settling cases. The funny thing is, there is a certain machismo that goes with being a trial lawyer. But let me clue you in on a little secret: management-side employment lawyers are *not* trial lawyers. We simply don't go to trial that often. Not because we don't want to; most of us find trials fun and exciting. But we don't usually go to trial because it's rarely in our employer clients' best interests. The risks are usually too high, especially when you consider that employees can win back their attorneys' fees.

If your employment lawyer brags about how many trials she's done, ask her why the hell she keeps going to trial. Is she afraid of settling, or is she just no good at it? Then find a new employment lawyer.

Settling cases is difficult, and it takes skill, empathy, patience, creativity, and persistence. It also takes strategy. And of course, compromise. The best definition of the ideal settlement that I've ever heard is where both parties leave equally unhappy. In an effective settlement, the employee gets less than he wanted, and the employer pays more than it wanted. But that generally ends up being a better result than going to trial.

Mediation

One effective method of bringing about a settlement is mediation, which is a form of "alternative dispute resolution." In a mediation, both parties agree to use a neutral person—the mediator—who facilitates settlement talks. The mediator has no stake in the outcome, and she doesn't make any decisions. Instead, her job is to try to get the parties and their lawyers to work together to reach a solution. Some mediators are former judges; others used to be employment lawyers. The best mediators are committed to getting a deal done.

Mediation can be fairly costly. The mediators generally charge a few hundred dollars an hour (up to about $500 for the best), and while there's often an expectation that both sides will split the costs, it's not uncommon for the employer to pick up the tab alone. But if a mediation avoids the need for a trial, it's money well spent.

Arbitration

Another form of alternative dispute resolution is arbitration. This is often confused with mediation, but they are very different animals. Arbitration is much less common in employment cases, and usually only happens when there is a preexisting contract providing for it if there is a dispute. In other words, the employee would have signed an agreement—often at the start of employment—waiving his rights to go to court or an agency and instead having the dispute resolved by an arbitrator.

The arbitrator is chosen by both sides from a list of potential neutrals. In effect, he acts like a judge. Unlike a mediator, his job is to make a decision at the end of the case.

Many employers and management lawyers think it's a good idea to have mandatory-arbitration clauses in employment agreements. They think arbitration is a good idea because it tends to be cheaper and faster than the agency-and-court system. They believe that arbitration ends up favoring the employer.

But they are wrong.

Arbitration is a terrible idea, for four reasons. First, the less-formal approach to litigating the case, dispensing with the evidentiary rules, means that the employee can bring in evidence that never would have seen the light of day in court. As I said before, rules of evidence are a good thing if you have a lawyer who understands them. Ignoring the rules turns the case into a free-for-all.

Second, there is no precedent in arbitration. In the court system, the judge generally has to abide by past decisions of earlier court cases, especially higher-level courts. Our legal system is based on the authority of precedent. But in arbitrations, there's no such thing. Yes, lawyers can cite to past arbitration cases for examples of what arbitrators have done in similar cases. But the arbitrator is free to ignore it.

Third, there is almost no ability to appeal a bad decision. I don't want to overstate this. While you can almost always appeal a bad decision at an agency or in a court, appeals typically have little chance of success. But it's even worse in the arbitration world. Yes, you can file the equivalent of an appeal in court to prevent the enforcement of an arbitration award. But you shouldn't bother: there's next to no chance of it succeeding.

My final reason is the most important (and why arbitrators want to smack me in the nose). Remember how I said a few paragraphs ago that arbitrators are chosen by the parties? That's the whole problem. If an arbitrator doesn't get chosen for cases, he can't make money. And if he gets a reputation as being too pro-employer, plaintiffs' lawyers will stop agreeing to use him. (Likewise, if he gets a pro-employee reputation, management lawyers will stay away.) Trust me: this happens. At our firm, we had a list of arbitrators that we would never use because we felt that they were too likely to side with the employee.

In court cases, judges are assigned, not chosen. So the judge needn't worry about acquiring a reputation of favoring one side or the other. But an arbitrator has some pressure to avoid that sort of reputation. This pressure naturally moves an arbitrator to try to come up fairly even-steven over time, with a rough balance of wins for both employers and employees. Sounds fair, right?

Wrong.

Coming out more or less fifty-fifty sounds like it evenly benefits both employers and employees, but in fact it drastically favors employees. Why? Because employees don't win half of the cases filed. At the various antidiscrimination agencies, the percentage of cases where probable cause is found tends to run in the 5- to 15-percent range. (There are no reliable figures from court cases.) There are a number of reasons for these relatively low success rates.

For example, discrimination claims are inherently difficult to prove; it's hard to get inside a manager's head and find a discriminatory bias. Also, many cases are merely disgruntled employees' weapons of last resort. Many fired employees bring their cases because of anger instead of an honest belief of having suffered discrimination. So a low success rate is to be expected. That's why a success rate approaching 50 percent, which is more typical with arbitrators, dramatically favors employees.

▧ **Note** Now some of you are thinking: "Hang on a minute. If the probability of success is so low, what am I worried about? Why am I even reading this book? Isn't there a game on?" What you're worried about is this: having a case brought against you is a problem in and of itself. Yes, you may have a decent chance of winning in the long run. But even if you win, you lose. The costs of an employment-discrimination case, in terms of money, time, energy, focus, and stress are enormous. That's why you're reading this. Plus the game's over. Your team lost. Sorry you had to find out this way.

So if your employment lawyer tries to talk you into arbitration agreements, ask her if she's thought about these points.

Trial

OK, so you didn't settle or mediate, and you weren't stuck with an arbitration agreement. And you didn't get the case dismissed by summary judgment. It's time for the trial. Better clear your calendar.

Scheduling Difficulty

Depending on the complexity of the case and the number of witnesses, a trial will typically take as few as three or four days and as many as fifteen. A week-long trial is about average.

The lawyers will have a final pretrial conference with the judge a few days before the trial is set to start. At this conference, minor housekeeping matters will be dealt with, such as evidentiary motions.

One of the frustrating things about trials is the scheduling. Courts usually want to avoid inactive time, when no case is being heard. Because so many cases settle, the courts usually schedule several cases for the same week, with an order of priority. The priority usually depends on the age of the case, and criminal cases get precedence over civil cases (because someone's freedom is on the line rather than just someone's money). That means that the lawyers need to be ready to start the trial on a certain date, knowing that the cases ahead of them would need to settle for their case to go forward. There's a lot of hurrying up and waiting.

Bring on the Jury

Once your case begins, the first day is usually taken up with empaneling the jury. This is a long and tedious process where would-be jurors are brought in from the jury pool. The jury candidates are then asked a series of questions, usually as a group. These questions are designed by the judge in consultation with both lawyers to weed out potentially biased jurors.

For example, one of the questions in your case would certainly be "Have you or a member of your immediate family ever been involved in an employment-discrimination case?" Jury candidates who raise their hands on that question will be shown the door.

Other questions will have to do with candidates' familiarity with the parties and the witnesses. So if you see your next-door neighbor or your cousin in the jury pool, you can rest assured that they won't be deciding your case.

Candidates who make it through this process are then tentatively seated in the jury box. Then both parties have the opportunity to issue "peremptory challenges." Each side has a set number of challenges—usually about a handful. This allows the lawyers to disqualify jurors without giving any reason. Essentially, the lawyers are saying, "I don't like the look of this juror."

This process turns lawyers into wannabe Jedi Knights, trying to intuit how a juror is going to rule based on looks, limited information (age, address, occupation, and employer), and a gut feeling. Lawyers can't use their peremptories to discriminate; for example, it's not OK to disqualify all the black jurors in a discrimination case brought by a black employee. Besides being morally wrong and illegal, that would also be too ironic in a discrimination case.

Court Is in Session

Once the jury is finalized, the court swears in the jurors and the trial begins. The employee's lawyer gives an opening statement, setting out what she intends to prove during the trial. Then your lawyer does the same.

The plaintiff's side then begins calling witnesses. More often than not, they'll start with the employee himself. His lawyer will ask him questions (the "direct examination"), getting him to testify about how the company screwed him over. When she's done, your lawyer will cross-examine him, trying to get him to show that it was really his fault he was fired.

This back-and-forth questioning continues until the plaintiff "rests." Then the employer's lawyer will move for a directed verdict. This is similar to the summary-judgment motion, but much less formal. Basically, it's a request that the judge dismiss the case because the plaintiff has failed to prove the elements of his claim, and that continuing the trial would be a waste of time because he now can't possibly win. These motions usually fail.

Then the defense calls its own witnesses, usually starting with the manager (unless the manager was already called by the plaintiff's lawyer). When the defense rests, the plaintiff has a chance to call rebuttal witnesses. Then both sides make their closing arguments, explaining to the jurors why they should vote their way. The jury then goes into a private room to deliberate.

Deliberately Uncomfortable

Waiting on the jury is a decidedly unpleasant experience for the parties and their lawyers. You basically have no idea what's going to happen, and you no longer have any control over the outcome. Plus you're physically, mentally, and emotionally exhausted. One senior lawyer told me that he felt roughly the same feeling of powerlessness as when his father was dying.

The jury could take hours to deliberate, or it could take days. And usually the amount of time taken has no bearing on how they'll rule. Finally, the jury returns and the verdict is read, with all the drama that you see in movies and on TV.

What the Employee Can Win

If the jury finds in the employer's favor, that's the end of it. Yes, the employee can appeal, but the odds of a successful appeal are minute, so it usually doesn't happen.

If the employee wins, then the jury also has to determine damages. There are two kinds of damages: compensatory and punitive. Compensatory damages are designed to make the plaintiff whole for the harm that he suffered as a result of the discrimination. They can include front pay, back pay, and damages for emotional distress. Punitive damages do not compensate for the harm suffered. Instead, they are damages designed to punish the employer. Not all statutes allow for punitive damages.

Lastly, the judge (as opposed to the jury) will award the winning employee his attorneys' fees. The employee's lawyer will make a fee petition, showing what her fees added up to and justifying why the employer should pay that amount. The employer can argue against paying the entire amount. For example, if the employee won only $10,000 in damages (which is essentially a nominal amount), the judge is going to be unlikely to award $200,000 in attorneys' fees.

But the judge will award something, which will make you feel like you're getting the insult after the injury. It's one thing to have to pay your own lawyers (who ended up losing). It's another thing to have to pay the lawyers who have been beating you up for the last two or three years.

Conclusion

These two chapters have taken you through the arduous process that is an employment-discrimination case. The main reason for writing this book is to help you fire people the right way so as to avoid ever having to refer back to these chapters.

In the next chapter, we'll talk about another type of claim employees can bring: wage claims.

A Big Payday

Wage Cases

As we've talked about in the past two chapters, discrimination cases are the weapon of choice for fired employees. But there are a couple of other types of claims that can really ruin an employer's day. And firing an employee is exactly the sort of thing that can make these claims come to light.

When an employee goes and finds himself a good employment lawyer, the attorney will generally have a checklist of questions to try to figure out what possible claims he might have. Many of those questions will have to do with his pay.

Wages and Hours

It's a fact of life that state and federal governments take the issue of paying employees very seriously. In some states, failure to properly pay wages can lead to criminal prosecution (although outside of child-labor issues, that's rarely done). In addition, the civil penalties often include multiple damages and awards of attorneys' fees.

Unfortunately, it's also a fact of life that many, if not most, employers regularly make some sort of mistake in the payment of wages. This isn't because employers are prone to taking advantage of employees. Instead, the mistakes come from ignorance and confusion about the overly complicated statutes that govern wage payments.

How to Lose a Wage-and-Hour Case

It's really quite easy to do: just screw up an employee's pay.

That's all. No fussing, no mussing. You see, unlike in most any other kind of employee lawsuit, your employment counsel has no lawyer tricks to defeat a wage claim. Either you paid the correct wages (and paid them correctly) or you didn't.

In a disability-discrimination case, for example, your lawyer can make technical, legalistic arguments about whether the employee is really disabled, whether he was otherwise qualified to do the job, whether a particular accommodation was reasonable, and so on. In a sexual-harassment case, your lawyer can argue that the sexual conduct wasn't egregious enough to alter the employee's working conditions, or that the conduct wasn't unwelcome, or that it wasn't even sexual conduct at all.

But in a wage case, if the right wages weren't paid, it's all over. You're on the hook for the lost wages, and probably the employee's attorneys' fees. In states like Massachusetts, you're even looking at automatic triple damages.

The message from the states is clear: don't mess with wages. Pay what you owe, pay it on time—especially around termination—and keep careful track of it. Otherwise, you're likely to pay a lot more.

State Wage Laws

Unlike discrimination laws, there's a wide degree of variance among the different jurisdictions. It's well beyond the scope of this book to give a comprehensive guide to the wage laws of every state. Instead, you should talk to your employment counsel and make certain that you're in full compliance.

But we can talk in general terms about wage issues that come up frequently no matter which state you're in. For example, many states have strict rules about the frequency of wage payments. Some states require weekly payments, or at least biweekly, sometimes depending on the employee's job level. Certain types of businesses—law firms are a good example—traditionally pay their professional employees on a monthly basis. But some states require you to get the employees' written permission first, and other states simply forbid the practice.

Related to that, some statutes require that wages be paid within a certain number of days after the work is completed. This causes all kinds of problems with a company that pays its employees on a semimonthly basis (as opposed to a biweekly basis). Many companies like the semimonthly pay schedule, where they pay employees on two set days a month (the first and the fifteenth are most common). It helps for monthly budgeting, because the payroll remains more or less the same each month.

By contrast, when you use a biweekly pay system, you will end up with two or three months in every year that have three paydays instead of the usual two—meaning a 50 percent bigger payroll during those months. On the other hand, employees might dislike the semimonthly system because it can mean extra days between paychecks during certain months.

Wage Claims

In some states, just as with discrimination claims, employees wanting to sue for wage-law violations first have to make an administrative filing with the state labor department or attorney general's office. Sometimes, the agency will first investigate the unpaid-wages charge, and then issue a right-to-sue letter. Once the employee has the letter, he can file his lawsuit in court.

Because the states take wages so seriously, there are very few defenses. For example, some wage laws prohibit employers from contracting away their obligation to properly pay wages. In other words, the employee could sign an agreement that her employer doesn't need to pay her on time, but that agreement isn't enforceable. If she later changes her mind—say, after getting fired—the employer is left holding a worthless piece of paper.

Vacation, All I Ever Wanted

Many state wage laws also protect employees' rights to vacation. Under these wage laws, a vacation policy is simply a promise to pay wages for certain weeks when the employee isn't working. Ironically, these laws don't require that the employer actually provide vacation in the first place. Nor do they mandate that the vacation time has to accrue over the course of the year. But once the employer takes on the obligation of providing vacation, the state laws treat vacation as being identical to wages. For this reason, it's critical that employers pay out any earned but unused vacation time when the employee departs the company.

For reasons passing understanding, most state laws treat vacation differently from other forms of paid time off, like sick days. Make sure your employment counsel explains to you the rules in your state, and then follow them carefully.

An Extra Added Bonus

One form of pay that is treated differently is the bonus. Wage laws generally recognize that bonuses are conditional and depend on the rules set out by the employer. For example, if the rule says that you need to be employed on December 31 to qualify for the year-end bonus, an employee who is fired at Christmas doesn't get one. (Of course, as I said before, don't do the Christmas termination, unless you're begging for a lawsuit. And want to look like a jerk.)

But there is a catch to this. An employee can argue that the real reason you fired her was to deprive her of the bonus that she otherwise would have been entitled to receive. To be sure, if she wants to sue to recover this, the wage laws won't help.

Instead, she would have to claim that the employer breached something called the "implied covenant of good faith and fair dealing." This is kind of a catchall common-law concept that assumes that parties to an agreement won't try to screw each other over on mere technicalities. When a party tries to unfairly get out of an obligation because of a technicality, this covenant protects the other side. The moral of the story: don't try to get cute with employee bonuses.

Commissioned Work

Another area that comes up in post-firing disputes is when employees earn sales commissions. State wage laws generally recognize that commissions are treated differently from normal wages, but they still count as wages and they still need to be paid to employees who earn them. The terms for qualifying for a commission are up to the employer, but as with a bonus, an employer usually cannot get away with firing an employee to deprive him of commissions that he's already earned and otherwise would have received.

Employee? What Employee?

One of the most common mistakes that employers make is classifying employees as independent contractors. Almost all of the time, under both state and federal law, they are actually employees.

It's understandable why employers would prefer to classify workers as independent contractors. Unlike with employees, companies aren't responsible for withholding taxes, paying unemployment insurance and Social Security payroll tax, and providing workers' compensation. Additionally, independent contractors don't enjoy all the same protections that employees do. For their part, the workers appreciate not having taxes withheld from their checks—which makes it easier to underreport their income on their tax returns.

But most of the time, "independent contractors" are actually employees. They usually don't have the degree of control and discretion required to be a truly independent contractor. A real independent contractor would be someone like the roving web site designer who does work at different companies and basically operates as his own mini-business.

But when the individuals work only for one company and perform the kinds of activities that are the main part of the business, they are almost certainly employees. For example, a lawyer working for a single law firm probably should be treated as an employee. When an employer gets this wrong, the state taxing authorities and the IRS can punish the company for failing to properly withhold.

Working Overtime

Many people think that overtime laws are designed to protect employees by keeping them from working too hard and for too many hours. They assume that requiring overtime pay for hours worked beyond 40 is to reward employees for their hard work. But that's not historically accurate.

Law of Unintended Consequences

In 1938, near the end of the Great Depression, the US unemployment rate was a staggering 19 percent. One way to try to encourage employers to hire more workers was to make it more expensive to have employees work more than a certain amount during a workweek. Thus the 40-hour workweek became US law with the passing of the federal Fair Labor Standards Act. (The Act also set a federal minimum wage and prohibited most forms of child labor, but that's beyond our discussion.)

Under the FLSA (which employment lawyers often pronounce "falsa;" rhymes with "balsa"), if an hourly employee works more than 40 hours in a single workweek, the employer is required to pay time and a half (150 percent of the normal hourly wage) for all hours exceeding 40. The New Deal thinking back in the Depression was that employers would be reluctant to pay overtime, and would instead hire new employees to pick up the excess work. And arguably, it worked, as unemployment fell dramatically after 1938. (There was also the little matter of World War II, which had a far greater effect on lowering unemployment.)

The problem is that the modern workplace is now dramatically different from how it was during the Depression. Because of benefits and payroll taxes, the cost of employing a new worker is at least 20 percent more than just the wages alone. Nowadays, it ends up being less expensive to pay some overtime hours from time to time than to hire an additional person. Yet FLSA remains on the books.

Exemptions and Exceptions

What is more, the Act has grown and changed over the course of the last 70 years. The statute has been amended many times, and the US Department of Labor further complicates the law by issuing arcane regulations to enforce the Act. The details of these changes are well beyond the scope of this book, and you would definitely fall asleep midway through. Instead, have your employment lawyer make sure you're in compliance.

But in the meantime, it's useful to have a basic understanding of the law.

As I said, if an hourly worker puts in more than 40 hours in a single workweek, each additional hour must be paid at the time-and-a-half overtime rate. Salaried workers for the most part aren't covered by this, as long as they're covered by one of the major exemptions to the law (and make at least $455 a week).

Employees generally fall into two categories: exempt and nonexempt. Nonexempt employees are entitled to overtime after working more than 40 hours in a single workweek; exempt employees are not. There are five major exemptions to the FLSA overtime requirement:

- **Executive:** The employee must supervise and manage at least part of a business, including overseeing the work of at least two other full-time employees.
- **Professional:** The employee must work primarily as the kind of professional who needs to complete advanced intellectual education. Examples include lawyers, doctors, some engineers, architects, and accountants.
- **Administrative:** The employee must perform office work that relates to the operation of a business, and must use discretion and independent judgment in doing so. For example, a salaried office

manager or an HR professional is likely to be exempt, but a salaried receptionist would not be.

- **Computer Employees:** The employee must work as a computer-systems analyst, programmer, software engineer, or other similarly skilled worker in the computer field who performs certain specific duties. Unlike the other exemptions, a computer employee can also be paid hourly as long the wage rate is greater than $27.63 an hour. (You know they must have picked that number out of a hat.)
- **Outside Sales:** Salespeople can also be exempt, but they have to be the types that work primarily outside the office. Inside sales-people do not qualify for this exemption.

Where the FLSA and its regulations really become difficult for employers is in the *exceptions* to the exemptions (I kid you not), and in other esoteric definitions such as "salaried nonexempt." Well-meaning employers who try to comply with the law are surprised to discover that they've been doing it wrong all along.

And it's very difficult to fix technical violations going forward. Once you discover that you've been improperly treating employees as exempt, it's natural (and admirable) to want to fix it right away. The problem is, it's almost impossible to fix the technical violation without employees realizing that they've been shortchanged on overtime, perhaps for years. You'll need to work with your employment counsel to handle the very delicate task of fixing the mistake without incurring a massive expense.

Interns

Many companies offer unpaid internships to college kids and other young people as a way of introducing them to a particular field and letting them get their foot in the door. It tends to be a fair exchange: the young people get hands-on experience and the opportunity to meet people who might help them get jobs in the future, and the company gets the services of eager kids willing to learn how it all works.

The problem is that the US Department of Labor and state attorneys general treat these kids as, well, *actual* kids. Fearing that employers must be taking advantage of the young people to fleece them for free labor, the federal and state governments have made it next to impossible to have unpaid internships. About the only unpaid internships that they'll allow are ones where college credit is received, or where the employer is a nonprofit or government entity.

About a year ago, I represented a company in the film and TV industry, where internships have long been a way of life. Eager young students and recent graduates jockey to get the chance to work in the industry of their dreams, thrilled to have the opportunity to get the real-world learning that their colleges can't possibly teach.

Unfortunately, a disgruntled former employee wrote an anonymous letter to the state attorney general, dropping a dime that the company used unpaid interns. As a result, the company may well be forced to pay hundreds of thousands of dollars in back wages to young people who were thrilled to work for nothing but the education and experience. Just another example of the damage that a disgruntled employee can cause.

▓ **Note** Ironically, I myself interned while I was still in law school—*for the attorney general's office.* Never got paid a cent. Appreciated the experience, though.

Classless Actions

Perhaps the most devastating weapon that unhappy former employees can wield is the class-action lawsuit. A class action is a lawsuit brought by a large group of employees who share certain characteristics. The thinking behind this litigation device is that it is fairer and more efficient to group similar plaintiffs together rather than require them to each fight his or her own lawsuit separately. That might sound good in theory, but I'm sure that no employer has ever been thankful for the existence of class-action rules.

Class actions can occur in other areas of employment litigation, such as discrimination cases, but they are far more common in wage cases. There exist certain kinds of plaintiffs' lawyers who specialize in going after employers with wage-and-hour class actions. Many of these firms operate like mills. (This might not be obvious to you, but I'm not a fan.)

The way it typically works is this: an unhappy (often recently fired) employee goes to one of these lawyers and wants to make some money off his former employer. The lawyer goes through a list of questions designed to spot possible claims to bring against the employer. When the lawyer discovers that the employer has a technically unsound pay practice, she then asks for the names and phone numbers of the employee's coworkers.

Once she has a few candidates who are willing to act as the "named plaintiffs," she can start the process of filing a class action. All similarly situated employees become members of the class, whether they want to sue the employer or not. (They can choose to opt out of the class, or in some jurisdictions, not opt in.) The employer is about to have a very bad day, followed by a whole bunch more.

As I said earlier, if you've messed up how you paid someone, even inadvertently, there's just about nothing you can do to successfully defend against a wage claim. With a class action, it's even worse, because you're in effect defending claims involving employees who never would have considered suing you. If you're in the wrong, the best thing you can do is quickly settle. And prepare to pay a lot of money.

Conclusion

Most employers are ethical, and are not intentionally violating state and federal wage laws. But unlike with discrimination cases, intent is not a factor in the analysis. It's one or the other: either you paid your people correctly, or you didn't. If you didn't, you're going to lose your case (unless you settle). So the lesson here is twofold: pay your employees correctly, and keep them happy enough to never want to sue you.

In the next chapter, we'll talk about another claim that fired employees might bring: the sexual-harassment case.

He Said, She Said

Sexual Harassment

Another weapon that an angry, fired employee can use against your company is the sexual-harassment claim. Even though the law of sexual harassment is related to employment-discrimination law, how this claim comes about after a firing is a little different. Generally, the employee isn't going to claim that she was fired *because* of sexual harassment (although there's one big exception that we'll talk about at the end of the chapter). Instead, the claim arises this way: "You fired me, eh? Oh, by the way: I was sexually harassed."

This scenario happens frequently enough that a brief discussion of sexual harassment belongs in a book about firing. The threat of a sexual-harassment claim is a very powerful weapon in the hands of an angry, recently fired (or about-to-be-fired) employee. In addition, anyone who previously complained about sexual harassment has a big blunt instrument in a potential retaliation claim.

Just What Is Sexual Harassment?

Over the years, I've taught sexual-harassment training to thousands of employees and managers. The most important thing I learned from that experience was that most people didn't really understand what "sexual harassment" actually means. In fact, the overwhelming majority of sexual-harassment incidents are caused not by evil, predatory harassers who want to harm their victims, but by clueless bozos—nearly all of them male—who don't know how to appropriately interact with women.

During my seminars, as I explained what sexual harassment really is, I would see the light bulb come on in the eyes of many of the employees. I could almost hear them thinking, "Damn! *I* do that sometimes. I didn't think *that* was sexual harassment." Often, some of the employees would even tell me that privately after the seminar was done.

As I mentioned a moment ago, sexual harassment arises out of employment discrimination. Technically, sexual harassment is a form of sex discrimination, under the thinking that the harassing treatment only comes about because of the victim's gender.

Note I'm using the term *victim* because that's the conventional term in this area of the law. Plus *harassee* just isn't a real word. I'm also using feminine pronouns for the victim and male for the harasser, because that's how it breaks down in the overwhelming majority of sexual-harassment cases. But the victim and harasser can be either gender; they can also be the same gender. It's just that the other combinations don't happen very often. Only about 10 to 15 percent of harassment claimants are male.

Some states have added separate sexual-harassment clauses to their employment-discrimination laws. Other states, plus the federal government, rely instead on judicial decisions interpreting harassment as being part of sex discrimination. So even though the definition of sexual harassment might be worded differently depending on what jurisdiction you're in, the law is basically the same throughout the country.

Despite the definitions, which are often very complicated and obtuse and filled with legalese, sexual harassment can be defined very simply. In fact, in three words: "unwelcome sexual conduct." To be more precise, you could add "relating to work."

Let's talk about what these terms mean.

Unwelcome

First of all, the behavior being complained of has to be unwelcome to fit within the definition of sexual harassment. If two people are flirting with each other at work, or kissing, or knocking boots in the supply closet, and this behavior is consensual for both participants, it is not sexual harassment. It may be inappropriate for the workplace, it may offend other people (even to the point of sexually harassing *them*), and it may even be reason enough to fire the participants. But neither employee can claim that the other one was sexually harassing him or her. (Well, that's not completely true. Neither one can *honestly* say that the other was committing sexual harassment.)

In other words, it's not sexual harassment if you willingly participate in it.

One of the cases I always talked about in my seminars illustrates this point well. It involved a bus company in Western Massachusetts that had a particularly informal work environment. These people apparently liked to have a lot of fun at work, and their tastes ran to the risqué. For example, the company put together an annual pinup calendar of employees in sexy outfits. If an employee had a birthday, the rest of the staff would chip in and buy him or her gag gifts that usually involved sex toys. Office parties were a real hoot, sometimes involving cakes decorated with naked people (made of frosting, I assume; not real naked people).

One employee, Jill, fully participated in this bawdy humor. She and the male company president would frequently exchange lewd remarks. She once helped make a costume for the president that was labeled "U.S. Sex Express." At one office party, she reached down and grabbed his, er, presidency in front of other employees and even the president's wife. (The wife apparently didn't have a problem with this.)

But when Jill got passed over for a promotion, she didn't take it well. She'd been told that she hadn't gotten the new job because she had some performance problems. So like many disgruntled employees, she sued. In her charge, she claimed that she had been sexually harassed at work, and that the sexual harassment had been the cause of her poor performance.

Jill lost her case at the Massachusetts antidiscrimination commission, which concluded that she had been a "willing and active participant" in the ribald behavior. She appealed all the way up to the Massachusetts Supreme Judicial Court, who agreed with the commission. The conduct she complained of wasn't sexual harassment *to her*, because it wasn't unwelcome.

One other thing about unwelcomeness: there's no requirement that the victim explicitly complain about the conduct. She might even feel pressured to play along with it. But if she can show that it was unwelcome to her, then it's sexual harassment.

Sexual

The second factor in the test for sexual harassment seems kind of obvious: the conduct has to be sexual in nature. Most of the time, it will be pretty obvious that the complained-of behavior has to do with some form of sex. But there can be some confusion over it.

For one thing, the victim doesn't have to show that the harasser was sexually attracted to her. For example, in a case that went all the way to the US Supreme Court, a man claimed sexual harassment when he began his job working on an oil rig in the Gulf of Mexico. Turns out, the workers on this particular rig had a tradition of roughly hazing new employees. The hazing was so shocking that the Supreme Court chose to leave out a description of the facts in its decision. But the lower court did describe the humiliating events, which included such activities as violating the man in the shower with a bar of soap and threatening other forms of rape.

When he sued for sexual harassment, the employer argued that it couldn't be that, because neither the male victim nor the male harassers were gay. But the Court said that the sexual orientation of any of them didn't matter; nor did their gender. But because the conduct itself was sexual in nature, it was indeed unlawful sexual harassment.

On the other hand, conduct that isn't sexual in nature cannot be the basis for a sexual-harassment claim. Determining this will often depend on the context of the workplace and the situation. For example, a supervisor affectionately patting a subordinate on the backside after a good workplace performance sounds like it would surely be sexual harassment. But turn on any baseball game and watch what happens after a player homers. In that context, slaps on the butt are not examples of sexual conduct.

Sometimes employees try to argue that the use of swear words is a form of sexual harassment, especially the "f-bomb." They claim that because that particular word technically refers to a sexual act, that it must therefore be sexual conduct. Fortunately for those of us with a less-than-pristine vocabulary, the law doesn't turn on that technicality. Using the f-bomb to tell people what you think of them or what you want them to do to themselves is not sexual harassment. Of course, if you use the word to tell someone what *you* want to do to him or her—*that* could well be sexual harassment.

Finally, plain-old, garden-variety harassment that isn't of a sexual nature is not sexual harassment. It isn't unlawful to be mean to someone at work. (That doesn't mean you should do that, though.)

Conduct

The third component of sexual harassment is the conduct. This can take many different forms. It can be physical conduct, with the most extreme form being some sort of unwanted sexual touching (all the way up to rape). Intentionally brushing up against someone, unsolicited neck rubs or hugs or kisses, or even encroaching upon a person's physical space are all examples.

Then there's verbal conduct. Making comments about a person's body in a sexual way is a typical example. There's the matter of degree, though. It's not sexual harassment to tell a coworker that she looks nice today. But going on and on about it, or getting into details about what parts of her looks nice— that can cross the line. Discussions about sexual activity, whether aspirational or historical, about the victim, the harasser, or someone else, can qualify. Sex-related jokes are frequently the basis for complaints.

Computers have magnified the opportunity for harassment. Internet porn, e-mailed jokes or stories, and even online versions of a sports magazine's swimsuit editions can all play a role in a sexual-harassment claim.

Even looks and gestures can be examples of sexual harassment, as long as they fit the test for unwelcome sexual conduct. As with so many things, there are degrees of seriousness. A single e-mailed sex joke is not going to lead to a winning sexual-harassment case, although a single grabbing of someone's hind parts might.

Relating to Work

Lastly, there needs to be a workplace component to the unwelcome sexual conduct. Obviously, if the conduct occurs at work, then this part is pretty straightforward. This also includes work activities away from the office. Where it gets a little grayer is during activities that merely relate to work. Office holiday parties, after-work drinks with colleagues, business trips, conventions: these are all possible venues for sexual harassment. Even if two work colleagues are away from the office for purely social reasons, if unwelcome sexual conduct occurs that could impact the at-work relationship, it's likely to be seen as sexual harassment.

Uh-oh: Latin Again

Finishing up our discussion of the definition of sexual harassment, you should know that the law recognizes two categories of sexual harassment.

The first category is in Latin, because that's how some lawyers like to talk. It's quid pro quo sexual harassment, which is a fancy way of saying "tit for tat." (Come to think of it, maybe it's in Latin just to avoid that potentially risky phrase.)

Quid pro quo harassment is when the harasser tries to make the unwelcome sexual conduct part of an exchange with the victim. Such as, "Go out with me and I'll give you that promotion," or "If you want this job, you have to sleep with me." This is the classic type of sexual harassment, and until the 1990s, it was the main type recognized by the law. You don't see too many examples of this anymore, because *everybody* knows that this type of conduct is unlawful.

The other category of sexual harassment doesn't have a Latin name; instead, lawyers and judges went with a ponderous legalese phrase: hostile work environment. This label is unhelpful, because it makes people think that there needs to be hostility for a claim to succeed. (There needn't be.) In fact, I once had an opposing lawyer argue in federal court that because his client's colleagues were mean to her, that she experienced a hostile work environment. Happily, the judge shot down that argument.

Hostile work environment refers to the more common sexual-harassment scenario where unwelcome sexual conduct becomes part of the work atmosphere itself. The focus then is on the environment, rather than on the incidents themselves. If the unwelcome sexual conduct gets to a point where it interferes with an employee's job, then she's likely to have a viable sexual-harassment claim. That's why a single bawdy joke (or "body" joke) won't carry the day in court, but a pattern of them may.

A Surge in Claims

Sexual-harassment claims became more common in the early 1990s. Part of the reason is because federal antidiscrimination laws became more favorable for employees, allowing them to get jury trials and win greater damages. But the real watershed was in 1991, when sexual harassment became a national conversation during the Clarence Thomas confirmation hearings.

It came up during the hearings that Anita Hill, a former subordinate of his, claimed that Thomas had subjected her to a pattern of unwelcome sexual conduct, causing her to experience a hostile work environment (including, ironically, at the Equal Employment Opportunity Commission, which investigates these claims).

Opinion on this particular he-said-she-said episode was sharply divided. But regardless of how you come down on the Hill-Thomas allegations, there's no question that the number of claims has risen since then, and the amount of money awarded to employees has skyrocketed.

The Hardest Claim to Defend

Sexual harassment is the hardest employee claim to defend against. Why? Because it's the claim most likely to make its way to a jury.

When management lawyers defend their employer clients, they try to get most types of employee claims narrowed or dismissed using an arsenal of legal tactics.

Lawyer tricks, in jaded terms.

For example, say I'm defending a disability-discrimination claim. Here are the different arguments I can make to try to get the claim dismissed:

- the employee's not actually disabled
- her condition isn't serious enough to meet the disability threshold
- she's not "otherwise qualified" to perform her job
- she refuses to accept the reasonable accommodations my client has provided
- the accommodations needed to allow her to do the essential functions of her job are not reasonable
- she's already claimed elsewhere that she's totally disabled, meaning she can't work, period

As you can see, there are a number of arguments I can use in a legal motion to try to get the claim dismissed. They're not easy arguments—disability cases are very tricky—but they are arguments.

Sexual harassment is different. I have fewer arguments I can make. Once the employee clears the hurdle of showing that the conduct actually was sexual harassment—meaning that it was unwelcome sexual conduct at work— she's off to the races. The only remaining issues are questions of facts—"he said, she said." And questions of facts are decided at trial. Once a sexual-harassment case gets to trial, the employee has a decent chance of winning, and a probable six-figure payout if she does.

The smart employer has a serious anti-harassment policy and regularly trains its employees and managers so they know what harassment is and how to prevent it. That's much more effective than lawyer tricks.

"Get Your Retaliation in First"

One of my favorite novelists is Lee Child, who writes the wildly popular thriller series involving a former military policeman named Jack Reacher. The Reacher character is very thoughtful and intelligent, but he is also an expert in fisticuffs. In his debut novel *The Killing Floor* (Jove Books, 2006), Child mentions some of Reacher's maxims for surviving a street fight. One of them is "Get your retaliation in first."

I bring this up because retaliation claims are one of the fired employee's strongest weapons in an employment-law street fight. We might amend Reacher's maxim for employer use: "Get your retaliation *defense* in first."

This is an all-too-common scenario: Your company has just been sued for sex discrimination, but your lawyer tells you that the discrimination claim stinks. You're almost certainly going to beat it. Good news, you're thinking.

Not so fast. Turns out something bad happened to the plaintiff after she complained about the bogus discrimination. Like getting fired. Now the company is stuck defending a much stronger retaliatory-discrimination claim.

Whenever an employee complains about sexual harassment or employment discrimination, she's setting the stage for a possible retaliatory-discrimination claim. If she then gets fired soon after her complaint, or suffers some other adverse employment action (demotion, disciplinary action, and so forth), she can argue that it was *because of* her complaint. And agencies and courts will often infer that because the firing followed shortly after the complaint, it happened *because of* it. That's, of course, unfair to the employer, but it's a fact of life.

This happened recently here in Boston. The state's Probation Department faced a sex-discrimination claim (among other things) from an assistant chief probation officer. The case went all the way to a jury trial, which as you know is unusual. The Suffolk County jury found in the Department's favor on the sex-discrimination claims, but ruled for the plaintiff in her retaliation claim. It awarded her $6,000 in compensatory damages, and ... half a million dollars in punitive damages. Plus, she was then entitled to her attorneys' fees.

In that case, after the employee had complained of sex discrimination, she was stripped of supervisory duties and reassigned to cover the front desk. In its defense, the Department said that her performance had declined. Maybe it had. But that's a weak defense in a retaliation claim.

When you're facing a potential discrimination lawsuit, you have to be extra careful to avoid doing something that could end up giving the employee a much stronger retaliation claim. It's a delicate situation to be in, but the wrong actions by the employer can be just the thing that the plaintiff needs to end up with a windfall.

While this doesn't mean that an employee who complains of discrimination or harassment becomes untouchable, it does mean that you have to be much more careful in how you proceed.

Conclusion

When you fire an employee, you want to be careful that the termination doesn't trigger a sexual-harassment claim that was otherwise dormant. Sexual-harassment claims are among the hardest to defend. You also want to protect yourself from a potential retaliation claim, which can bootstrap an otherwise-lousy lawsuit into a cash cow for the fired employee.

So now we've covered the various claims that are the worst-case scenarios after firing an employee. In the next section, we turn to ways that you can lower the risk of these worst-case scenarios before they happen.

Lowering Your Risks

Part IV discusses what steps you can take to avoid employee lawsuits, and even to avoid having to fire employees in the first place. We'll cover how you go about establishing one of your most important relationships as an employer: the one with your employment counsel. I'll give you my thoughts on employee handbooks and employment policies, and why overlegislating the workplace is such a bad idea. We'll discuss how hiring well can help lower the chances of needing to fire employees in the future. And I'll introduce you to the concept of "gruntled employees," who are much less likely to sue you.

Lawyering Up

"Don't Take This the Wrong Way …"

A while back, we finished up a case where we represented a start-up company. The founders had been wrongly accused of taking trade secrets from their employer in a bid to set up a new competing business. We ended up with a terrific result, getting the lawsuit dismissed and allowing them to continue their careers with no money changing hands. We did it effectively for what turned out to be a very reasonable fixed price.

After it was over, the clients were very appreciative. They thanked us for our work and our results. In an e-mail, one of them expressed more gratitude, and then added this:

> Don't take this the wrong way, but I hope I never have to speak to you again professionally.

Huh.

Now I know what he meant, and I know that he meant it half tongue-in-cheek. But just half. As good a job as we'd done for him and his colleagues, as much value and caring and support as we had given him, it was—overall—a negative experience for him.

And this wasn't the first time I'd had this expressed to me over the course of my career. A longtime client would call after a months-long hiatus, and I'd go, "Hey, it's been a long time" and he'd go, "I know. It's been nice." Ouch. Now I know that my client isn't saying that he dislikes talking with me. It's just that he'd rather not *have to* talk to me.

I understand that.

Maybe it's the nature of the work employment lawyers do: people usually aren't very happy when they need employment-law help.

A Necessary Evil

So I appreciate that none of you is ever going to come home at the end of the day and say to your spouse or significant other: "Great news, honey! We just hired a new employment lawyer!" Never going to happen.

An employment lawyer is a necessary evil for your company. The fees you pay to lawyers and law firms show up on your company's income statements as expenses. They do not put money in your pocket. All they seem to do is take money out.

To be fair, a good law firm can actually help increase your company's profits. Profits, of course, are simply your income minus your expenses. While employment lawyers are highly unlikely to help you increase your income, they can help you cut down on your expenses. If you spend $50,000 on employment lawyers who help you settle a lawsuit for another $50,000, where the lawsuit was likely to cost you $400,000 in expected fees and damages at trial, then those lawyers have shaved $300,000 off your expenses. That goes straight to your bottom line.

But I know, I know. You're not interested in that argument. I don't blame you. You don't like to spend money on lawyers, but you know you need to. This chapter is about how to make that process less painful and more pleasant—how to pick the right lawyers for your company, and how to make dealing with them as easy as possible.

What Size Firm Should You Pick?

As with most things in life, law firms come in small, medium, and large. Before choosing your employment counsel, you should give some thought to what size firm you want representing you.

Large Firms

Most large firms (that is, firms having more than a hundred lawyers), have dedicated employment-law departments. Actually, that has begun to change over the last decade or so. Many large firms have begun to roll their employment departments into larger litigation groups.

Part of the reason is economic; employment departments don't tend to be the brand-name moneymakers for big firms. More commonly, they are support arms for the firms' corporate departments. The corporate lawyers tend to bring in the companies as clients. When the company has an employment-law issue come up, they ask their corporate lawyer if the firm has someone who can help with that. That's how most large-firm employment groups get their business.

In any event, nearly every big firm will have at least a handful of lawyers who specialize in employment law. And the lawyers at these firms will almost exclusively represent employers. It's fairly unusual for large-firm employment lawyers to represent employees.

Medium-sized Firms

While all big firms have employment lawyers, that's less likely to be the case with your medium-sized firms. Some medium-sized firms will have a dedicated employment lawyer or three, but others try to get the job done by using business-litigation lawyers to do their employment work. More on this in a bit.

Small Firms

Finally, there are the boutiques. In most large cities, you will find a handful of small employment-law firms. Typically, these firms will do nothing but employment law. These boutiques will almost always specialize in representing one side or the other. My firm, Shepherd Law Group, only represented employers. Other firms will focus on representing employees.

So if you have a choice of law-firm size, which should you choose? Since I worked my whole legal career in small firms, you might expect me to wave that particular banner. But that would be oversimplifying. I've worked with excellent lawyers in big firms, medium firms, and small firms. But there are differences.

Pros and Cons

Unsurprisingly, large firms tend to be more expensive. They tend to bill out at the highest rates (anywhere from $300 to $800 an hour, depending on the location of the office and the experience level of the particular lawyer). They also tend to take more of a blunt-instrument approach to litigation. They know they have the resources, so they tend to be unafraid to use them. They often will "big firm" the other side with enormous discovery requests and greater numbers of depositions. Their attitude sometimes is that if the client can afford to hire them, the client must not be afraid to spend the money.

But because the large firms pay their lawyers much more than their small counterparts, they tend to attract the top candidates from the top law schools. Many of their new lawyers start working at the firm after serving in a coveted judicial clerkship. There's something to be said for wanting to use a firm that hires "the best and the brightest."

On the other hand, I've heard employers say that they prefer to hire big firms for big cases, thinking that it will intimidate the small-firm lawyers that the employee hired. I've got news for them: never going to happen. As someone who has gone up against (and beaten) four of the fifty largest firms in the country (in noncompete cases, where management-side firms typically work on both sides), I can tell you that small-firm lawyers are *never* intimidated by the size of their opponents.

Put it this way, if I lose a case to one of the largest firms in the country, the reaction will be "Well, they're one of the largest firms in the country. What are you going to do?" On the other hand, if I win, the accomplishment seems even greater. It's like playing with house money. The intimidation factor is completely overblown.

My employee-side friends say the same thing. They're always going up against top firms. If the size of their opponents had them quaking in their boots, they should be in a different line of work.

You can do well with large firms and with small firms. With small firms, you might end up knowing the lawyers better, whereas with larger firms, you may sometimes deal with lawyers you haven't met. On the other hand, you might have trouble reaching your small-firm lawyer if she's tied up with another client, while the large firm will always be able to find someone to help you.

At small firms, the junior lawyers tend to get more experience faster, mainly because they have to. At larger firms, the more-junior lawyers are likely to have less experience (but cost considerably more than their small-firm peers).

Bottom line: there are pros and cons for both. But it's important to find lawyers you're comfortable dealing with.

Picking Sides

For some unknown reason, you will sometimes hear employee-side lawyers say that they also do "some management work." On the other hand, management lawyers will almost never say that they also do plaintiff-side work.

In my opinion, you're better off with a law firm that represents management exclusively.

That said, I can tell you from my own experience that there's a benefit to having practiced on the other side. As I mentioned, for the first year after I started my firm, I needed to take cases representing employees, even though all my previous clients had been employers. The simple fact was that it is much easier to get new employee clients than it is to get new employers. Since I didn't take any clients with me from my old firm (although a few followed me to my new firm years later), I needed to do some plaintiff's work to pay the bills.

Even though I didn't care for working on that side of the table, I gained a real understanding of the employee-side practice. Conversely, one of my favorite employee lawyers spent years working in house as a management lawyer. This became a real selling point for her in her employee-side practice. Her knowledge of the management-side playbook gave her a distinct advantage. That's why I've referred dozens of employees to her over the years.

What's So Special About Specializing?

One of the first things that my first law-firm boss told me was that employment law was not rocket science. And she was right; it's not. Employment law lacks the deep mysteries-of-the-universe intellectual challenge of quantum mechanics.

It's also a particularly finite field. A new lawyer practicing employment law full-time in a boutique should be able to get to a comfort level handling clients' questions in about two years. After four years, a full-time employment lawyer has probably seen most every type of case and situation, and should be fully comfortable with the entire practice area. It's no coincidence that I started my own employment-law firm after I'd been practicing in the field for four years.

Part-time Lover?

But that said, notice that I keep saying "full-time." I've seen countless attorneys "dabble" in employment law (and everything else). Trust me when I tell you that you can't keep on top of all the developments and nuances in employment law if you only dabble in it.

When you're considering lawyers, take a look at their web site profile and see what practice areas they work in. If they list more than one or two, run the other way. (If they don't have a web site profile, run even faster the other way.) When you see a lawyer who "specializes" in six or eight or ten different practice areas, you're seeing a lawyer who doesn't specialize at all. Lawyers like that—and unfortunately, they abound—tend to list any practice area in which they've ever had a single matter.

This isn't me being an employment-law snob. (What a ridiculous thing to be snobby about.) This is common sense. Let me put it to you this way. Let's say you're looking at the profile of a lawyer who lists six different practice areas. And let's give her the benefit of the doubt and say that she legitimately practices in all six areas (including employment law) more or less equally. Fine. Maybe that breadth of experience will serve her well as a general-practice lawyer in a small town with very few attorneys.

But if she divides her time evenly among her six practice areas, that means she only spends one-sixth of her time practicing employment law. In other words, all things being equal, a full-time employment lawyer would spend 500 percent more time on employment law than the attorney with the six fields. That's pretty significant.

You want to work with an expert, and an expert is someone who specializes in employment law full-time. It's similar to seeing a medical specialist. If you have something serious going on with your heart, you're going to want to go see a cardiologist. You're not going to visit a general doctor who "dabbles" in ears, eyes, gastrointestinal tract, the brain, knees, and—oh, yes—hearts. Right?

Not to Belabor the Issue

Sometimes you'll hear people refer to "labor lawyers" as opposed to "employment lawyers." Let me clear up any confusion over this.

Back in the day—say, 40 or more years ago—there was really only one type of lawyer who did work related to the workplace. They were called "labor lawyers." Much if not most of their work came from dealing with unionized workplaces. The two sides were management, obviously representing the employers, and union, ostensibly representing the employees (but actually representing the unions themselves).

But over time, state and federal governments increased the scope of employees' individual rights, affording them the opportunity to protect themselves without the need of the union. At the same time, US manufacturing diminished considerably, lowering the number of workplaces where unions traditionally thrived. These two developments led more lawyers to focus on individual employment rights instead of union-related activity. These lawyers became known as "employment lawyers," while the lawyers who dealt with unions remained "labor lawyers."

Today, it's something of a generational thing. Many lawyers in their fifties and sixties had started out as labor lawyers but over time became employment lawyers. When speaking to nonlawyers, they may still describe themselves as "labor lawyers"; but to other lawyers, they'll correctly call themselves "employment lawyers."

Note By the way, what's the deal with lawyers calling everyone else "nonlawyers"? Is there any other occupation that does that? Am I a "nonplumber" to the pipe-and-wrench set? Discuss among yourselves.

Today, there are very few labor lawyers; most workplace people are really employment lawyers. This makes sense, since only 6.9 percent of the US private sector belongs to a union (as of January 2011). Many younger employment lawyers have zero labor-law experience; in fact, it's a dying specialty. Employment lawyers in their forties are somewhat in the middle. For example, early in my career, I did a decent amount of labor-law work. This was because my firm had been founded by labor lawyers who had become employment lawyers. Once I started my own firm, though, my labor-law business dropped off. So I never considered myself a true labor lawyer, and I never wanted to.

In choosing who's going to help you with your workplace issues, decide whether you need experience dealing with labor unions. If so, make sure your firm has someone who works as a classical labor lawyer. If not, then just focus on employment lawyers.

What to Look for

Once you've decided what size firm you want to work with, and you've located the right kind of specialists, you still need to find a lawyer who is a good fit for you and your company.

It's important that your employment lawyer is a "people person." You would think that anyone going into this field would have to have that quality, but it isn't so. The best employment lawyers are empathetic and sympathetic, and they are good readers of people and their motivations and emotions. These traits are far more important to being a good employment lawyer than are intelligence and the ability to read cases and statutes. (Those things are table stakes anyway.) You need to find someone who has good judgment and common sense, and the only way you can determine this is by meeting him or her in person.

You want to work with an employment lawyer or firm who's skilled and experienced at settling cases. As I said earlier, this doesn't mean that they're afraid to litigate, or aren't good at it. On the contrary: to be a good at settling cases, you have to be good at litigating them.

On the other hand, some would-be clients ask the lawyer how many cases she's tried, thinking that the more she's done, the better she is. As I wrote before, though, a management lawyer who tries a lot of cases is a lawyer who appears to have problems resolving her clients' issues. Real lawyers settle cases.

It's also important that you find someone who is going to be willing to learn about your company and industry. In fact, they should have already read up on your company by the time you first meet them. There's no excuse anymore for a lawyer not to take an hour and study your company's web site and Google links before the pitch meeting. If they don't understand your company and the business you're in, that's going to seriously hamper their ability to do great work for you.

How to Work with Them

At my firm, it was our goal to have our clients think of us as if we were part of the same company, just located in a different building. A lot of lawyers and law firms pay lip service to the notion of being "part of the team," but it's an important factor. When an employee crisis comes up, you want your lawyer to be able to immediately understand it—and its potential impact— on your company.

The more comfortable you feel with your employment lawyers, the more effective your relationship with them will be. Not surprisingly, communication is a big part of this. You need to be confident that your lawyer will be responsive. The most common complaint you hear about lawyers, even more than fees, is that they don't return calls fast enough. That has to be a priority for them if your relationship is going to work.

When to Call Them

Short answer: right away. Or sooner.

I can't tell you how many times throughout my career that I've wanted to ask a client—or have actually asked, "Why didn't you call me sooner?" It is always better to call sooner rather than later. When a client calls to say that they've fired an employee who had some health issues and now he's filing a claim, that's too late. Sure, the lawyer can help defend the disability-discrimination claim, and that's important.

But if the employer calls months earlier, when the crisis (and potential lawsuit) was still just an "issue," the employment lawyer would be far more likely to be able to make a difference. The lawyer can help the employer deal with the unhealthy employee, better positioning the termination or even preventing the firing altogether.

I've talked to many employers who've told me that they often delay calling their outside counsel because they don't want the meter to start running on lawyer fees. That's understandable. We'll talk about fees in a moment. But in any event, it's very important to call your employment lawyer as soon as an employee issue arises.

Whose Job Is It Anyway?

This part might be controversial, but I feel that it's critically important. Lawyers and clients must have a clear understanding of what their respective roles are. A good lawyer will spell this out to the client at the beginning of the relationship.

The lawyer's job is to do what's best for the employer. Seems obvious, doesn't it? But it doesn't always work out that way. Because sometimes what the client *wants* you to do is different from what is best for the client. Too many lawyers will bow to pressure from the client and do what the client asks. But in that instance, the lawyer is not doing what the lawyer is supposed to do.

In other words, the customer is *not* always right.

If you think about it, how could the client be expected to always be right? The client isn't the employment-law expert. Otherwise, there'd be no need for the lawyer.

Over my career, I've gotten into a number of heated arguments with clients who wanted me to do something that I felt wasn't best for the company.

Sometimes it was about a position to take in a litigation. Often it was about settling a case. Most of the time, the employer was acting out of understandable emotion. The lawyer's job is to help the client get past the emotion and instead take whatever action is best for them.

Strategy and Tactics

I find that the best way to look at the respective roles of the client and the lawyer is to consider strategy and tactics. The big-picture strategic choices are usually the province of the client. The ultimate decision whether to fight the case or to settle, how much to settle for, whether to fire or not fire an employee—these are all client decisions. (As long as they're thinking rationally instead of acting out of emotion.) How to litigate the case, how to deal with the opposing counsel or the court or witnesses, whom to depose and what questions to ask—these are all the lawyer's responsibilities.

I once had a client get upset with me because the employee's lawyer had asked me for an extension to file something and I granted it—without consulting the client. It was our firm's policy to always grant extensions. Not doing so is an obnoxious, *lawyerly* move. Plus the opposing counsel can always petition the court for the extra time, which the judge will surely grant, making me look like a tool.

But the client didn't like the former employee, and he didn't like the opposing counsel, either. He didn't want me giving the other side *anything*. I explained that we didn't operate that way. That it was our firm's policy to grant extensions. That if we really needed the cheap advantage of depriving the other side of extra time, then our case was too weak in the first place.

The client backed off a bit, chastened, then lamely said, "Well, you still should have checked with me first." To which I said, "No. That's not your job. It's not your call. It's my call as the lawyer."

Lawyers need to be unafraid of doing their job, instead of letting the clients do it for them. It's a hard lesson for many lawyers to learn.

Tell Me How to Do What I Want to Do

On the other hand, clients also don't want to work with lawyers who see their role as always saying "no." This isn't exactly a new sentiment, either. The legendary financier J. P. Morgan once said:

> I don't know as I want a lawyer to tell me what I cannot do. I hire him to tell me how to do what I want to do.

That was over a hundred years ago. Yet I'm sure the problem is even worse today. Lawyers, acting out of fear (of being wrong) spend their time issue-spotting and telling clients about the risks of their chosen course of action. What clients want is what Morgan wanted: help in achieving their goals. Today, many lawyers have no idea of their clients' goals and dreams, and would never consider offering something as unlawyerly as "business advice."

Some even advocate for this. Former lawyer and *Inc.* magazine columnist Norm Brodsky is dead set against lawyers giving business advice:

> The attorney's role should be to advise clients of the potential
> legal consequences of whatever decisions they make. Period.
> End. I have been known to fire lawyers who insist on arguing
> with me about business issues.

In his defense, he's probably right that lawyers give bad business advice, but only because they're not trained to do it.

But I believe that the best lawyers *do* give business advice. Any Googling chimpanzee can (eventually) find the various employment statutes that govern a company's workplace. But a top employment lawyer can take those laws and put them into the context appropriate for his or her client's business. Said another way, the best employment lawyers give business advice with employment-law advice as its foundation.

Lawyers' Fees

One of the biggest complaints about lawyers concerns their fees. And the complaints are completely justifiable.

This happens to be an area I know a lot about. In early 2011, I founded a company called Prefix, LLC (prefixllc.com) to teach lawyers and other professionals how to price the knowledge that they sell, rather than just tracking and billing time. I also do a lot of speaking and writing on the topic.

Most lawyers bill by the hour, a business model that was created in 1919. (Not exactly an innovative approach.) Because it's very difficult for lawyers to estimate how much time something is going to take, it's almost impossible for a client to know in advance what a service is going to cost. In fact, it's just about the only thing that you have to agree to purchase before you know what the price is.

Imagine going to a car dealership and saying, "I like the red one—how much?" and having the dealer say, "It depends. We'll send you an invoice at the end of the month." You'd never buy a car that way, and yet almost everyone buys legal services in that manner.

In the Alternative

Fortunately, the legal industry is now being dragged kicking and screaming into the twenty-first century. Many lawyers and law firms are starting to talk about "alternative billing," or "alternative fee arrangements" (AFAs). Personally, I hate these terms. The word "alternative" has a connotation of disrepute and seaminess, as in "alternative lifestyle." Plus it overcomplicates everything: many lawyers and even clients are now attending complex two-day seminars on AFAs.

But if I read another article about "alternative fee arrangements" or hear of another two-day seminar explaining all the various and complicated AFAs out there, I'm going to try to swallow my tongue.

Lawyers beholden to the Prohibition Era model of billing and the consultants who court them keep talking about how complex and tricky AFAs are. The clients and other lawyers who read these articles and go to these seminars walk away shaking their heads and surrender to sticking with the old billable-hour model. Maybe with a discounted rate, please.

Two Types of Fees

But I'm here to tell you that it is not at all complicated. In fact, if you have seven seconds, I can tell you about all the different types of law-firm fees. Ready?

There are two:

1. Time-based pricing
2. Solution-based pricing

That is all.

No, really. It's no more complicated than that. Time-based pricing is what nearly every law firm does, where the price of the legal services depends on the time spent doing the work and the rate of the "timekeeper."

▧ **Note** In truth, I'm being generous here, because it's not really "pricing" at all. Pricing is when you tell the client what something will cost them before they buy it; time-based law firms don't do that at all.

Under the time-based-pricing model, the one invented in 1919, every activity is worth the same amount on a minute-by-minute (or really, six-minute-by-six-minute) basis, regardless of how important the task is. With few exceptions, every client is charged the same per hour, regardless of their differing needs. The only measurement of value is the amount of sand that has dropped in the hourglass.

Solution-based pricing is when a law firm sets a price based on the value of the solution to the client. It's that simple. I'm not saying it's easy, because it's not. It takes a lot of thought and preparation and understanding and empathy and experience to figure out how much this particular client values this particular solution at this particular moment. But that's OK because we're professional knowledge workers, not pieceworkers in a pin factory.

Clients—simple question: do you want the price of your legal work to be based on the time lawyers spent, or on the value you place on the solution? It's one or the other.

(See, I just spared you that two-day seminar on AFAs. You're welcome.)

Experts Know What It Costs

To figure out how good your lawyer is, give him or her the following test. It only has a single question, so it will only take about three seconds to administer. On the other hand, it will take considerably longer to answer. And it should.

Here it is:

> **Question One:** How much will this cost?

That's it. Only five words, but it's the whole ballgame. If your lawyer can't correctly answer it, then you've got the wrong lawyer.

Now for the Teacher's Guide to the test:

- Every case, every matter, every job will have a different answer.
- The answer your lawyer gives you won't necessarily be the same as the answer he or she gives another client.

- "It depends" is not an acceptable answer. Neither is "Well, there are variables ...."

One of the commonest complaints I hear from CFOs and general counsels is that law firms pitching their wares always talk about how good they are and how experienced they are. Unlike other vendors, they never talk about how they're going to create value for the company. That's because the law-firm business model doesn't provide a means for doing that. In the billable-hour system, costs are passed on to the client, meaning that there is no incentive to reduce them. Meaning that they won't.

A fixed price avoids that problem, and requires the law firm to be effective and efficient. But a fixed price also requires the law firm to know and understand the value of its services, something it can only do well if it really knows its business.

Many lawyers have insisted to me that you can't put a fixed price on litigation. "There are variables," they whine. "We can't control the costs. What if the other side hits us with a bunch of discovery? What then?"

What then indeed.

If your law firm knows its business well, then it should know the value of the service it provides. Hiding behind a fear of variable costs is an admission that they don't really know their business. An airline doesn't say "there are variables" when charging you for your ticket. And yet headwinds, storms, airport congestion, and overtime can dramatically increase the airline's cost of a particular flight. But your ticket price won't change after they sell it to you.

The Red Sox won't say "there are variables" when selling you a ticket for tonight's Yankees game. Yet Sox-Yankees games tend to be much longer than other games; plus maybe it's raining lightly with more bad weather expected. A longer game, especially one with rain delays, means increased costs for the Red Sox in wages, overtime, electricity costs, and so on. But your ticket price won't change after they sell it to you.

The Red Sox know their business. The airline knows its business.

Does your law firm? Give it the one-question test.

Conclusion

Picking the right employment lawyer or law firm is one of the most important things you can do to help protect your company from workplace problems and lawsuits. Developing a strong, trusting relationship with excellent communications will go a long way to keeping you out of trouble. Make sure your employment lawyers are specialists, and make sure both they and you understand your respective roles.

In a perfect world, you'll find employment lawyers who will actually price their knowledge and expertise instead of merely tracking and billing their time. If you find lawyers you like but who don't know how to price, send them to me at prefixllc.com. I'll teach them how.

Next, we'll talk about how to handle your employee handbook. But it might surprise you to learn what I tell you to do with it.

Throw Out Your Personnel Handbook

Perhaps more than any other chapter, this one might make a lot of managers and HR professionals uneasy. It goes against conventional management wisdom, as well as decades of common practice. So buckle up.

The Trouble with Policies

The trend among employers these days is to have more policies, and more-detailed policies. And employment lawyers like me (well, not really like me) have made it worse, by advising employers that way. Some management lawyers might tell you that these policies are a good tool for companies because they protect them in future litigation.

But I disagree. I think that this growing tendency to hyperlegislate the workplace is actually *bad* for employers. It does nothing to protect against future litigation; instead, I'm convinced that it actually *fosters* it.

You can tell a lot about what kind of employer a company is by looking at its personnel policies and employee handbook. After I'd been practicing for a

while, it got to the point where I could tell if a prospective client was someone I even wanted to bother working with. One look at their personnel
manual and I knew whether they were my kind of employer.

This tended to save a lot of trouble and wasted time, because if they were
the type of company that legislated their employees to death, they weren't
going to be comfortable with my brand of management advice. Better to go
to a more lawyerly lawyer who actually advocated restrictive policies.

Unlike my more-lawyerly colleagues, I say that there are three reasons why
it's bad for business to have a policy-driven workplace:

1. It means that you're playing defense instead of offense.

2. It means that you're giving up your managerial discretion.

3. It means that you're not treating employees like individuals.

Playing Defense Instead of Offense

We talked about this a bit in Chapter 1, but it's important enough to touch
upon again. Employers who hyperlegislate their workplaces either do it out
of ignorance or out of fear. Neither is good.

Ignorance is less common. Some employers just think that it's customary to
have detailed policies designed to cover every possible workplace scenario.
Perhaps they've seen this in other workplaces, and now believe that this is
the norm. "Employees need employee manuals, don't you know, so let's put
a lot of effort into this and address every conceivable topic."

More common are the manuals that arise out of employers' fear. By fear, I
mean this: The employers have been burned before by employees who have
taken advantage of managers' kindness or naiveté. In the past, a bad employee
has been given an inch and taken a yard, so the employer swears that it won't
make that mistake again. Take advantage of sick leave to go to a ballgame? *I'll
show you. Mandatory doctor's notes!* Lying about attending a uncle's funeral and
instead going to Disney World? *Never again! Mandatory death notices, and limits
on which relatives qualify for bereavement leave.*

Sound crazy? Sure. But unfortunately, it happens all the time. And then it's
the baby-and-bathwater thing. In their fear-driven effort to prevent being
taken advantage of again by bad employees, these managers make life miserable for all the good employees. Next thing you know, there are workplace
rules up the ying-yang, and no one likes working at the company anymore.
The bad employees have won.

This is similar to retail stores that have had problems in the past with shop-lifting. They lose a few CDs here or sunglasses there and they decide, "Never again!" So they make it impossible to open CDs by wrapping them in impene-trable plastic wrap, or they place stickers and chains on the sunglasses so it's impossible to try them on. In the end, customers stop buying the CDs and sunglasses, and then they stop shopping at such unpleasant places. All to pro-tect against the one percent of customers who would actually shoplift. That's just bad math.

Employers with their fear-based policies and rulebooks are using the same type of bad math. They are focusing on the relatively small number of bad employees who would take advantage of an employer, policy or no policy. But all these policies make it unpleasant for all the rest of the employees— the good employees—who now are less likely to want to work there.

These employers are playing defense instead of offense. These managers are letting the bad employees drive workplace decisions instead of making those decisions themselves to empower the good employees. It's the tail wagging the dog.

The Better Part of Valor

The second reason why it's bad to hyperlegislate the workplace is because it causes management to (often unwittingly) give up their ability to use their discretion. And using discretion is a critical managerial skill.

Of course, it's much easier to be a manager, at least in the short run, when you don't have to worry about exercising your discretion. Of course, being that kind of manager isn't exactly going to win you any awards.

When I say "discretion," I mean the ability to adapt to a situation as the need arises. It's important to have this ability if you ever hope to lead people, and that's line number one in any manager's job description. When a situation comes up and the rules, such as they are, would lead to an injustice (or any other bad outcome), the manager's role should be to adapt to the situation.

Law and Equity

This reminds me of a lesson I learned in law school. Professor Dan Coquil-lette was teaching a course on English Legal History, a topic that would be useful in my daily practice for my entire career. (Yeah, totally lying there.)

The professor, who is one of the nicest guys you'll ever meet, was explaining the difference between law and equity.

Law, he said, was when a walled city had a rule that the city gates had to be closed from sunset to sunrise. On the other hand, equity came into play if citizens were caught outside the gate after sunset and an enemy brigade was closing in on them. Equity called for opening the gate despite the law rule for keeping it closed after sunset. This, by the way, is very much an English concept (and now American, too); Continental European legal systems depend almost exclusively on law concepts.

Note Actually, it's wrong to say that I didn't use my English Legal History every day. If it weren't for that course, you wouldn't be reading this book now. No exaggeration. Professor Coquillette, who previously had been the dean at Boston College Law School, gave me the recommendation that led to my getting a job as an employment lawyer after graduation. If he hadn't, I never could have written this book.

So a manager's ability to use discretion is similar to the concept of equity. It's the decision to open the gate after sundown for the employee caught outside as the enemy approaches. It's for the times when simply following "policy" or company rules would lead to the wrong result. This is why you have managers in the first place. Otherwise, you could replace them with machines that simply measure whether the rules are being followed. (Actually, too many companies have already done this. The machines are called "bad managers.")

Progressively Worse

It's the lack of discretion inherent in progressive-discipline policies that makes them so bad for employers. In a typical progressive-discipline policy, an employer is *required* to give a series of progressively stronger punishments to a wayward employee before being able to fire him or her. And who requires this? The policy, which the employer itself created. If the employer hadn't created this policy, managerial discretion would have carried the day. But a progressive-discipline policy takes discretion out of management's hands.

This cuts both ways. Sometimes an employer would recognize that a problem employee is just too much of a problem, and would prefer to let him go, but can't—because of the policy. On the other hand, sometimes an employer is faced with an employee who is worth saving, but because of the policy, she *must* receive the next level of discipline spelled out in the rule. Both situations are problems for the employer, because both eviscerate the role of managers and their ability to use discretion.

But many will cry out that this managerial discretion will inevitably result in employees being treated differently. And HR people and employment lawyers are always telling us that you can't treat employees differently or you'll get sued.

Ironically, that leads right into the third reason why it's bad for business to have a policy-driven workplace: because it means that you're not treating employees like individuals.

Employees Are Individuals, Like It or Not

I understand why managers and HR pros feel the need to treat employees the same. It's our fault, and by "our," I mean "lawyers.'" Lawyers have been telling employers for years that the danger in treating employees differently is that it raises the possibility of employment-discrimination lawsuits, and that you want to avoid those at all costs. But most lawyers are thinking just about the "law" aspects of employment; most don't consider the "management" aspects. And treating employees all the same is a bad management approach.

When you treat employees equally, you end up treating them equally badly. Not exactly a recipe for success.

The Most Important Lesson

Employees are people, and all people want to be treated as special. That's not to say that all people want "special treatment." They just want to be treated like the individuals they are. Like they matter. Like they're not just replaceable cogs in a machine.

In lawyers' understandable and praiseworthy desire to protect their employer clients from expensive and disruptive litigations, they've overlooked the basic human need that **each employee has to feel like he or she matters.** Of all the things I've learned over the course of my career, this is the single most important lesson. (Hence, the boldface.)

I appreciate that this approach is going to make many of you nervous. Most human-resources professionals have been hearing the mantra their whole careers that you must never be seen as giving one employee preferential treatment. That if you make exceptions to policies, those exceptions will end up being fodder for a future discrimination case. That if you enforce rules (or choose not to enforce them) arbitrarily, that this will be used as evidence against your company. I know that's what employment lawyers tell you. And I understand the sentiment behind that advice. But it's all wrong.

You're not increasing your chances of facing an employment-discrimination case if you treat employees as individuals. Instead, you raise your chances of going to court if you treat employees as members of groups. This leads to notions like "the company pays men more than women" or "the company promotes whites ahead of blacks." Those are the notions that will (rightly) buy you plenty of time talking to your employment litigators. But treating employees as individuals will actually *lessen* the chances of getting sued because employees will realize that you *don't* view them as machines, but as individuals.

How many times have you heard (or said) this line? "I can't make an exception for you or else I'd have to do it for everyone." People in management and HR—well-meaning people, mind you—trot that one out all the time. I say "well-meaning" because I'm sure that most of the time they'd prefer to make the exception, but that they feel they can't.

But the logic behind that statement is completely unsound. There's no legitimate basis for the notion that an exception made for one employee must then be made for every other employee. *That's* why they call it an exception!

It's the opening of the gate after sundown. It's recognizing that the employee with the issue is an individual with unique circumstances and concerns. There is absolutely no reason to assume that the next employee who comes along is going to share those circumstances and concerns. Instead, the next employee will have her own circumstances and concerns. And you'll treat her as an individual, too. And if she doesn't get the exception she wanted, that's part of your discretion.

It's possible that she'll point out that the other guy did get the exception he wanted. "So what?" you'll say. "You're not him. Your circumstances are different from his. And his situation is none of your business, so you needn't be worrying about it." If employees understand that you treat them all as individuals, they will be much less likely to think that you're favoring one group over another.

Tito's Way

I mentioned early on that I'm a big baseball fan. Actually, that's not completely accurate. I'm a big Red Sox fan. For most of my life, this meant constantly being set up for a letdown. Year after year, impressive teams of well-paid superstars would tantalize for much of the season, only to collapse when it mattered most.

But that all changed in 2004, at least temporarily. That year, a scrappy Red Sox team that was pushed all the way to the brink—down three games to zero in the American League Championship Series against the hated New York Yankees—did the impossible and battled back to win the pennant and then the World Series. No team had ever come back from a 0–3 deficit to win a four-game playoff series. Then they swept the Cardinals in the World Series, ending an 86-year Boston drought.

One of the things that had changed that year was the addition of Terry Francona as manager. Francona had been a decent player (and son of another player) whose playing career was cut short because of injury. He worked his way up through the coaching ranks until he became a manager. Before taking over the Red Sox at the start of 2004, his managing record had been unimpressive. But he brought with him an attitude and a philosophy that served the team well.

He was not the classic major-league manager. He never yelled in the clubhouse or knocked over the postgame dinner spread. He never called out his players in interviews with the media. He never appeared too down after losses, nor too up after victories.

One of the hallmarks of the 2004 was the individuality of the team members. They were far more laid back and colorful (and hairier) than the corporate, clean-shaven Yankees. Some criticized Francona for allowing the unruliness, arguing that he was coddling the multimillionaire divas.

But Francona has no use for unnecessary rules. His rules are basically "show up on time," "do your job," and "support your teammates." And he's maintained this philosophy ever since. In his eight-year tenure as Red Sox manager, he led the team to two World Series championships and five playoff appearances.

In a 2010 interview with Charles P. Pierce of *The Boston Globe*,[1] Francona explained why having a rules-oriented clubhouse didn't make sense for them:

---

[1] "The Calmest Man in the Clubhouse," *Boston Sunday Globe*, May 23, 2010.

I want there to be an atmosphere where they want to show up every day and do the right thing. We can have rules out the [expletive], but if they want to do the right thing, we'll be a better team.

Just so you know, the *Globe* bleeped out the word, not me.

Back in the first chapter, I mentioned the bereavement-leave policy at Alabama Agricultural & Mechanical University as an example of the kind of rules-oriented behavior that dooms an employer to having unhappy workers. Rather than let the Alabama A&M managers use their discretion in letting employees take time off to mourn the passing of a family member, its HR department concocted a stupefying policy that spells out under precisely what limited circumstances an employee could take a bereavement leave.

Contrast this with the way Francona and the Red Sox dealt with a family situation that came up for their star second baseman Dustin Pedroia in July 2009. His wife went into the hospital because of some late-pregnancy complications. Francona excused him from the game to go be with his wife. That might not seem like a big deal, but it is a major break with baseball tradition. (The Sox did end up getting shut out by the Oakland A's in that game.) As the *Globe*'s Dan Shaughnessy wrote:[2]

> The episode is a perfect demonstration of Terry Francona's managing style and the evolution of old-fashioned hardball rules. In the bad old days, players heard about family emergencies and baby deliveries via Western Union. Management did not encourage players to leave. Ever.
>
> ...
>
> Players' families come first [under Francona]. It earns him a lot of loyalty in his clubhouse.

There was no consultation with HR to see if the personnel manual allowed for a certain number of days off in this situation. It was just a question of doing the right thing for the individual employee in a unique situation.

An Organizational Belief

Now some of you might correctly point out that federal and state leave laws often mandate that companies allow time off for family-medical situations. Fair point. But there's a big difference between using discretion to help out an employee and merely following bureaucratic employment laws.

---

[2] "Pedroia Benefits from the Embrace of Hardball's Softer Side," *The Boston Globe*, July 8, 2009.

Let me give you another Red Sox example. In 2010, the young daughter of Sox first-base coach Ron Johnson was severely injured in an automobile accident. A car hit the horse she was riding; the girl ended up losing her leg. Johnson sped home to be with his family and ended up being away from the team for much of the season.

But there was no question about letting Johnson have that time. While I don't know firsthand, I have no doubt that no one in the team's HR department was counting the days off against his Family and Medical Leave Act allotment. Likewise, I'm confident that the team paid Johnson despite his not being at work, even though the FMLA only requires unpaid leave.

The *Globe* asked Sox general manager (and Francona's boss) Theo Epstein about Johnson's leave. Epstein's quote[3] tells you everything you need to know about the team and its feelings about Johnson's time away:

> His priority is with his family, and that's an organizational belief, that at times of crisis, family comes first. He's doing a great job supporting his family through this tough time.

You'd do well to adopt that organizational belief: "Family comes first." I'm happy to say that our law firm had it from the start (yes, long before I read this Epstein quote). Do you really want to work in the kind of an organization that is more concerned with policies and rules and counting available leave days than in one that stands up and does the right thing for one of its team members?

Update I wrote most of this chapter before the team's epic September 2011 collapse. For four and a half months—from mid-April to the end of August—the Red Sox were the best team in baseball, winning at an amazing .659 clip. Then the wheels fell off. They became the first team in history to miss the playoffs despite having a nine-game lead in September.

Francona and Epstein both left the team under a cloud shortly after the season ended. Even Ron Johnson ended up getting fired. I wondered whether this material should stay in the book. In the end, I decided that the lessons were no less valid given what happened. Sometimes, even the best management philosophies can't save a team—or a company—from having a bad run. Smart management and pro-employee organizational beliefs won't guarantee you playoffs or profits, but they will improve your chances.

---

[3] "Delcarmen Dealt to Rockies for Prospect," *The Boston Globe*, Sept. 1, 2010.

Focusing on a Technicality

Here's a stark example of the opposite type of workplace.

In 2008, I received an e-mail from a woman who had come across my blog post on *Gruntled Employees* talking about the Alabama A&M bereavement-leave policy. Her father had just died, and she had called her company to inquire about bereavement leave. She was told that the company's policy was to grant three days' leave for an employee who lost an immediate family member so that the employee could attend the funeral. But the woman's father had requested that there be no funeral service held.

So the company told her that she could not have the time off. No funeral, no funeral leave.

This is what happens when managers and HR people focus on rules instead of people. Common sense should have told whoever gave this employee the news that while there was no actual funeral service, the woman had still lost her father. The point of bereavement leave is supposed to be so that the employee can grieve with her family and take care of all the arrangements that come with a death. That there was technically no service defined as a funeral is completely irrelevant.

You Can't Plan for Everything

One of the fundamental beliefs underlying the writing of detailed personnel handbooks and employment policies is the notion that you can plan for anything and everything, and that you should. But the human experience is too random, and the lives of humans are messy. They don't lend themselves to planning. Just ask the Soviets.

But people will still try. The policy drafters will try to imagine every possible scenario that could come up in various management issues. Then they try to draft for each scenario. "What if the employee's relative doesn't have an actual funeral?" they'll ask each other, probably in some endless policy-drafting committee meeting. "Then we should ask for a letter from the funeral home confirming that." Or some nonsense like that.

But no matter how adept the policy-drafting committee is at anticipating different management situations, things will come up that were never planned for. And once again, managerial discretion will be called upon to solve the problem.

Better Off Without the Handbook

I've got to be honest with you. Over the years, my firm made a decent amount of money drafting employee manuals and personnel policies for clients. And it was pretty easy work. It's not like we'd start from scratch with every new handbook gig. Over the years, we'd gather different policies that we'd written and that we were happy with. We'd start with a base manual, and then make adjustments and customizations for the specific client.

But it was probably my least favorite type of work I ever did as a management lawyer. Part of it was the boredom factor. I mean really: how excited can one possibly get over drafting a new internet-usage policy?

But the bigger problem was that I often felt that the manuals were unnecessary. Clients believed that they needed them, and they'd specifically call us looking for us to give them one (or update their existing one—an even worse job). But our question to them often came as a surprise:

"Do you really need one?"

Perhaps they had trouble believing that a lawyer would question the opportunity to bill some hours. (Of course, for the last five years, my firm didn't bill hours. But you get my drift.)

But it was a serious question. While it's understandable and appropriate for an employer to make sure that its employees know what the rules are, a comprehensive employee handbook with Hammurabi-esque edicts on employee conduct can cause more harm than good.

Gaming the System

One problem with handbooks is the creation of an impersonal, rigid structure that encourages employees to "game the system." Employees are smart when it comes to getting what they want. If a policy creates a loophole that allows more time off if you call it "personal time" instead of "sick time," you will see a rise in personal-time usage. This is not my being cynical; this is my recognizing that employees, like all humans, are (often) rational, self-interested actors.

A few years ago, my firm was asked by a large local employer to help them deal with a massive Family and Medical Leave Act problem they were having. It turns out, over the course of the previous year, fully one-fourth of the company's employees had taken FMLA leave. What is more, this shocking statistic represented a huge jump over previous years, when the percentage of workers taking FMLA leave was in the low single digits.

The first thing we asked was if the company had made any significant human-resources changes before the numbers shot up. Unsurprisingly, it had. Management had adopted a new policy that made it harder to take traditional sick leave. Sure enough, before the change, too many employees had been taking sick leave—roughly 25 percent.

Once the policy was changed to make it harder to get sick leave, the savvy employees gamed the system, and took advantage of the FMLA policy. Oops.

A Matter of Trust

Finally, a thick manual of dos and don'ts sends a message that you don't trust your employees, or that you consider them wayward children. Some policies may be necessary to spell out, like how vacation accrues. And some policies are legally mandated, like sexual-harassment policies in some states.

But too many policies are the result of HR professionals and employment lawyers hyperlegislating conduct in the workplace. For example, dress codes or bereavement policies that go on for more than a sentence or two. You're better off without this paternalistic nonsense.

How do you think employees will react to this sort of managerial attitude? Most employees aren't stupid. They'll quickly figure out what it means. It means you don't trust them. And I've got news for you: People resent it when you don't trust them. Plus it begs the question: If you don't trust them, why are they your employees in the first place?

Treating Employees Like Children

Besides showing that you don't trust them, a policy-driven workplace also makes it seem like you're treating your employees like children. Specifically, like children who don't know any better, and who can't think for themselves.

My wife and I have two young kids, so like many parents we don't get out very often. So when my mother and father offered to take our daughters for the weekend, we had some important decisions to make. We wanted to go out for a couple nice dinners in Boston. So do we go to an old favorite, a place where we knew that we were likely to have a good experience? Or do we get adventurous and try something new? Since we had two evenings to cover, we decided to do both.

Friday night, we went to a new (for us) place. The food was really quite good (the chef is world famous), but the service was indifferent. We kept overhearing waitstaff complaining about coworkers—"I'm not working with Aziz again!" The overall experience was *meh.*

On Saturday, we blew off adventurous and returned to our favorite Boston restaurant, a hip, cool Italian place called Sorellina. What a difference. The food, as always, was excellent. But it was the service that makes it stand out.

We arrived very early—5:30—so that we'd have to time for a movie afterward. They had just opened for the day, and the management and staff were having their daily pre-meal meeting. Now many high-quality restaurants have a daily meeting like this, but this got me thinking: maybe companies in other industries would benefit from having a daily "pre-meal" meeting.

Every person we dealt with was gracious, polite, genuine, eye-sparkly (to borrow a term from Tom Peters), and warm: the hostess, the bartenders, the waitstaff, the busboys, and the general manager. They did things without being asked, like splitting the (fantastic) tuna tartare appetizer into two beautiful dishes so that we could share it, or bringing my wife an extra wineglass so that she could try a sip of my Shiraz. We never felt rushed, nor did we ever feel ignored. It was a terrific team performance.

Our waitress, Katrina, was bright, charming, and knowledgeable, with an arch sense of humor. (It took great restraint for me not to ask whether people comment on her name. The hurricane? Too soon. "Walking on Sunshine"? Also too soon.) She told us that she had been working there for three and a half years. She also pointed out that many of the servers had been there as long or longer.

During the meal, the general manager, Dominick Minots, came over to chat with us. No particular reason—even though we've been there a bunch of times over the years and even had the Shepherd Law Group holiday party there in 2007, we weren't exactly regulars. He asked how we were enjoying our meal in a way that showed that he actually cared about the answer. I asked him about the long tenure of their staff, mentioning that it was unusual in the restaurant industry. His answer resonated with me.

"We don't treat our employees like children," he said. Everyone was accountable to each other, to the restaurant, and to the guests. For them, team was the key concept. Not in a there's-no-I-in-team sense, but in a sense that the team worked together to make the guests' experiences as enjoyable as they can be. And it showed.

How many companies can honestly say that they don't treat their employees like children? Too many worry about policies and rules and personnel manuals. How can an employer expect someone to feel accountable and have a sense of responsibility when it legislates all aspects of the employees' conduct?

If you want your workplace to provide world-class results like Sorellina, start by treating your employees like grown-ups.

The World's Shortest Employee Handbook

So for the strategic employer who views its workers as its most important asset and wants to promote an atmosphere of professionalism and trust, let me propose the world's shortest employee handbook:

"Respect others."

Now, wait. Before you accuse me of breaking out the zither and the folk songs, hear me out. As I've said many times before, our roles as HR professionals, employment lawyers, and managers all boil down to the notion of showing employees respect. You could say that disgruntled employees are just gruntled employees who have been dissed. Employees you don't treat with respect are the ones most likely to sue you (see Chapter 7 on Retained Dignity). And I'm not making these pronouncements based on a Pollyanna-ish view of the world. Instead, I'm making these observations based on years of defending employers from lawsuits. End of self-defense bit.

Think about it: what policies in your typical handbook can't be distilled into the two words "respect others"?

- Policies about harassment and discrimination and office romance are all about respecting coworkers.
- Policies about trade secrets and computer usage and even attendance are all about respecting the company.
- Policies about dealing with customers or answering the phone or about handling complaints are about respecting the customers.
- Even policies about drugs and alcohol are all about respecting yourself.

Employees who follow this Rule Number One (and Only) will be valuable members of your team. Employees who fail to respect others should no longer be, unless you feel they deserve another chance.

Two words. Think of how much paper you'll save.

But It's the Law

There is one exception to my minimalist take on employment policies: when a state or federal law requires you to have a written policy. In that case, the statute trumps my antipolicy policy. For example, some states (like California and Massachusetts) require employers to have written sexual-harassment policies. Similarly, the federal government recently amended the Family and Medical Leave Act to require employers to post a written notice about employees' FMLA rights. You need to check with your employment counsel to see what policies are required in your jurisdiction. But just because your state might require certain policies doesn't mean you should start firing up the policy generator.

Conclusion

Having a workplace ruled by personnel policies and employee handbooks means taking power away from management. It means that you're playing defense instead of offense, worrying more about protecting the company from bad employees instead of encouraging good employees. It means giving up managerial discretion. And it means not treating employees as individuals.

Next we turn to one of the most effective ways of avoiding lawsuits brought by fired employees: hiring well in the first place so you don't have to fire.

Hiring to Avoid Firing

In the science-fiction classic *The Terminator* (1984), an artificially intelligent network of machines known as *Skynet* is under attack in 2029 from a human resistance group led by John Connor. To protect itself, Skynet sends a cyborg (Arnold Schwarzenegger) back in time to 1984 to assassinate Connor's mother, Sarah (Linda Hamilton), before her son is born. You could say that Skynet has a *very* preventative program for dealing with troublesome resistance leaders.

Employers could learn from Skynet and adopt their own preventative program for dealing with troublesome employees. Actually, it's a lot easier than depending on sentient machines and time travel, and much more successful, too.

It's called hiring thoughtfully.

The Best Defense

It's a battered old sports cliché to say that the best defense is a good offense. But the nice thing about battered old sports clichés is that there's usually a fair amount of truth and wisdom in them. Firing problem employees, as we've discussed throughout this book, is about playing defense. As managers, you're reacting to the problem employees to protect your company.

But there's an awful lot you can do on the other side of the ball. Hiring the right people to work for you is about playing offense. Here you're being proactive instead of reactive.

We talked about this a little way back in Chapter 2 when we discussed the importance of having the right team. (Yes, more sports metaphors.) But that was in the context of why you needed to get rid of troublesome employees. This is different. Now we're talking about getting the right people from the start.

How do we do it? First, we start with the concept of talent.

Taking a Dip in the Talent Pool

"Human resources" is a terrible term. The best you can say about it is that it's a mild improvement over the sterile and antiquated "personnel." In 1989, the American Society for Personnel Administration changed its name to the Society for Human Resource Management "to reflect its broadened scope and influence in business and political worlds internationally." But many feel that "human resources" still has an artificial, impersonal feel to it that belittles the importance of the role. And I agree.

Top business gurus Tom Peters and Seth Godin have both railed against the HR moniker and suggested replacing it with "talent," as in "the Talent Department." In a post called "Marketing HR" on his eponymous blog, Godin writes:

> Understand that in days of yore, factories consisted of people and machines. The goal was to use more machines, fewer people, and to design processes so that the people were interchangeable, low cost and easily replaced. The more leverage the factory-owner had, the better. Hence Personnel or the even more cruel term: HR. It views people as a natural resource, like lumber.[1]

Godin concedes that changing the name to "Talent Department" might make people uncomfortable because it sounds like spin control. But if we're going to insist that the function of "human resources" is as important as we say it is, then we should be prepared to defend a more highfalutin name. Many leading companies have already done this: Apple, Citigroup, Deloitte, and even a law firm, Sheppard Mullin, all have chief talent officers.

---

[1] Seth's Blog, "Marketing HR," http://sethgodin.typepad.com/seths_blog/2008/02/marketing-hr.html, February 2008.

Your company—whether it's a hospital, a software company, a bank, a paperboard mill, or a law firm—doesn't work without the talent that makes it work. So put someone in charge of finding and keeping that talent, and then recognize that person's job with the proper title: chief talent officer.

Moving HR to "C" Level

And that's the other piece of the puzzle, raising the altitude of HR to "C" level.

Most companies have a handful of executives who report directly to the CEO: the chief operating officer, the chief financial officer, the chief information officer, the chief marketing officer, and the chief legal officer (usually called the general counsel). But rare is the company that has its head of human resources sitting in the "C-suite."

This makes no sense. Every company depends upon having the best people—the best talent—it possibly can to succeed. Without top talent, who actually does the operations, finances, technology, marketing, or legal stuff? Why do most companies relegate the recruiting, managing, and retaining of talent to an administrative position that usually reports to the CFO? HR professionals often—legitimately—lament not having "a seat at the table," and for good reason. Most companies fail to recognize the strategic role that HR should play.

Tom Peters beats the drum for elevating HR to its rightful place in his excellent book *Re-imagine! Business Excellence in a Disruptive Age* (DK Publishing, 2003). Like Seth Godin, Tom advocates for changing the name of HR to "Talent Department." (Or even the slightly more exuberant "Seriously Cool People Who Recruit and Develop Seriously Cool People.") He writes on page 256:

> I have long believed that human resources people should sit at the Head Table. I'm a fan of HR. It is . . . after all . . . an Age of Talent.

> Problem: All too often "HR folks" are viewed (all too) correctly as "mechanics." Not as . . . Master Architects . . . who aim too . . . Quarterback the Great War for Talent.

Tom loves ellipses and capital letters nearly as much as he loves exclamation points. But his ideas for building HR into a strategic arm of the company, with a Chief Talent Officer reporting directly to the CEO, are visionary.

Most companies say that their employees are their most important assets. If that's true, they should put the person in charge of developing them at the right altitude: at C level.

Dump the "Personnel" Stuff

There's another reason why many companies and their employees lack sufficient respect for HR professionals. They spend too much of their time dealing with what I call "personnel stuff": I-9 forms, dress-code exceptions, sick-day tracking, floating-holiday calculation, progressive-discipline rules, snow-day cancellations, dental-plan waiting periods. This administrivia is the tail wagging the dog of HR. Even the most forward-thinking, strategy-minded HR chief has no time left to do the important work—developing and implementing the company's talent strategy—after dealing with all the personnel stuff.

Get rid of it.

Outsource it. Send it offshore. Offload it to companies who provide these services as an "outside personnel department." Clear your desk of the nickel-and-dime stuff. Then you can focus on finding, developing, managing, inspiring, and retaining the best talent your company can get.

Getting the Right People

Once you have your Talent Department in its rightful place, then it's time to go out and get that talent. And most companies go about that crucial task the same way.

They run ads in local newspapers or on online job boards like Monster or Craigslist. They gather up résumés and cull them based on schools attended and past work experience. If the position is senior or important enough, they use an outside recruiting firm. Then they bring in the people who made the first cut to have brief interviews with someone in HR or recruiting. After a callback with the head of the department with the open position, references are checked and an offer is made.

The problem with this approach is that it doesn't focus on the most important thing: the individual. Résumés and job applications and brief serial interviews don't give each candidate a chance to showcase what makes him or her the right individual for the job. Instead, hordes of random applicants are processed into a few viable candidates leading to the hiring of a person who fits a checklist of education and experience but may or may not be a good fit for the job and the company.

Companies need a better way to discover the right individual for the job. It's not about the education and work experience; those are just table stakes that you expect from every candidate. Instead, it's about who that person is as an individual, what his or her passions and dreams are, and why working for your company in this particular job will make him or her happy.

Let me give you an example of how one company does it: Starbucks.

So You Want to Be a Barista ...

So it's Sunday and it's hot and I'm taking the family to the local pool. But I need my caffeine fix, and I'm trying to figure out the mechanics of sneaking an iced triple venti latte into the pool area without getting caught. I decide it's worth the risk, so we stop at the nearby Starbucks en route to the pool.

While I'm waiting for the barista to make my order, I notice a small table with a little sign and a pad of employment applications. As an employment lawyer, I'm always interested to see how businesses go about hiring new employees. I'm curious, especially with national employers, to see how many technical violations of state law (in my case, Massachusetts) the application has. I counted just two, which is pretty good. (Massachusetts has a lot of obscure technical application rules. Make sure you check with your employment counsel about your state's rules.)

But here's what the application does right. More than right. In fact, better than just about every other application form I've ever read.

After asking all the usual job-application questions, it asks the following:

1. Have you ever visited a Starbucks Coffee location? Where? Describe your experience.

2. What do you like about coffee?

3. Why would you like to work for Starbucks Coffee Company?

4. Describe a specific situation where you have provided excellent customer service in your most recent position. Why was this effective?

Now the first and third questions are pretty basic. They probably get a lot of lame answers, which help weed out the barista pretenders.

But the second question and the fourth question are brilliant, and should be emulated by all employers.

Starbucks is all about two things: coffee and customer service. To attract the best employees, Starbucks looks to hire people who "get" coffee and "get" customer service. Judging from the top-quality service I received every day at the Starbucks near my old Boston office, where the "partners" (as the company calls all its employees) made an extra effort to remember my name and my order, it seems to be working.

What questions can your company put on its job applications to make sure you attract employees who get what your company is all about? Use this opportunity to learn a great deal about how the interests of the applicant and the company intersect.

Geeks at the Apple Store

Another great example is the people who work at the Apple Store. Beyond their matching t-shirts, which serve to identify them as employees, they are as diverse and eclectic a bunch as you will find anywhere. Men, women, older people, twentysomethings, black, white, foreign, American, pierced and tattooed, or really pierced and tattooed. But they all have one thing in common: they love Macs. (And iPhones and iPads and iPods.)

They're passionate about them, and about Apple as a company. They would hang out there even if they weren't being paid. They have tons of tacit knowledge about the products they sell, and they love to share that knowledge. They're geeks who probably had difficulty fitting in at other jobs but feel at home in the Apple Store.

I don't have firsthand knowledge of the Apple Store hiring process, but I'm confident that they make certain that candidates share that passion or they quickly get shown the door.

 Note Just to be clear, I'm not using "geeks" pejoratively. I'm an Apple geek myself. Heck, I'd probably work at an Apple Store if I didn't have this book to write—on a Mac.

Personality and Passion

The lesson from Starbucks and Apple is to hire people based on their personalities and passions. Now you might retort that I've chosen two well-known consumer brands as examples, and that there are plenty of jobs that don't require passion. Like working in a paper mill. Or a bank. Or being an employment lawyer. But if you think that about your company, maybe it's *you* who shouldn't be working there. People can find passion in any job, and in any workplace.

Earlier this year, I was selected to come in for jury duty at the Middlesex Superior Court in Woburn, Massachusetts. A couple hundred people get herded into the jury-pool room to wait and see whether they're going to get called up for possible selection in a case. Trust me: no one wants to be there.

The room was overseen by a uniformed court officer named Richard, whose job it was to inform all of us about the many rules and tell us what to expect on this most boring of days. The guy had obviously been doing this for years, and had to give the exact same speech every single workday.

And he was a riot.

He could have been doing stand-up comedy. He had an unexpectedly irreverent approach and pitch-perfect deadpan delivery. At eight on a cold, snowy morning, he had 200 strangers who were involuntarily stuck there laughing and smiling at each other.

Richard must have realized that his job was to turn a necessary but irritating day for Middlesex County citizens into a more pleasant experience. And he had passion for that, which showed in the way he did his job. Plus, knowing the court system as I do, I guarantee that no one told him to do his job that way. He came up with it on his own.

If Richard can have passion for that job, then you should be able to find passion for any of the jobs in your company.

Finding the Right People

It takes more work to find the right people. But you can be smart about it. Starbucks' customized job-application form is a great example. Other companies are turning to video applications, asking candidates to submit a two-minute video explaining why they want to work there. An applicant can demonstrate a world of personality in two minutes.

Note Some employment lawyers will have a conniption over this idea, because video applications will reveal the candidate's race and national origin. Yeah, well, so will meeting them in person. Get over it. If you think your managers or HR people are going to discriminate against people based on their videos, you've got the wrong people in those roles.

The last time I placed an ad for a new lawyer in the local trade newspaper, I instructed candidates to explain in a short note "why you'd be the best fit for this job and this firm." I meant this as an invitation for candidates to tell me about themselves and how the things that my firm was doing (trashing timesheets and billable hours, reinventing the law-firm business model, helping client employers have gruntled employees) were the kind of things that excited them.

The ones who ignored this request were cut without a look at their résumés; attention to detail was a must for this position. The ones who sent in generic cover letters that they had probably used a few dozen times before? Well, they'd have the chance to use them again. And the guy who boasted about his "tremendous litigation experience" (despite having been a lawyer for only two years) and how lucky we'd be to have him? We decided to take our chances without him.

But the best candidates were the ones who showed that they'd done some homework about our firm, and then explained how what we were doing fit in with their own identity.

Breaking Bread

Another part of the hiring process that we did differently was with interviews. We had no interest in doing a series of short, meaningless interviews where the candidate was nervous and the interviewer was bored.

Instead, we had longer, more-casual conversations that were designed to learn more about personality than about past accomplishments. And before we would make an offer, we would usually go out for a meal or for drinks with the person. Anything to get away from the artificiality of rote interview questions like, "What would you say your biggest weakness is?"

Yes, this makes the hiring process more involved and time-consuming, but it gives the employer a much-better shot at finding the right people to hire.

What to Look For

So how do you know the right talent when you see it? Remember: past accomplishments and skill sets are merely table stakes for candidates. Without those, a candidate shouldn't even get through the door. Instead, what you're really looking for is a culture fit, which is the best determinant of a successful employment. You want candidates who truly want to work there, and who will want to spend time with you and your coworkers, and with whom you will want to spend time. If you're just looking at work experience and qualifications, you're missing the opportunity to bring in the right people.

Here are what I think are the ten most important traits to look for in a job candidate:

1. **Differentness.** You don't want an office full of cookie-cutter dupli-cates. Instead, your team will be stronger when you have a truly di-verse workforce. And not just race and gender, but also background and life experiences.

2. **Sense of humor.** You're more likely to enjoy working with people with a good sense of humor, who know when to laugh and who can bring the funny from time to time. They don't have to be comedi-ans, but they do need to know how not to take life—and them-selves—too seriously. A good sense of humor is also a leading indi-cator of intelligence.

3. **Optimism.** I'm not talking about Pollyanna-ish types who are na-ive and unrealistic. I'm talking about people who have positive atti-tudes, and can help lift coworkers up instead of bringing them down. Life's tough enough without someone telling you how tough life is all the time.

4. **Eye sparkle.** This is a Tom Peters term. It's that look you see in a person's eyes that shows that they're alive and thoughtful and en-gaged. It shows warmth and empathy and fun. It says that the lights are on and someone is indeed home.

5. **Connectivity.** Look for signs that the candidate knows how to in-teract with other people. Ask about his or her friends and family. This is why going out for drinks or lunch is such a good idea. Some-one who connects well with people will be an asset to your team.

6. **Creativity.** Even if the job isn't what you would normally consider a "creative" position, it's better to have creative people. They tend to be more positive and engaged, looking for better ways to solve the customers' problems.

7. **Perseverance.** The workplace should be a marathon, not a sprint. You want to find people who will stick with it, even when it gets dif-ficult. Look for signs that they follow through with things that they start. Someone who jumps around a lot from job to job might be deficient in this area.

8. **Initiative.** Few things are more frustrating than having an employee who sits around passively and waits to be told what to do. I'd rather have someone who oversteps his or her bounds and needs to be reined in than someone who doesn't show any initiative.

9. **Self-confidence.** This is a critically important trait. It's difficult to teach, although it can be developed and fostered. You're better off hiring a candidate who believes in herself. Then she'll also be more likely to believe in your company. Self-confidence is contagious.

10. **Passion.** This goes back to the coffee question on the Starbucks application, and the Apple geek factor. If you know that the candidate is passionate about something—anything—then it's easier to believe that he or she will care about the company, the customers, and their problems.

You might not agree with everything on this list, and you might list other traits that are important to you or to your company or industry. That's fine. Just make sure that you go into the hiring process with a strong idea of what you're looking for in a candidate. It will make your task much easier, and it will improve your chances of getting the right people for your team.

Conclusion

Getting the right talent into your company is one of the most important things you can do as a manager or employer. When you start with the right people who are there for the right reasons—because they believe in your company—you've already gone a long way to reducing your odds of facing an employee lawsuit.

In our final chapter, I'll talk about how to keep your employees happy. Because happy employees never sue their employers.

Gruntled Employees

We sent my two daughters, ages 8 and 11, to a new day camp this summer. The other camps they had gone to in the past had been fine, for the most part. But "fine," when used to rate an experience, is just shorthand for "there were no major problems, but it sure didn't wow me."

But this camp, called LINX Camps in Wellesley, Massachusetts, was by no means just "fine." As soon as we arrived the first day, we could tell that there was something different about this camp.

The first counselor we met made Disney World employees (or "cast members") seem like undertakers. She greeted us with a huge, smiling *"Hi!"* and said that her name was Beth. She then immediately turned to our girls and asked them their names. Then she started telling them how much fun they were going to have. She didn't talk down to them like some people talk to kids; she *engaged* them, and talked to them like they were going to be friends.

But what really struck me about this first encounter was how much energy and enthusiasm this young woman had. It made a wonderful first impression on us, and more importantly, on my kids. They went from being a little apprehensive about their first day in a new place to being totally "psyched" (as they put it).

That first impression continued as we met more counselors and administrative people. Turns out, Beth wasn't unusually enthusiastic, at least not compared to the other employees. They were all like this. And it wasn't just a first-day-of-camp thing. Over the next few weeks, every time I went to the camp for drop-offs or pickups, I was blown away by how *into* their work these camp staffers were. It was clear that they were having fun, and that they truly enjoyed their jobs and their coworkers.

A few times when I was at the camp, I remarked to a counselor that they all really seemed to love their jobs. Every time, the counselor would agree enthusiastically and explain how they all got along and were treated well by management. This was not the sort of workplace where everything was written down in rulebooks and people were micromanaged. Instead, the camp was governed by founder Joe Kahn's guiding principles of safety, fun, and learning. And it worked extremely well.

I was so struck by the consistent energy at this camp that I pored through its web site to learn more about it. Sure enough, when you go to the camp's employment page, you immediately see this quote from Josh Schiering, the executive director:

> The key to having happy campers is having a happy staff!

But rather than just being a tagline on a web site, LINX Camps made it their practice.

"But I Don't Run a Summer Camp"

OK, fair point. You're saying that it's a lot easier to have fun at a summer camp where young people play games in the sunshine with happy kids. But what if you're stuck inside under fluorescent lights in an office tower doing tax work or inside sales or employment law?

Doesn't matter. People can have fun and be happy in any workplace. It's all about having the right leadership, and hiring the right people. And it's about remembering that employees are people, and people like to have fun.

I hate those cynical workplace cartoons and e-mail jokes that complain about the drudgery of work. You know, the ones that say it's not supposed to be fun; that's why they call it "work." In fact, when I Googled the phrase "that's why they call it work," I got about a quarter million hits (September 2011). That's disappointing. It tells me that there are a lot of unhappy people in the workplace.

Now some of you might disagree with me and say that *business* needs to be taken care of at work, and that fun is a luxury, and that you work so you can have fun when you're not at work. And you're right.

But there's no reason why you can't do both. As long as your company has standards for accomplishing the tasks that need to be accomplished, there's no reason why it has to be drudgery. People are more engaged in their work when they like being there, and when they like being around their coworkers. Don't you want your employees to be more engaged?

Happy Birthday

Many years ago, when I first went away to school, I remember being bummed out that no one knew it was my birthday. When I mentioned it to my mother, she asked in a way that only mothers can: "Well, did you tell anyone it was your birthday?" I hadn't, of course. Now I do. And it makes the day more fun. (Coincidentally, I'm writing these words on my actual birthday. So now I've told you, too.)

Some people don't make a big deal out of birthdays. Some think birthdays should be limited to friends and family. Some workplaces even have policies restricting or forbidding the at-work celebration of birthdays. Wow. What fun places to work those must be.

Last year, my work colleagues wished me "happy birthday" with a funny group card, a homemade loaf of banana bread, a bookstore gift certificate, and then drinks after work. And trust me: this had nothing to with my being the boss. We did similar things for everyone's birthday. It made our workplace seem like more of a family, and that's a good thing in my book.

People like to be reminded from time to time that they're special. Making a point of celebrating a person's birthday is one way of doing it.

Managers: if your workplace doesn't celebrate your employees' birthdays, why not? Because of expense? Give me a break: people can chip in a few bucks, or it can come out of petty cash. Because it's a distraction from work? Please. The goodwill that you generate by treating your employees as people—as special people—will more than make up for any expense or lost productivity. Add everyone's birthday to the calendar, and do something nice for them on their special day.

Employees First, Customers Second

Of course, making your employees feel special is about more than just celebrating their birthdays. It's about treating them with respect and compassion. It's about finding ways to make them happy and keep them happy. And it pays off in revenue.

The June 2007 issue of the *Harvard Business Review* carried an article by two professors from Manchester (UK) Business School, Gary Davies and Rosa

Chun, called "To Thine Own Staff Be Agreeable." The professors had conducted field interviews with 4,700 customers and employees of 63 businesses. They learned that service companies were more likely to enjoy sales growth if their employee satisfaction exceeded their customer satisfaction:

> Our research shows two things: Employee and customer views strongly correlate, indicating that the former influences the latter; and year-on-year sales growth positively and significantly correlates with the size of the gaps between employee and customer views. The more the staff's view outshines the customers', the greater the sales growth, because, we believe, employee views tend to transfer to customers through the aptly termed process of emotional contagion.

"Emotional contagion" describes the way that employees' good feelings rub off onto the customers. This emotional contagion is what I witnessed at the LINX Camps, and what I strove to achieve in my law firm.

The professors also found that employee satisfaction was most influenced "by the perceived quality of both training and management and by how much autonomy workers have." In other words, treating employees with respect led to greater employee satisfaction.

Bottom line for managers and HR: employee satisfaction can actually be used as a metric to provide a leading indicator for company growth. And this satisfaction doesn't have to cost your company very much.

Employee Satisfaction for $2.40 a Day

When Apple introduced the iPhone in the summer of 2007, there were about a zillion stories written about it. But to me, as an employer evangelist, one of the most interesting stories was that Apple gave each of its employees a free 8-gigabyte iPhone. I first read about this in John Moore's excellent marketing blog, *Brand Autopsy*. In his post on "Marketing to Employees," Moore described the Apple employee giveaway:

> I am a huge proponent of companies spending marketing money on employees. It's simple. Astonish employees and they will, in turn, astonish customers. Giving every full-time employee a $600 (retail value) iPhone is an astonishing act that will only help to feed the already vibrant evangelical corporate culture within Apple.[1]

---

[1]Brand Autopsy, "Marketing to Employees," www.brandautopsy.com/2007/06/marketing-to-em.html, June 27, 2009.

John's key line—"astonish employees and they will, in turn, astonish customers"—jibes with the British study showing employee satisfaction as a leading indicator for company growth. And it didn't cost Apple that much to astonish its employees.

Think about it: each 8 GB iPhone retailed for $599 when it was introduced in 2007. Giving each Apple employee a $599 bonus would be nice, but it wouldn't really generate any excitement. And if you convert that $599 to a raise, it works out to less than 30 cents an hour for full-time employees, or $2.40 a day. Big whoop.

Instead of giving employees a 30-cent raise, Apple gave them a status symbol (which it was back then) and a story to tell their friends and family. The lesson for employers: find creative, surprising ways to reward your employees, instead of just giving a standard 3 percent merit increase. Your employees in turn will reward you with better performance.

A few weeks after the iPhone launched, I took a page from Apple's playbook and gave my firm's employees their own iPhones. I saw firsthand the effect it had. My team was surprised and delighted. For months afterward, they would tell friends that their employer had gotten them free iPhones. Even the *Boston Business Journal* wrote a piece about it. For a relatively small expense, I was able to show my appreciation to my team members and make them feel special.

Gruntled Employees

Some of you might be wondering, "What does this have to do with firing employees?" Fair question. The answer is simple: *everything*.

As I said at the beginning of the book, and several times throughout, employee lawsuits are the weapon of last resort for disgruntled employees. So it stands to reason that the most effective way to avoid employee lawsuits is to avoid having disgruntled employees. Instead, you want "gruntled" employees.

Note What kind of a word is "gruntled"? OK. It isn't much of a word. But it should be. If disgruntled employees are more likely to sue their employers, you need to know how to keep them ... gruntled. Right? In fact, the *New Oxford American Dictionary*, which is my dictionary of choice (and available free on any Mac) actually does call it a word, describing it as a recent (1930s) back-formation from "disgruntle." It describes it as an "adjective, humorous" and says that it means "pleased, satisfied, and contented." Works for me.

I've been talking about gruntled employees for the last five years, when I started the *Gruntled Employees* workplace blog (gruntledemployees.com). And even before that, since I began advising managers 17 years ago, I've been preaching a message about how happy employees don't sue you. And it's true. Consider this carefully calculated statistic from my litigation career:

> One hundred percent of the employment cases I litigated were brought by employees who were angry at, hurt by, or unhappy with their employer.

That's what litigation is all about. It's a universal truth: people don't sue people they like. Even the greediest employee plaintiff in the world doesn't sue *just* to make money. There has to be strong emotion involved, or the litigation doesn't happen. Never once in all the cases I handled did I deal with a suing employee who was all "it's nothing personal; it's strictly business" toward the employer. Litigation is *always* personal. People don't sue people they like.

Gruntled employees are happy employees. Gruntled employees like their coworkers. They may not want to go out to dinner with them or socialize with them all the time, but they at least get along with them.

And more importantly for our discussion, gruntled employees like their employers. And people don't sue people they like.

So how do you keep your employees gruntled?

What You Can Do

It's not just about giving employees free iPhones or recognizing their birthdays.

It's about treating them as individuals, with their own personal passions and dreams and failings and strengths and opinions and beliefs and backgrounds and experiences.

It's about treating them with respect, and recognizing that they work there voluntarily, and can always choose to go work somewhere else.

It's about giving them autonomy: showing them the standards of performance they need to reach and giving them guidance to help them reach those standards, but also giving them the freedom to do the work without being micromanaged.

It's about making the workplace a place that's not just about work, but also a place that's about fun and learning and interestingness.

It's about bringing together a group of people who work together as a team, who treat each other like family, and who are fiercely loyal to each other. They don't all have to be friends or go out to dinner together, but they do have to treat each other with courtesy and respect.

These are the things that make employees gruntled, and gruntled employees don't sue. And these are all things that are in your power as managers and employers.

Conclusion

The workplace is never perfect. Problems will arise. You'll make mistakes in hiring employees, or people will end up letting you down. At some point, you will have to make the difficult decision to fire an employee.

But how you treated that employee from the start and how you treat him or her during the termination will make a tremendous difference in whether that employee decides to sue you over the termination. If you work to have gruntled employees, you will end up with fewer employee lawsuits.

Appendixes

Firing Checklist

Here is a handy checklist to help you make sure that you've thought through everything and prepared for this most difficult of managerial tasks. (Chapter 6 takes you through the actual firing process in detail). You can also download a free PDF of this checklist from the book's web site at firingatwill.com/checklist.

Before the Termination

- ☐ Don't fire when angry. Take enough time to make sure that you're not making the decision for emotional reasons.
- ☐ Choose the appropriate day and time to minimize additional pain. For example, don't do it right before Christmas, or on the employee's birthday, or when everyone else is going to be milling around.
- ☐ Choose a location in the workplace that offers privacy, with the door closed.
- ☐ If you're concerned about an angry or violent reaction, have security or another coworker nearby and ready.
- ☐ Have the employee's final paycheck ready for the meeting. Include pay for the entire day of the termination, as well as any other money owed. Make sure your payroll people keep the termination secret.
- ☐ Make sure you include pay to cover any accrued but unused vacation.
- ☐ If the employee has computer access, make arrangements to have her locked out of the system while you're in the termination meeting.

Not before and not after. And make sure the computer person keeps the termination secret.

☐ Prepare what you're going to say in the meeting, but don't write out an actual script.

☐ If appropriate, prepare a severance agreement to give to the employee. For an example, see Appendix C.

☐ Gather up any material that your state requires you to give to terminated employees. Often, this includes information on unemployment benefits and health-insurance continuation (COBRA).

☐ Decide how much notice you want to give, and how much transition time you need during which the fired employee will stay on. Hint: the answer should almost always be "none."

During the Termination

☐ Have a witness in the room unless you absolutely trust the employee you're firing.

☐ Don't beat around the bush. You're here to fire the person, not talk about the Red Sox or the weather.

☐ Speak about the firing as a done deal. Don't give the employee a false sense of hope that he might be able to change your mind and save his job.

☐ Choose the right way to say it. "We've decided to let you go" or "It's time for us to go our separate ways" are better than the lawyerly "We're terminating your employment."

☐ Resist the temptation to get into a debate about the employee's performance or conduct. Now is not the time for that, and you'll just end up making the employee defensive.

☐ Tell the truth and nothing but the truth, but not necessarily the whole truth. There's no need to go through every transgression the employee had. The less said, the better. Telling untruths, even white lies to soften the blow, is a risky proposition.

☐ Be firm but gentle, empathetic but steadfast. Remember that your goal is for the employee to leave with as much Retained Dignity as possible (refer to Chapter 7).

☐ If you're offering a severance package, present the agreement to the employee. Don't get into the details, other than to say what you're offering her. Focus on the severance as a way to help the employee with her transition. Explain that she should take some time to review the severance details in the letter. Do not talk about the release you're seeking.

☐ Give the employee whatever other documents the state requires.

After the Termination

☐ If you're not worried about violence or theft or other disruption, you can let the employee return to her office or station unsupervised. If you are concerned, have someone walk her out with as much dignity and as little drama as possible. Offer to send her stuff home.

☐ If you've offered to write a letter of reference, do it right away. You don't want this hanging over your head, and you don't want to extend the time for having contact with the employee. On the other hand, if you've also asked her to sign a severance agreement, you might decide to wait until she returns it before giving her the reference.

☐ Inform other employees about the termination on a need-to-know basis. This should be a private tragedy, not a public spectacle. Don't worry overly about gossip, and don't do anything that would further embarrass the fired employee.

☐ Arrange to have the employee's phone answered by the appropriate person. Instruct that person about how to handle questions about the fired employee.

☐ Arrange to have the employee's e-mail forwarded to you or another appropriate person. You can then forward personal e-mail to the fired employee for a reasonable time, while keeping the business e-mail.

☐ If the firing was for a reason like theft or disloyalty, or if you have any reason to think that litigation might ensue, have your IT people make a disk image of her work computer. Resist the temptation to immediately reassign the computer to someone else. The hard drive may contain evidence that could help you in future litigation.

Firing Around the World

I wrote *Firing at Will* primarily for US employers and managers, which makes sense since my experience is as an American employment litigator. I am no kind of expert in international employment law, and I have never said otherwise. But today, more companies have a global reach and employ people all over the world. Over the years, I would occasionally advise American employers about workplace issues in other countries, and I also helped foreign companies from time to time.

Small World

One thing is clear: the world is getting smaller. I once had to review the noncompete agreement of an individual in Amsterdam whom an American employer client of mine was about to hire away from a competitor. After doing some research online, I came across an article on Dutch noncompete law written by an American lawyer working in the Netherlands. I figured I could save some time by reaching out to her.

She was surprised and pleased to get a call from a US lawyer about the obscure article she had written. She certainly knew her topic well, and was very helpful and forthcoming. She saved me hours of legal research and also was able to give me the inside-baseball knowledge that I never would have found in my computer research. Then, as we were winding up our chat, she asked me a question that she should have asked me at the beginning: what was the name of the individual's current employer—my client's competitor? So I told her.

"Oops," she said. (The word apparently has the same meaning in Dutch.) My client's competitor turned out to be a client of hers. "I should probably get off the phone now."

Small world indeed.

Postcards from Around the World

While the laws that I talk about in the book are specific to the United States, many of the management concepts are universal and can be used anywhere. Hiring to avoid firing, maximizing Retained Dignity, keeping your employees gruntled—these are all things that employers can do to protect and grow their companies no matter where in the world they are.

What follows are some selected highlights of the major differences between the United States and certain other countries. Since there's no way to get into any kind of detail about another nation's complete set of employment laws in a few paragraphs, employers operating in those countries need to make sure they get themselves excellent employment counsel with the proper expertise in their jurisdiction.

United Kingdom

Given that US law owes so much to its British common-law heritage, it would be fair to assume that British and American employment law would be quite similar. But while there are many overlapping concepts, such as antidiscrimination laws, the two systems treat employees quite differently. Some of the differences can be attributed to the stronger "nanny state" approach that Labour governments established over the second half of the twentieth century. Other differences come from the increasing importance of European Union law.

The biggest difference is that the United Kingdom, like most other countries, does not recognize the American concept of employment at will. Instead, all British workers are contractual employees. The contracts don't need to be in writing, and their terms can be explicit or implicit (and buried in workplace rules, handbooks, or other writings). Of course, having all employees be contractual makes it more difficult to fire employees.

Unlike in the United States, where wrongful-termination claims tend to be weak, employees in Britain have strong statutory protection against "unfair dismissal." Once an employee has worked a year for the same employer, he or she obtains the right not to be unfairly dismissed. If the employee is then fired and brings a claim for unfair dismissal, the burden rests with the employer to prove that the dismissal was indeed fair. This can only be done by proving that the employee was incapable, lacked qualifications, committed misconduct, was laid off ("made redundant"), broke the law, or was fired for "some other substantial reason."

In other words, it's a far cry from the American at-will concept of "any reason or no reason at all." In the United Kingdom, the employer must be prepared to justify the termination with good reasons. There are also substantial notice requirements and procedural rules.

Redundancy dismissals are handled differently, with mandatory payment based on years of service (as long as the employees have worked there for at least two years).

Since it is much more difficult to fire workers in Britain, employers in the United Kingdom need to be even more careful in their hiring and managing decisions.

Australia

Employers Down Under face the same sort of challenges that their British cousins face, as opposed to the relative freedom to fire that their American counterparts enjoy. Vague standards of fairness and reasonableness govern whether dismissals are justifiable. What is more, Australian employment law has gone through massive changes on a national scale over the past decade.

The Fair Work Act 2009 (don't know why it's not "of 2009") made sweeping changes to Australian employment law, effectively federalizing most rules governing workplaces (except in Western Australia). If an employer terminates an employee who has been there six months (or a year, if at a small business), the Orwellian-named Fair Work Australia agency can determine whether the dismissal was "harsh, unjust, or unreasonable." The agency will take into account whether the employer had a "valid" reason for dismissal that was related to the employee's capacity or conduct, whether the employee had notice and an opportunity to respond, and whether the termination was procedurally sound.

As in the United Kingdom, different rules apply to redundancies (layoffs). Under those rules, many employers are subject to strict notice requirements and must often give employees redundancy pay.

Besides claims for unfair dismissal, there are also claims for unlawful termination. These include terminations for discriminatory reasons, union activity, medical leave, and other statutory rights.

One benefit that Australian employers enjoy compared to American companies is a short filing deadline. Unfair-dismissal claims must be filed within 14 days of the dismissal, and unlawful-termination claims must be brought within 60 days.

Canada

Canadian employers have more freedom to fire employees than British and Australian companies. As in the United Kingdom, employees are generally presumed to have a contract, whether explicit or implied. The big issues for Canadian employers are just cause and notice.

If the employer has just cause to fire an employee—say for theft or insubordination—then notice isn't a problem. But if an employer wants to fire a worker without just cause, the employee is generally entitled to "reasonable notice." How long this notice period is depends on which province the employer is located in.

For example, in Ontario, the Employment Standards Act requires employers to give a week of notice for every year of service, up to eight weeks' notice. In other words, if you want to fire someone who's become difficult after working there for eight years (but whose termination doesn't rise to the level of "for cause"), you have to give her eight weeks' notice. Of course, no employer wants to have an already-fired employee with no incentive to perform well hanging about for two months. So then the employer has to give pay instead of notice.

Again, as in the other countries, employees enjoy the usual protections against discrimination and so forth.

Germany

This probably won't come as a big surprise, but the German workplace is heavily regulated. As with other countries, there is no concept of at-will employment; all employment is contractual. But unlike in other nations, German employment contracts must be written, with the start date, pay rate, work location, work to be performed, and vacation all spelled out.

Most German contracts are unlimited in duration. An employer can give a limited employment contract for a specific time period, but only if there is an "objective reason" for the time limitation. If the period is two years or less, though, that restriction doesn't apply.

Employees generally can't be made to work on Sundays and holidays. They also can't be made to work more than eight hours a day, and people on average work between 35 and 40 hours a week. Women can't be fired during pregnancy and in the four months after. Maternity leave is paid and starts no later than six weeks before the due date and ends eight weeks after the birth. Both men and women can take up to *three years* of unpaid parental leave per child, during which they can't be fired. Employees are also entitled to 24 days of vacation, although five or six weeks is more common.

Although German employment law seems determined to make sure that workers work as little as possible, it ironically also makes it difficult to fire employees. Companies must give employees advance written termination notice, and the notice period is defined by statute and ranges from four weeks to a whopping seven months, depending on the employees' length of service.

Employees who have been with the company six months or more enjoy special statutory protection against "unfair dismissal." Under this statute, the employer has to prove that the termination was based on a compelling business reason or because of specific bad conduct about which the employee was warned in writing beforehand. And mass layoffs have to be approved in advance by the government.

Japan

Employment in Japan is generally governed by two statutes, the Labour Contract Law and the Labour Standards Law. Employers are usually required to give employees written terms and work rules.

Typically, employees are given a three-to-six-month probationary period, during which it is somewhat easier to fire them. After the probation ends, employees can be fired only for "reasonable and socially acceptable grounds" such as a poor performance or bad behavior. Under the Labour Standards Law, dismissals that aren't based on "objectively" reasonable grounds are "null and void as an abuse of rights."

Because Japanese courts are reluctant to conclude that the grounds for dismissal were "reasonable and socially acceptable," it is common for employers to ask workers to resign in exchange for severance. There is a strong belief in the notion of second chances, where employees who underperform or misbehave are given the chance to improve. In fact, many companies allow three written warnings before termination. Three strikes and you're out, just as in *besuboru*.

Employers usually must give 30 days' notice before dismissing an employee, or offer payment in lieu of notice. While the law doesn't require severance pay, it is common for Japanese employers to give a month's pay for every year worked. Mass layoffs, which used to be prohibited, are still strictly regulated and need to be formally justified.

China

China's employment-law system is more like the other countries in this appendix than it is like the US system. It's governed by the relatively new (2008) Labor Contract Law.

Once again, there is no concept of employment at will. All employees are contractual, and the contract must be in writing. The contract is for a specific term, and it is very difficult to fire an employee during that term, except during an initial six-month probationary period.

Employers must specify workplace rules and responsibilities. Except in cases of serious misconduct, employers must give 30 days' notice before terminating employees. In general, employers have to pay one month's severance pay for each year worked.

Conclusion

Although it often doesn't seem that way to employers, the American workplace system based on at-will employment offers more freedom to control who works for you than anywhere else in the developed world. This is something that we tend to take for granted. While firing employees in the United States is a challenging task made more difficult by the threat of litigation, it's much harder overseas. As you're wrestling with the issues we've covered in this book, keep in mind how much more difficult it would be outside the United States.

Sample Documents

Here are a few sample documents relating to some of the topics we've covered in the book. I'm including them just to give you some ideas about what these things should look like. That doesn't mean that I'm recommending that you copy and paste them into your documents. That would be silly. These documents were designed for the specific situations we faced in our law firm. You need to have your own employment counsel draft specific documents for your specific situations. OK? Promise? Fine. Now you can look at them.

Here's what we have:

- offer letter
- severance-agreement letter
- employment agreement
- reference letter (reduction in force)
- agency position statement

These documents are also available for free on the web site at firingatwill.com/samples.

Sample Offer Letter

As we discussed in Chapter 1, it's very important to have your employees be at will. To make sure that happens, you need to start at the beginning. The wrong kind of offer letter could create an unintended contract that destroys the at-will nature of the employment. Here's a sample (names changed) offer letter that I wrote for a client a few years ago.

Dear Fred:

It is my absolute pleasure to extend you this offer to join the Agency Zero team in the role of Account Director. I am highly confident that you possess the skills and experience necessary to succeed in this challenging role.

Here are some of the details of the job offer:

- **Employment at will.** This is an at-will position. This means you are not obligated to stay any longer than you want, and you can leave for any reason or for no reason at all. I sincerely hope that will not happen anytime soon. Naturally, Agency Zero has the same freedom to end the relationship.
- **Pay.** Your starting base salary will be at an annualized rate of $45,000. You will be paid semimonthly ($1,875 twice a month). As a creative professional, you will be exempt from federal overtime law. Bonuses and raises will be at the firm's discretion and will be based primarily on your performance and the firm's performance.
- **Commissions.** In addition to your salary, you will have the opportunity to earn more money by bringing in new business to the firm. For any new client that you are responsible for bringing to the firm, we will pay you a commission of 5 percent of the revenue actually paid by the client during its first twelve months of working with us. To remain eligible to receive commissions, you must still be actively involved in maintaining our relationship with the client.
- **Work schedule.** Account director is a full-time salaried position. Our regular office hours are from 8:30 a.m. to 5:00 p.m. weekdays, but from time to time you will need to perform work at other times including weekends.
- **Vacation.** You will be entitled to take three weeks of paid vacation per calendar year. The vacation time will accrue monthly. The more advance notice you give, the better we'll be able to accommodate

your vacation-schedule requests. Because we believe it's important to recharge your batteries periodically, we'll want you to take the vacation during the year you earn it; the time won't carry over into the following year, unless our scheduling prevents you from taking some of your time.

- **Holidays.** The seven major ones are paid days off: New Year's Day, Presidents' Day, Memorial Day, Independence Day, Labor Day, Thanksgiving, and Christmas. The minor holidays (MLK Day, Columbus Day, Veterans Day, and Thanksgiving Friday) will be ad hoc: if we close those days, you will receive them as paid holidays also.
- **Volunteer time.** Because public service is so important to us, we will pay you for up to two days (or four half-days) per year for volunteer service you provide. We will need to approve the time in advance.
- **Insurance.** We will provide you with individual health-insurance coverage and contribute half of the monthly premium.
- **Nonsolicitation and confidentiality agreement.** In exchange for this job, you will need to sign a nonsolicitation and confidentiality agreement that protects our secrets and our customer relationships. As you know, these agreements are standard in this industry.

Because the firm is still small, you will have a great opportunity to get in on the ground floor. You will enjoy much more responsibility than you would at a large firm, and you will be instrumental in growing a first-class public-relations firm. I know you will make a great addition to this agency and that your contributions will be an integral part of our growth and success.

Welcome to Agency Zero, Fred. I think we'll accomplish a lot together. It should be fun.

Very truly yours,

Maxwell Zero

President

Sample Severance-Agreement Letter

In Chapter 6, we talked about the actual mechanics of firing an employee. One important consideration is whether to give severance pay. It's often a good idea because it can help soften the blow.

Ideally, when you give an employee severance pay, you in return get a promise not to sue from the employee (a waiver and release). The tricky thing is this: there are laws that govern what must be included in a waiver for it to be enforceable. You want to make sure you follow those laws; there is nothing worse than paying severance in exchange for a waiver and release and then finding out that it was invalid. On the other hand, you don't want to make the waiver seem so lawyerly that it scares the employee from signing it.

Here's a sample from my practice. It was written for a Massachusetts employee who was under the age of 40. Releases for employees aged 40 and over have additional required language. Your state may also require different language. Don't use this letter; have your employment lawyer draft one. (But this can serve as stylistic model.)

Dear Betty,

As we have discussed, your employment with Prancing Pixel ends today. To ease the transition, we would like to offer you the severance package described in this letter. Please read this letter carefully, as it explains the terms of your benefits under this severance agreement.

Under the severance package being offered to you, you will receive the equivalent of four weeks' salary less tax withholdings and other appropriate deductions. The severance pay will be paid as part of Prancing Pixel's regular payroll cycle.

If you are enrolled in Prancing Pixel's medical and dental plans today, you may continue your participation in those plans under the Massachusetts mini-COBRA law, which we will provide you information about. Otherwise, your participation in all employee-benefit plans of Prancing Pixel will end as of today, under the terms of those plans.

In return for the severance benefits described above, you release and forever discharge Prancing Pixel, its subsidiaries or related companies, officers, directors, members, employees, and agents from any claims known or unknown that arise on or before the date you sign this agreement. These claims include wrongful discharge, breach of contract, and any claims under the Civil Rights

Acts, the Massachusetts Fair Employment Practices Act, the Americans with Disabilities Act, the Employee Retirement Income Security Act, and any other federal, state, or local legislation or common law relating to employment or discrimination in employment. But this release does not include your right to enforce the terms of this agreement, nor does it have any effect on your eligibility for unemployment or workers'-compensation benefits. Prancing Pixel will not contest your application for unemployment benefits.

By signing this letter, you are saying that you have not filed any lawsuits, claims, or charges against us in any court or with any administrative agency.

It is important to keep the terms of this agreement confidential, and you agree to do so. But you may discuss it with your immediate family and your legal and financial advisors as long as they also keep the terms confidential.

As you know, we need to be able to protect our confidential information and our important client and business relationships. You agree not to disclose or use any confidential or proprietary information or trade secrets.

If you have any Prancing Pixel property, you agree to return it today. If you discover any other Prancing Pixel property in your possession after today, you agree to immediately return it as well. This includes all documents, materials, and information related to Prancing Pixel's business and all keys, access cards, and all other property of Prancing Pixel in your possession. By signing this, you are affirming that you have not kept any copy of any Prancing Pixel documents, materials, or information (whether in hard copy, on electronic media, or otherwise).

This agreement and general release will be governed by Massachusetts law without regard to conflict-of-laws principles. If a court rules that any of its provisions are invalid, the rest of this agreement will not be affected. Any action relating to this agreement may be brought only in a court in Massachusetts, and both parties consent to personal jurisdiction in Massachusetts.

If you choose not to sign this agreement, it will be void in all respects and you will not receive the severance benefits discussed above. Your employment by Prancing Pixel will nonetheless have terminated as of today. If this agreement is acceptable to you, please sign the enclosed copy and return it to me. You may take up to seven days from today (until November 5, 2010) to consider, sign, and return this agreement. You and Prancing Pixel agree that any changes to this offer, whether material or not, that you and Prancing Pixel agree to in writing after this seven-day period has begun will not serve to restart the seven-day period. We advise you to consult with an attorney before signing the agreement.

This agreement contains the entire understanding between you and Prancing Pixel and replaces any earlier agreements, oral or written, relating to your employment by Prancing Pixel or the termination of your employment, except any written agreements between you and Prancing Pixel regarding confidential information. This agreement may not be modified except in writing, signed by both parties. This agreement will be binding upon your heirs and personal representatives, and the successors and assigns of Prancing Pixel.

Betty, please accept our sincere best wishes for your future.

Very truly yours,

Millard Fillmore

President

Accepted and Agreed:

_____   _____

Betty Dole   Date Signed and Returned

Sample Employment Agreement

If for some reason you do have to use an employment agreement that includes a termination-for-cause provision, at least put some thought into it (and have your lawyer do so, too.) Too many employers cut and paste boilerplate cause language into agreements, making it almost impossible to fire employees unless they commit crimes against humanity and are convicted by the World Court in The Hague. Here's a sample agreement I drafted for a client.

Solid Bases Employment Agreement

Parties. In this Agreement, the terms "you" and "your" refer to Patrick Sewall, and the terms "we," "us," and "our" refer to Solid Bases, LLC.

Background

- We are in the business of providing custom-engineered Aeroposts ("products") to our customers.
- You are an individual.
- Both you and we wish to have you act as our Sales Support and Account Manager.

Therefore, in consideration of the mutual covenants contained in this Agreement, the parties agree as follows.

Terms and Conditions

I Your Basic Obligations

You will use your best efforts to support our sales force as directed by the General Manager and the Sales Manager. You will use your best efforts to solicit orders for the sale of products by representing the products in a clear and professional manner. You will make the solicitations and any resulting purchase orders using the procedures, prices, terms, and conditions that we specify from time to time. No sale or purchase order will be final until we approve it. Your job may require travel from time to time.

I.I   **Marketing Activities.** We will provide you with marketing materials and technical support to assist in your efforts to get sales. You may only use the marketing materials that we either provide you or approve in writing in advance. Examples of marketing materials include videos, brochures, computer presentations (e.g., PowerPoint shows), photographs, and documents, among others.

We are entitled to terminate this Agreement and void your commissions if you use unapproved marketing materials.

1.2   Other Manufacturers and Distributors. While selling for us, you will not make any negative comments about any competing manufacturers or distributors or their products. Nor will you make any sale, or seek to make any sale, that is contingent upon the customer buying another company's products.

1.3   Pricing. At the start of each month, we will give you the schedule of prices for that month. While we expect those prices to remain the same for that month, we reserve the right to change the prices if we decide it's appropriate. You will use the most recent pricing we give you unless we first give you written approval to use other prices. The pricing schedule may include discounted prices (or "floor prices") for larger-quantity sales. You may use your discretion to offer a price lower than the list price but not lower than the discount price for that quantity. If you wish to offer an even lower price, you must first obtain our written approval, which may be contingent on reducing or even eliminating your commission for that sale.

1.4   Delivery. While we will try to deliver products as quickly as the customers need them, we will not be responsible for meeting delivery deadlines that you promise unless we first approve the deadlines in writing. Because delays in manufacturing and delivery are sometimes inevitable, you will avoid promising delivery deadlines without first consulting us.

1.5   Confidential Business Information and Trade Secrets. You recognize that we have confidential business information and trade secrets ("our secrets"), and that to help you sell products we will from time to time share our secrets with you. You agree that sharing our secrets with others may give our competitors an unfair advantage over us. You also agree to maintain our secrets and not to share them with anyone during or after your engagement with us, unless we expressly authorize you in writing beforehand.

1.6   Professionalism. You agree that while working on our behalf, you will conduct yourself in a professional manner and will maintain a professional appearance. At no time will you work on our behalf while impaired by alcohol or any drug.

2   Our Basic Obligations

While you are our Sales Support and Account Manager, we will compensate you as follows:

2.1   **Salary.** We will pay you a base salary at an annualized rate of $50,000 a year.

2.2   **Commission.** In addition to your salary, we will also compensate you with a commission when we sell products to a customer. For any sale made to an existing customer while you are our Sales Support and Account Manager, we will pay you a commission of 2.5% of the value of the sale. An "existing customer" is any customer who is no longer a new customer, but who previously was a new customer to whom an independent sales representative made a sale. A "new customer" is any customer who has never purchased any product from us before, or who first became our customer in the previous 180 days. To qualify for commission under this paragraph, you must be actively involved in the maintenance of our relationship with the customer; it is not necessary for the sale to be the direct result of your personal marketing efforts. We will pay you the commission within 45 days of our receipt of the customer's payment for that sale.

2.3   **Health Insurance.** We will not provide you with a group health-insurance plan, but we will reimburse you for all your individual or family health-insurance costs up to $300 a month. This is not subject to the deferral described in paragraph 2.2.

2.4   **Vacation.** You are eligible to take two weeks' vacation per calendar year, with 2005 being prorated based on your number of months worked. Because we believe it is important to take regular vacations to recharge your energies, you may not carry over vacation from one calendar year to the next, nor may you "cash in" vacation time for extra pay.

2.5   **Profit Sharing.** We will also compensate you with two percent of our profits while you are our Sales Support and Account Manager. We will distribute your share of profits under the Solid Bases Financial Operating Procedures ("the Procedures") contained in the Addendum to our Operating Agreement. If there is any conflict between this paragraph and the Procedures, the Procedures take precedence. Please understand that the Procedures can be changed at any time without notice.

3   Term

The term of this Agreement will begin when the parties have signed it and will end when a party terminates it under paragraph 4.

4   Early Termination

4.1   **By Us For Cause.** We may terminate this Agreement without notice if you take any action that is illegal or unethical or that reflects badly on us, or if you fail to follow our instructions. If we terminate this Agreement under this paragraph, we will only owe you whatever unpaid commissions remain from sales completed before the termination date, plus any deferred salary.

4.2   **By Us Without Cause.** We may terminate this Agreement with 30 days' notice for any reason or no reason at all. If we terminate this Agreement under this paragraph, we will only owe you whatever unpaid commissions remain from sales that your team completed before the end of the 30-day notice period, plus any deferred salary. Additionally, we will pay you commissions on sales to existing customers under paragraph 2.2 for six months after the end of the notice period, and we will waive the "active involvement" requirement of that paragraph.

4.3   **By You For Cause.** You may terminate this Agreement without notice if we cease doing business. You may also terminate this Agreement if we fail to pay you commissions after you have given us written notice of our failure to pay and 30 days to cure this failure. If you terminate this Agreement under this paragraph, we will only owe you whatever unpaid commissions remain from sales completed before the termination date, plus any deferred salary.

4.4   **By You Without Cause.** You may terminate this Agreement with 30 days' notice for any reason or no reason at all. If you terminate this Agreement under this paragraph, we will only owe you whatever unpaid commissions remain from sales completed before the end of the 30-day notice period, plus any deferred salary.

4.5   **Relocation.** If we move our headquarters far enough that it would add more than a hour to your average commute to the office, you may terminate this Agreement with 30 days' notice and receive three months' salary continuation as well as commissions on sales to existing customers under paragraph 2.2 for the next six months (and we will waive the "active involvement" requirement of that paragraph). We will also pay you profit sharing under paragraph 2.5 for the next six months.

5   Assignment

We may assign our duties or interests under this Agreement to any parent, affiliate, successor, or subsidiary that we may have. We must notify you in writing of any assignment within 30 days. You may not assign your duties or interests in this Agreement.

6   Nonsolicitation of Employees, Sales Representatives, and Customers

6.1   **Of Employees and Sales Representatives.** You agree that, during the term of this Agreement and for two years after, you will not solicit or take away, or attempt to solicit or take away, any of our employees or sales representatives, either for your own business or for any other person or entity, nor will you induce or encourage any employee or sales representative to sever his or her relationship with us. You also agree that during this period, you will not hire or assist in the hiring of, directly or indirectly, any employee or sales representative of ours.

6.2   **Of Customers.** You agree that, during the term of this Agreement and for two years after, you will not solicit or take away, or attempt to solicit or take away, any of our customers, either for your own business or for any other person or entity, nor will you induce or encourage any customer to sever his, her, or its relationship with us. You also agree that during this period, you will not hire or assist in the hiring of, directly or indirectly, any employee or sales representative of ours. Further, you agree that even if you are solicited by a customer of ours to provide services to that customer or client, you will refuse to do so for two years following the termination of this Agreement.

6.3   **Noncompetition.** During the term of this Agreement, you may not perform work or other services—directly or indirectly, whether for compensation or not—for a business that competes with us, nor may you solicit, encourage, or assist any of our employees or sales representatives to do so.

7   Miscellaneous Provisions

7.1   **Entire Agreement; Modification.** This Agreement contains all the terms and conditions agreed on by the parties. Any previous agreements between the parties are replaced by this Agreement.

This Agreement can be modified or changed only by a new written agreement signed by both parties.

7.2   **Waiver.** A party's waiver of enforcement of any of this Agreement's terms or conditions will be effective only if in writing. A party's specific waiver will not constitute a waiver by that party of any earlier, concurrent, or later breach or default.

7.3   **Severability.** If any part of this Agreement is held invalid or unenforceable, the rest of the Agreement will continue in full force.

7.4   **Survival.** The covenants in paragraphs 1.5 and 6 will survive the expiration or termination of this Agreement.

7.5   **Counterparts.** This Agreement may be executed in any number of counterparts, each of which is considered an original.

7.6   **Choice of Law.** This Agreement is governed by and must be interpreted under Colorado law, without regard to its choice-of-law provisions.

7.7   **Notices.** Notices provided for by this Agreement may be delivered in person, via a reputable express carrier, or by registered or certified mail (postage prepaid) to a party's address stated below. Notice sent by US mail is deemed delivered three days after deposit with the US Postal Service. Notice sent by a reputable express carrier is deemed received on the day receipted for by the party or its agent. Either party may change its address as listed below by giving written notice to the other party.

7.8   **Headings.** All headings are for reference purposes only and must not affect the interpretation of this Agreement.

Dated: _____

Solid Bases, LLC, a Colorado limited-liability company
(referred to as "we" throughout)

by Jesse James

_____

Its General Manager and Principal

_____

Patrick Sewall (referred to as "you" throughout)

Address

Sample Reference Letter (Reduction in Force)

Reference letters of the "To Whom It May Concern" variety are a mixed bag, in my opinion. Many employees seem to think they're important, often including them as a requirement in a settlement. But I don't believe that employers pay much attention to these. They rarely say anything useful, and more-experienced employers know that they're often negotiated over.

Additionally, many employers are squeamish about writing reference letters. There's a fairly common myth that employers are constantly being sued for giving out references for lousy employees. But I can report that in 17 years of representing employers, I never once encountered or even heard or read about an actual claim for "negligent reference" against an employer. It's the Loch Ness Monster of HR.

If a manager really liked a departing employee, she would offer to make phone calls on the employee's behalf, or allow prospective employers to call her directly. A form letter is for employees you don't really like.

But there is an exception. When you have to do a reduction in force, it may be impossible to make phone calls for everyone laid off. In this case, a form letter like this one may well be appropriate—and appreciated.

Naturally, you should customize it as much as possible.

[River Bank Letterhead]

To Whom It May Concern:

[Employee] has been employed by River Bank since [DATE]. During this period, [he/she] demonstrated all the qualities that employers look for when seeking promotable employees.

[He/She] has an excellent capacity for quickly grasping new theories and applications and is proactive about looking for and taking on additional responsibilities.

[Employee]'s dedication to her job is displayed by [Personalized example]. [His/Her] competence is such that [Personalized example of leadership skills, work under pressure, creativity, etc.]

It's unfortunate for River Bank that because of economic constraints, we had to reorganize and lose valued employees like [Employee]. I highly recommend [him/her] for any position or career that [he/she] chooses to pursue.

If you have any additional questions, please do not hesitate to contact me.

[Letter writer's name]

[Title]

River Bank

Sample Agency Position Statement

This is an example of a letter-style position statement as described in Chapter 11. It's from an actual reply I filed several years ago at the Massachusetts anti-discrimination agency. As you can imagine, all the names have been changed (except mine).

Dear Ms. Jones:

Respondent Wormwood Finance, LLC submits this statement in response to the Complaint of Bob Smith alleging discrimination based on his alleged disability.

Smith cannot demonstrate that he was unlawfully discriminated or retaliated against under Massachusetts law. Wormwood did not discriminate or retaliate against him on the basis of his alleged disability. To the contrary, Wormwood had multiple conversations with Smith regarding what type of accommodations would be necessary to ensure that he would be able to continue working. They then made several accommodations including: (1) providing him with an air mattress in a private office so that he could lie down during work hours, (2) renting a parking space so that he would not have to take public transportation to work (see Exhibit A), and (3) allowing him to leave early and take paid days off (well in excess of his allotted sick time) if his back was hurting or if he needed to seek medical attention.

Despite these accommodations, Smith was unable or unwilling to perform the essential functions of his job and he has not provided any evidence to the contrary. Smith's charge of discrimination and retaliatory discharge should be dismissed for lack of probable cause.

Background

Smith started working for Wormwood on April 22, 2008. Wormwood is a small investment company located in Boston. Smith was hired to perform the duties of a financial analyst. As an analyst he was expected to produce accurate and timely daily profit and loss reports for all funds, as well as many other duties (see Exhibit B). The position of financial analyst is a full-time position. As a full-time employee Smith was expected to work a minimum of 40 hours a week.

Just two months after he started working for Wormwood, Smith began to complain that he was having some back pain. After taking several sick days, he requested, and was granted, the ability to leave early and seek medical attention if necessary, and the ability to leave his desk during the day in order to stretch his back—so long as someone knew where he was in case he was needed. Additionally, Wormwood agreed to pay the full cost of renting a nearby parking space so that Smith would be able to get to and from work easier (see Exhibit A). In fact, in his December 2008 self-review, Smith acknowledged the accommodations that were being made to help him and thanked Wormwood for its understanding. (See Exhibit C.)

On January 8, 2009, John Peters met with Smith (see Exhibit D) to further discuss additional options that would help him to continue working. As a result of that meeting, Wormwood purchased an air mattress so that Smith could lie down during work hours in order to stretch his back if necessary. Smith failed to take advantage of this accommodation and did not use the air mattress despite a statement made to his doctor on January 23, 2009, claiming that "lying down seems to be the only position that alleviates his pain." (See Exhibit E.)

But Smith did take advantage of the option to leave his desk: he was spotted numerous times chatting with the receptionist and making personal calls from another employee's private office. And during those times, Smith had not informed anyone that he would be away from his desk, as he had agreed to do when taking breaks for his back pain. These absences tended to last 30–45 minutes at a time. Smith also took advantage of the flexible scheduling Wormwood offered him (see Exhibit F). Wormwood business hours are between 8 a.m. and 5 p.m.; as the security log shows, Smith was frequently late for work and frequently left early. His multiple absences from work and from his desk compounded his inability to perform the essential functions of his job.

When he did show up for work, he underperformed. Smith was frequently reprimanded for failing to perform the tasks he was asked to do and for failing to be proactive on the tasks that he did undertake. Examples abound: an e-mail from one of Smith's supervisors shows how it took Smith 35 days to do a simple task, despite repeated reminders (see Exhibit G). Other e-mails show how he failed to follow a direct order (see Exhibit H), failed to meet a deadline (see Exhibit I), repeatedly failed to perform assigned duties (see Exhibit J) failed to be proactive in his work (see Exhibit K). Smith's supervisors and coworkers were forced to bear the burden of performing the essential functions of his position because of his frequent absences and tardiness and failure to perform effectively when he was at work.

Despite the multiple accommodations that Wormwood provided, Smith remained unable or unwilling to perform the essential functions of his job. On February 28, 2003, Wormwood terminated Smith's employment for a legitimate business reason: that he was not performing the essential functions of his job.

Affirmative Defenses

In compliance with 804 CMR 1.10 (8)(d), Wormwood asserts the following additional defenses in response to the allegations contained in the Complaint:

First Defense

Smith has failed to establish a prima facie case with respect to claims made based upon his alleged disability.

Second Defense

Smith fails to present sufficient evidence upon which a fact finder could form a reasonable belief that it is more probable than not that Wormwood committed an unlawful practice.

Third Defense

The Complaint fails to state a claim upon which relief can be granted.

Fourth Defense

To the extent Smith failed to mitigate, minimize, or avoid any damages allegedly sustained, any recovery against Wormwood must be reduced by that amount.

Fifth Defense

Every action taken by Wormwood with respect to Smith's employment was taken for a legitimate business purpose and was consistent with principles of law. Wormwood has acted, at all times in good faith, reasonably and justifiably.

Sixth Defense

Smith is not disabled within the meaning of the ADA, nor is he handicapped within the meaning of G.L. c. 151B.

Seventh Defense

If Smith is disabled as alleged in his Complaint, any such disability was reasonably accommodated.

Eighth Defense

Smith's claim for damages is barred by the doctrine of waiver, laches, estoppel and/or unclean hands.

Very truly yours,

Jay Shepherd

Counsel for Wormwood

I

Index

Firing at Will

I always like to know how things are made, so I assume that there are others who share this interest. Here's what I can tell you about the making of this book.

The body type is Gill Sans MT 11/12. The headings are Utopia, and Helvetica Neue Condensed is also used in places.

I wrote the book primarily using Writer from Information Architects on an iMac, a MacBook Air, and on an iPad. I then imported the text into Apress's custom templates in Microsoft Word.

The website theme was also developed by Information Architects and runs on WordPress, hosted by GoDaddy.

CPSIA information can be obtained at www.ICGtesting.com
Printed in the USA
LVOW040218071211

258184LV00003B/2/P